LEADERSHIP DISPATCHES

HIGH RELIABILITY AND CRISIS MANAGEMENT

Series Editors: Karlene H. Roberts and Ian I. Mitroff

Series Titles

LEADERSHIP DISPATCHES

CHILE'S EXTRAORDINARY COMEBACK
FROM DISASTER

Michael Useem
Howard Kunreuther
Erwann Michel-Kerjan

STANFORD BUSINESS BOOKS

An Imprint of Stanford University Press

Stanford, California

Stanford University Press
Stanford, California

Library of Congress Cataloging-in-Publication Data

Useem, Michael, author.
    Leadership dispatches : Chile's extraordinary comeback from disaster /
Michael Useem, Howard Kunreuther, and Erwann Michel-Kerjan.
        pages   cm — (High reliability and crisis management)
    Includes bibliographical references and index.
    ISBN 978-0-8047-9387-2 (cloth : alk. paper)
    1. Chile Earthquake, Chile, 2010 (February 27)   2. Earthquake
relief—Chile.   3. Emergency management—Chile.   4. Leadership—
Chile.   5. Chile—Economic conditions—21st century.   6. Chile—
Politics and government—21st century.   I. Kunreuther, Howard,
author.   II. Michel-Kerjan, Erwann, author.   III. Title.   IV. Series:
High reliability and crisis management.
HV600 2010 .C5 U57   2015
363.34'9580983—dc23
                                                        2014034995

    ISBN 978-0-8047-9449-7 (electronic)

Typeset at Stanford University Press in Helvetica and 10.5/15 Minion

Special discounts for bulk quantities of Stanford Business Books
are available to corporations, professional associations, and other
organizations. For details and discount information, contact the special
sales department of Stanford University Press. Tel: (650) 736-1782, Fax:
(650) 736-1784

CONTENTS

LEADERSHIP DISPATCHES

PROLOGUE:
A QUIET SUMMER EVENING

> What we saw was just incredible!
> —President-elect Sebastián Piñera

It had been another sunny day. Millions were enjoying their summer vacation at the beach with family, hiking in the mountains with friends, visiting museum exhibitions, having fun at theme parks with the kids, or maybe just relaxing at home. It was Friday night, and those not already on holiday were happily at the start of a seemingly carefree weekend.

LITTLE DID THEY KNOW

With temperatures in the 70s, the terraces of restaurants were packed; fresh food would be cooked and local wine served. Casual strollers enjoyed live music near every corner. We could be in a lively quarter of New York, Los Angeles, Paris, or nearly anywhere in the world at the start of a late summer weekend that everybody was savoring and somehow wishing would never end.

Little did these vacationers and weekenders know that what was about to happen would change their lives forever. It would bring a severe test of the nation's resilience, challenging the effectiveness of the country's institutions and the determination of its national leaders, the president above all.

Deep below the earth's surface, some twenty miles down, two massive tectonic plates had been slowly converging for more than a century, and the gathering strain had finally become virtually untenable for the planet. It had reached a breaking point.

By 3:30 a.m. on that Saturday most restaurants and streets had emptied except for a few late-night revelers. The tectonic plates below finally snapped at 3:34 a.m., violently rocking the earth's surface for nearly two minutes. The released energy was so great, NASA later estimated that the event moved Chile's capital, Santiago, eleven inches to the west and even tilted the Earth's axis by three inches. A quiet summer night had come to a shocking end.

LIVING ON THE RING OF FIRE

The earthquake on February 27, 2010, devastated Chile. It could seem like a nightmare or the script of an epic sci-fi movie. But for millions it was all too real. This book is about what came next, how an entire country woke up at the end of the summer to face one of the most devastating natural events most would ever experience. The story we are about to tell, however, is an affirmative one. The country came back quickly and fully, and the courage and determination of its people and their leaders in that recovery have been, by many measures, exceptional. It thus offers a rare account for anyone facing big risks on how best to embrace resilience and bounce back.

Chile is located on the western side of South America, bordering the Pacific Ocean and Argentina. Twice the area of California, Chile extends 2,600 miles from tip to toe—double the distance from New York to Miami—though it averages just 110 miles east to west. Its great vertical extension comes with a near perfect but very unwelcome alignment along the world's "ring of fire." Rimming the Pacific Ocean, this great semicircle is the most earthquake-active line in the world, running up the spine of Chile through the western United States, across Alaska, and then down through Japan. In other words, what happened in Chile could one day occur in the United States, Japan, or almost anywhere else on the ring.

To many readers, Chile still remains best known for having suffered almost two decades of General Augusto Pinochet's dictatorship in the 1970s and 1980s after the violent coup of 1973. Yet Chile is a very different country today from what its past might suggest. Democracy was restored in 1990, and the country had become one of the fastest growing economies in Latin America. It boasted a market-based economy with a broad and generous social safety net. In striking contrast to the United States and many other Western economies, it ran a surplus rather than being deeply in debt. And of special importance for dealing with a national crisis, while Chilean presidents can serve multiple four-year terms, they cannot serve two consecutive terms. As such they can focus their time and energy on the tasks at hand without having to worry about the consequences for their re-election, though of course it may also unduly shorten their task horizons to what can be achieved in the four years that they have.

The February 27, 2010, seismic event, now widely referenced in Chile as F27, was not just another earthquake. It released five hundred times more energy than the earthquake in Haiti six weeks before. F27 was a monster event, the sixth greatest earthquake ever recorded on earth.

Although the Chile earthquake did not retain international news attention for long, it devastated schools, hospitals, roads, homes, and businesses across a vast swath of the country's midsection, paralyzing the country for weeks. The economic damage proved massive: losses were 18 percent of the country's gross domestic product (GDP), nearly a fifth of what the entire country produces in a year. That would be the equivalent to $2.7 trillion in economic losses in the United States, more than twenty times greater than that inflicted by Hurricane Katrina in 2005, America's most costly disaster to date. Recalling how poorly the recovery from Katrina was managed in New Orleans despite days of advance warning, one can only wonder how an event twenty times more devastating than Katrina could be managed.[1]

There is a final but central element to the story, and that is the peculiar timing of the event. The F27 earthquake came just days before a change in national government, with Sebastián Piñera soon to take the presidential sash from president Michelle Bachelet. The president-elect was awakened that night like so many others in Chile: "All the communications were gone," he said, "but I understood immediately that it had been a very huge earthquake."

Late that same night, the incoming president met with his cabinet-to-be at campaign headquarters to map out a path to recovery. "We immediately realized that we had a huge task," recalled the future interior minister. Since the election of January 17, the president and his ministers-to-be had been focusing on plans to revive the economy. Now, just twelve days before inauguration, they faced a giant unanticipated calamity.

For most countries around the world, it might take years, if not decades, to recover from such massive devastation. But six weeks later, all of Chile's schoolchildren had returned to classes. By the end of the year, Chile's economy was back on track, delivering a strong 6 percent annual growth rate at a time when the world economy was still reeling from the 2008–9 financial crisis.

A TWO-PART RECIPE FOR AN IMPROBABLE COMEBACK

The early years of the twenty-first century have come with an unprecedented series of crises and catastrophes. These events have triggered a growing interest among all of us—citizens, business leaders, and government officials—in finding better ways to prepare for catastrophic risks and discovering ways to bounce back when rare but high-impact hazards become a terrible reality.

Because Chile's management of the historic F27 disaster and its leadership of the recovery years are not widely appreciated outside the country, we have compiled this account. Chile's experience offers a compelling and tangible tutorial on the leadership actions required of those facing big risks anywhere.

We want to know how Chile prepared and responded. What were the key drivers of its unlikely comeback? Who took charge, and how did they lead? How did past experience factor into their actions? Our focus is on Chile's national resilience, and we ask how the country's leaders—in government, business, and civil society—made their recovery decisions and then implemented them.

The country mobilized to help the injured and bury the dead. It then turned to repairing hospitals, reopening schools, and rebuilding homes. But Chile did not stop with the immediate rebuilding. Its national leadership, spearheaded by a doggedly determined president, insisted that the country think longer term, that its comeback go well beyond what the country had in place prior to the earthquake.

Moreover, Chile's comeback was in keeping with the country's deeply rooted institutional values that have placed exceptional emphasis on the effectiveness and fairness of the state, at least since the end of the military dictatorship from 1973 to 1990. Indeed, Chile's national leadership would not have had nearly the impact it had after the earthquake without the country's institutional backbone, the values that placed longer-term objectives and collective fairness ahead of short-run concerns and parochial interests. We find that a two-part recipe proved vital for the comeback, a mutually reinforcing combination of *able national leadership* and *strong institutional practices*. Each depended upon the other. At the core of both was strategic and deliberative thinking that transcended the tactical and intuitive thinking that can dominate much of our everyday conduct.

In what follows, we will learn about a new administration that took charge just days after the 8.8 magnitude quake, committed to rebuilding a better country without busting the national budget. We will witness an administration that capitalized on a preexisting set of institutional practices and partnered with private and nonprofit enterprises to achieve a turnaround that everyone wanted, even if short-term sacrifices were required. Chile's recovery is a story of how political leaders worked with civil society and market forces both to assist those in need and to restore national growth. It is an account of how one country with a checkered past has now come to be considered one of the most stable and capable in Latin America. Many developing countries might have stalled or gone into reverse after a calamity of this scale. Chile shifted into high gear.

The three of us were invited by the nation's president, Sebastián Piñera, to take a close look at Chile's recovery. His government opened its doors and records to our research team. The president, his cabinet ministers, and others gave freely of their time to numerous discussions. We traveled with the president to the earthquake zone and gathered data from a host of sources in Chile and internationally. We were also guided and informed by our ongoing work with the World Economic Forum's annual *Global Risks Report* and its Global Agenda Council on Catastrophic Risks.[2]

In focusing on the leadership decisions that defined Chile's response to the F27 earthquake, we sought to understand what worked well and what fell short, with an emphasis on the former. We have found, from working on risk management and leadership development with a variety of companies and countries, that positive actions can be much more effectively instructive than missteps or shortcomings. Our purpose is to extract enduring lessons for leaders and managers elsewhere. We do not intend to convey an overly optimistic account—or an overly pessimistic account for that matter—of what the president and his administration did. Rather, we seek to learn from their experiences and transmit lessons for others to apply in preparing for and reacting to crises.

Having worked with a number of government officials and business leaders in the United States and other countries, we believe that Chile's lessons are broadly applicable to a wide range of organizations and national settings. In recovering from the massive earthquake and tsunami in Japan in March 2011, from Hurricane Sandy hitting the northeastern United States in October 2012, or from Typhoon Haiyan's devastation of the central Philippines in November 2013, for example, we believe that the leaders in those countries could have usefully turned for instructive guidance to Chile's leadership experience in the wake of F27.

But this is not just a story about dealing with natural calamities. Large-scale catastrophes and extreme events of many kinds have been on the rise in recent years—from technological meltdowns and environmental disasters to financial crises, disease pandemics, international terrorism, and cyber threats. It is thus an auspicious moment to seek ideas and guidance from leaders who have already faced and rebounded from a catastrophic event. If their experiences can be appreciated and the transferable principles extricated, leaders in other countries will be in a much better position to prepare, confront, and overcome their own unthinkable calamities in the future and to make a difference for the global community.

Part I

TAKING CHARGE
TO LEAD A COMEBACK

1 TWELVE DAYS BEFORE ENTERING THE PRESIDENTIAL OFFICE

The reality of my life has changed.
—Interior Minister-Designate Rodrigo Hinzpeter

"Oh my God, it's not stopping," recalled a *Time* magazine reporter in Santiago who had been in a bar when the earth started moving. Glass shards everywhere, patrons were clambering out the shattered windows, others rushed for the door.[1]

Visiting Santiago from Oregon, Sylvia Dostal had booked a room on the twenty-third floor of the capital's Marriott Hotel. "I had been in earthquakes before," including the deadly 6.9-magnitude event in 1989 near San Francisco, "but this was different," she said. "The building was swaying AND moving up and down!"[2]

Near the epicenter, 210 miles south, Osvaldo González was on a river island with dozens of relatives when the earthquake happened. He began shuttling family members off the island in a boat, as did his cousin, Osvaldo Gomez, with another boat. But then, after several successful crossings, recalled González, "I never imagined what was about to happen." A thirty-foot wave surged up the river just as he was momentarily at the shore, but his cousin was still midstream when it hit. González saw his cousin's boat wafted high on the crest of the enormous swell.[3]

Karina Murga had been partying in a nightclub in the nearby city of Constitución: "It was about 3:20 in the morning. We were close to the beach, celebrating a cousin's birthday," she said, "when the ground started to shake. At first it was soft, but then it got strong, so strong we couldn't hold ourselves up." Some yelled, "Tremor, tremor!" Others, "Earthquake, tsunami!" When Murga emerged outside, she recalled, "You couldn't see anything. There was a cloud of earth—horrible—you had to yell people's names to know where they were, because you couldn't see them."

Katrina Murga's six-year-old daughter, Carla, had been left for the night with friends. "I yelled, 'My daughter! My daughter! I need my daughter! I have to go get my daughter!' Like a crazy woman, 'My daughter!'" Murga would soon reunite with her unscathed six-year-old. Osvaldo González would never find his cousin.[4]

THE PRESIDENT AND INTERIOR-MINISTER-TO-BE

Although more than two hundred miles from the epicenter, the capital city's shaking also aroused the president-elect's interior minister-designate, Rodrigo Hinzpeter. He and the new president would be taking power in less than two weeks. But as the first signs of the calamity's enormity became shockingly evident, the future minister quickly appreciated that the new administration's leadership of the country was about to be profoundly tested and redefined. It would have to address a whole new order of very unexpected business.

The designated minister of the interior and public safety (as Rodrigo Hinzpeter would be formally entitled)—the premier member of the presidential cabinet who would become vice president if the president were abroad or incapacitated—talked with his wife, checked on his three children, and attempted to call his mother. Telephone lines were dead or jammed, but after many redials, he found that his family was well and safe. Yet he also soon realized that tens of thousands of other families were suffering, and that any return to the anticipated governing path was not in the cards: "The reality of my life has changed." Hinzpeter's portfolio included public order and internal security, direction of all domestic policies, and oversight of regional authorities throughout the country. Every element would be affected.

Hinzpeter raced across the near-empty streets of Santiago at 4:30 a.m. to the party's campaign headquarters, where the future government had been readying itself ever since its victory at the polls on January 17. Plans for stimulating growth and creating jobs had been on the table yesterday, but today they would be swept aside for the urgency at hand. "We were waiting to start the government," recalled the future minister. "In a few days the government team would have to start working, so from the very beginning we had no time to lose" and "we had to understand what happened to the country."

The interior-minister-to-be had managed to learn a little about the country's condition before exiting his home, before all power had been severed. But now in the car, with a working radio, as he sped across the darkened capital he was hearing spot reports indicating that the destruction was severe and extensive. "I began to understand that it was a really big mess," he recalled, "more than I imagined when I was at home." Panicked citizens were already in long queues at gasoline stations, he saw, though to no avail, since the station pumps themselves were powerless.

Hinzpeter called the president-elect to compare what little data they had gleaned so far; they agreed to meet later that morning at an agency of the Ministry of Interior, the National Emergency Office, abbreviated as ONEMI (La Oficina Nacional de Emergencia del Ministerio del Interior—National Office of Emergency of the Interior Ministry). Similar in charter to the U.S. Federal Emergency Management Agency (FEMA), ONEMI was responsible for responding to large-scale national crises.

The soon-to-be-inaugurated president and interior minister entered the National Emergency Center at 11 a.m. The enormity of the moment was becoming all too evident. "The earthquake had been huge," recalled the president. "It had affected six regions where more than 70 percent of the Chilean population lived, and the consequences in terms of life had been very huge." He added, "We already knew that more than 500 people had been killed and that the economic damage had also been massive."

Sebastián Piñera and Rodrigo Hinzpeter returned to their campaign headquarters both to consult and to instruct the incoming cabinet, even though technically none of them had official responsibility yet. The president asked the minister-of-finance-designate, Felipe Larraín, to forecast the total costs of reconstructing the country; the future housing minister, Magdalena Matte, to estimate the number of homes destroyed; the future minister-of-public-works-elect, Hernán de Solminihac, to assess the damage to public infrastructure; and the future minister of the presidency, Cristián Larroulet, to look at the legal tools used with prior earthquakes to finance the reconstruction.

Rodrigo Hinzpeter decided that they would have to see the impact of the quake for themselves. "The country was in a very bad situation and many people were suffering," he recalled, but driving to the most affected region, several hundred miles to the south, would be impossible. The country's only north-south artery, the legendary Pan-American Highway, had been completely severed. Invoking for the first time the fact that they were the incoming administration, slated for investiture on March 11, Hinzpeter called one governmental office after another to borrow a helicopter—only to learn that all had been committed. He finally obtained a small helicopter from the Policia de Investigaciones (the FBI equivalent).

Landing at 3 p.m. in the devastated town of Talcahuano—where 80 percent of the residents had been left homeless—the president-elect and minister-designate drove along the waterfront and then down a main avenue. They were stunned by what they found—but also deeply moved by what they learned. "We were completely in shock, but our shock was smaller than the shock of the persons in the street," recalled Hinzpeter. Even then, the residents' concerns for the plight of others, not just themselves, were remarkably in evidence. "People believe other people suffer much more than they do," Hinzpeter found. Although traumatized, inhabitants were asking about the event's impact elsewhere, pressing to know how others had fared, dwelling less on their own plight. The cause of the disaster itself was not yet clear to many. "What happened?" some implored the president. "Was it a bomb or an earthquake?"

It soon became plain to the incoming officials what residents needed most at the moment: "Clear leadership that explained to the people, short and easy, what happened to the country," the minister-designate concluded, "not just what is happening to them but also what is happening to the other people. People want to know what happened to the *rest* of the country." So the president-elect and the nation's current and future leaders would have to focus, Hinzpeter resolved, on providing "immediate, simple, short information" about both the local area and the entire country.

The incoming officials also began to anticipate what else might follow—in the eyes of those most affected. "People need to know if they are likely to face new dangers in the immediate future," recalled Hinzpeter, "and how they will receive emergency aid." Residents sought face-to-face guidance and reassurance. And as the scale of the disaster unfolded, the minister-designate recalled, "People need to see their leaders hands-on."

Sebastián Piñera and Rodrigo Hinzpeter then traveled to the regional capital city of Concepción, one of the hardest hit of all, where they stumbled on one of the most astonishing products of the calamity. The Alto Río building on Avenida Los Carrera, a main thoroughfare, had completely toppled. The earthquake had turned this fifteen-story condominium—just a year after its opening—from vertical to horizontal. It now lay along a roadway over which it had towered the day before. Most distressing of all to the visitors, appeals for rescue could still be heard from residents trapped in the debris. "When we tried to approach the building and penetrate it," recalled the president-elect, "we heard the cries of the people that were caught there asking for help."

A passing fireman recognized the two horrified observers and urged them to call in a canine search-and-rescue team from Santiago. Hinzpeter contacted the national agency he was soon to oversee but was informed by the incumbent interior minister himself that no canine teams could be made available. Piñera and Hinzpeter would later learn that some of the residents whose cries they had heard that afternoon were among those who did not survive. Eight people perished inside the ruins, the last body not finally extricated for nearly two weeks.

The impact of the personal stocktaking was one of both anguish and action, and as the president-elect and the future minister flew back to Santiago that evening, they concluded that the first order of business was to mobilize governmental assets not only for rescuing trapped survivors but also for restoring basic necessities. Supermarkets had been destroyed, water conduits were severed, and hospitals had collapsed. A rising desperation was already evident in the streets, and some would turn to looting in the hours ahead.

"The most important dialogue that we had" on the helicopter flight home, Hinzpeter recalled, "was our conviction that the city was out of control, so there was a need to call the army to get control of the city that night." Darkness was approaching on the first day of the disaster, and yet there seemed to be no public authority in the streets. The future minister concluded, "You have to make an immediate assessment of what is the reality on site, because otherwise you make bad decisions since you don't have the information. You have to guarantee the basic needs of the people immediately, which are security, food, health, and housing."

Meeting with his incoming cabinet that same evening in Santiago, Sebastián Piñera plunged into national recovery. Yet he would do so, he pledged, without relaxing any of his campaign pledges to jump-start the economy. He concurred with his incoming interior minister's appraisal of the herculean task ahead but quickly added that he was not going to set aside any of his platform promises to spur growth and generate jobs. Still suffering from the 2008–9 world economic crisis, the country required a public stimulus. "The Chilean economy was in very bad shape," recalled the president. "The rate of growth was very low. The job creation capacity was very low. The unemployment rate was very high. The investment rate as a percent of GDP was falling down. Productivity was negative. Poverty was increasing."

The minister-designate countered that at least they ought to consider scaling back some of their campaign promises, but the president-elect declared that he would accept no compromises. Hinzpeter pushed back again: "I was thinking that we would have to rebalance our program." But the president replied, "Minister, you are wrong, we have more work, we will not change our program, and I will tell that to the nation in the next few days." The new administration would stand by its campaign commitments to restore the country to a 6 percent annual growth, create a million jobs, increase an investment rate of 20 percent of GNP to 28 percent, and reduce poverty.

The president-elect decided to embrace two orders of business, one well established in the campaign, the other forced by the natural calamity. He would pursue what had been promised before the earthquake—but now also what had been required by the earthquake. "We knew that we would have to face very difficult situations," said the president, citing three simultaneous winds all blowing in the wrong direction: an international financial crisis stemming from the collapse of Lehman and AIG, the stagnant economy, and now the February 27 catastrophe.

The president-elect decided and declared that evening that the country would fully "recover our growth capacity," and then he and his lieutenants set about analyzing how they could achieve both goals at the same time. For the immediate recovery, they would mandate themselves to restore essential services—civil order, water, and electricity—within a week; social services—including public schools—by winter's start on June 21; and all else by their four-year regime's end. One week, four months, and four years: "By March 11, 2014," the president contended, "the reconstruction process will be over."

To jump-start the recovery, Piñera raised a host of questions for himself and the cabinet members. "What do I have to accomplish? How can I get there? What are the phases? What are the resources that we need?" Most important, "How can I fund it, and who would be responsible for what?" Creating a strategy for addressing these challenges that very evening, he assigned responsibilities to specific cabinet members, and then made clear to all that each would have to deliver. "Look, we have to do it," declared the president. "We cannot fail!"

THE RECIPE FOR RECOVERY

In formulating both a near-term plan and long-term strategy for overcoming and then transcending the calamity, the new administration's actions offer an instructive look at how those with greatest responsibility for a country, company, or community can best attack the extraordinary challenges of coming fully back from calamity and instituting more safeguards against future disasters. Chapters 1 to 3 constitute the first part of our account, "Taking Charge to Lead a Comeback." Chapter 2, "One of the Most Intense Events Ever Recorded," characterizes the scale and magnitude of the earthquake. To appreciate the recovery process, Chapter 3, "First Order of Business," offers a portrait of the comeback.

In Part 2, "How They Did It," we frame the key concepts, leadership characteristics, and actions taken to accelerate Chile's recovery from the earthquake. "Frameworks for Action" (Chapter 4) focuses on the defining capacities of leadership and national institutions. We give special consideration to the importance of thinking deliberatively and acting strategically, and formulate operating principles that tie several tiers of leadership together and are of special concern during a crisis.

In "Presidential Leadership" (Chapter 5), we characterize those personal capacities that the newly installed president brought to the reconstruction process. Here we focus on Sebastián Piñera's decision to take charge, to build a team with a host of management skills but comparatively little political experience, and to set forward unequivocal directives—his mission intent—for his top lieutenants.

"Tiered Leadership" (Chapter 6) assesses how other cabinet ministers executed the president's strategic directives. Focusing on the actions of the ministers of Housing, Public Works, Health, and Interior—four of the ministries with greatest responsibility for the country's comeback—we witness how vital their detailed execution of the president's strategy proved to be, and how the president assiduously worked with each to ensure that his mission's intent was in fact fully executed through them.

We see in "Financing Recovery" (Chapter 7) that funding the comeback would prove an enormous challenge, since the F27 event came with a price tag of $30 billion, the equivalent of $2.7 trillion loss in the United States when measured in terms of percentage of GDP. A price tag of that magnitude had not been anticipated, nor were reserves available to cover it. Through deft management of the country's budget, the finance minister, backed by the president, drew on a portfolio of actions, notably new temporary tax revenues, budget reallocations, and utilization of a national copper fund. Markedly absent was significant new indebtedness, contrary to the way the U.S. government has financed all its most recent disasters. As a result of the Ministry of Finance's sound strategy, Chile's international credit rating did not suffer, in sharp contrast to severe downgrades by Standard and Poor's and Moody's of Japan's rating after its March 2011 earthquake. In fact, Chile's financial management of the disaster received high marks from rating agencies and the International Monetary Fund.

Fundamental to Chile's swift comeback were insurance payouts remitted by private insurers backed by reinsurers (the insurers of insurers) outside of Chile, as we report in "Insurance Payouts for Recovery" (Chapter 8). The significant amount of earthquake insurance coverage and rapid payout of claims provided a swift influx of capital to stimulate recovery and push national growth. In the end, more than a quarter of the cost of Chile's recovery was borne entirely by private insurance and reinsurance, similar to the fraction covered by the insurance industry in the United States after Hurricane Sandy in 2012.

A set of major companies, foreign governments, and international agencies also stepped forward with significant in-kind or cash contributions, as detailed in "Private Giving for Recovery" (Chapter 9). Although estimated to be less than $1 billion in total value, and although relatively modest against the $30 billion damage to the country, we find that these outside sources provided important supplements to funding provided by public agencies and private insurers in Chile.

With sufficient financial resources for the comeback, a take-charge attitude cascaded through the administration's ranks, but that brought unanticipated consequences, described in "Execution and Expectations" (Chapter 10). With limited public experience in the cabinet, the nation's leadership produced soaring hopes for near-term timetables that it could not meet.

We see in "Vulnerability and Readiness" (Chapter 11) that Chile's past experience with seismic events has resulted in a set of national institutions and cultural mores in place to make the country resilient in the wake of such events. In other words, a basis for Sebastián Piñera's leadership of the recovery actually predated his presidency. Indeed, we find that it was the distinctive combination of national leadership and institutional tradition that helped produce the country's comeback from the F27 calamity.

Just as the national government's financing of the recovery was made far easier by virtue of a strong private insurance market, the state-directed recovery was also supplemented and expedited by nongovernmental organizations, the focus of "Civil Action" (Chapter 12). Here we see the importance of three such organizations to the nation's recovery.

The third and final part of the book, "What They—and We—Learned," draws out the implications of Chile's extraordinary comeback for leaders of other countries and organizations. In "Long-Term Disaster Recovery" (Chapter 13), we step back to give special attention to the role of deliberative thinking and strategic action. Although some narrowly conceived and short-term decisions were taken by the nation's leaders, the president and his ministers worked hard to incorporate broadly defined long-term solutions.

An early application of what the nation's leaders had learned from the F27 event came just five months later, as documented in "Rescuing Thirty-three Miners" (Chapter 14). A cave-in had trapped thirty-three miners some two thousand feet below the surface in northern Chile, attracting the world media's attention for weeks. Sebastián Piñera and his cabinet would be tested yet again, though now with the F27 experience under their belts. They were already steeped in strategic thinking and deliberative decision-making even though complete recovery from the earthquake still had several years to go. Here we find that the joint leadership of the president and minister of mines would make the ultimate difference for the miners trapped for more than two months. We witness many of the same leadership capacities that accounted for the F27 comeback, further underscoring the actions required for taking charge whatever the disaster or crisis.

In the concluding chapter, "Leadership Dispatches" (Chapter 15), we identify the most enduring ideas and principles that have emerged from the account that can prove useful in entirely different settings. Conceptual thinking about risk and response is essential for those most responsible for risk management in countries, companies, and communities. Chile and the Piñera administration have thus furnished a compelling test and illustration of what can really matter in the wake of a calamity. We conclude with a set of leadership principles from their experience for those who are facing large-scale risks of all types and who seek to forge far-reaching recoveries when extreme threats become a terrible reality.

2 ONE OF THE MOST INTENSE EVENTS EVER RECORDED

The earthquake was so massive that it moved the country and even the
planet: Santiago shifted west by 11 inches, the Earth tilted by 3 inches.

When the 8.8-magnitude earthquake devastated Chile on February 27,
2010, world attention was still riveted on recovery from the massive earthquake that had devastated Haiti on January 12. That 7.0 magnitude event
had flattened the capital, Port-au-Prince. Destruction was everywhere, but
local leadership almost nowhere, and the international community rushed
in to assist the rescue, aid the injured, and shelter the homeless.

Then, just six weeks later, the far stronger event rocked Chile for 100
seconds. The epicenter was just 65 miles off Concepción, the country's
third largest urban concentration, and 210 miles southwest of its capital,
Santiago. The Haiti event released energy the equivalent of 480 kilotons of
TNT, enormous itself, but the Chilean quake released the equivalent of 240
megatons, 500 times more energy. It was felt by 12 million inhabitants of
the nation's 17 million.

The F27 earthquake was indeed so massive that it actually moved the
country, and even the planet. Santiago shifted 11 inches to the west, Chile's
coastline rose, its central valley sank, and the Earth's axis tilted 3 inches.
During the following weeks, Chile experienced 1,300 aftershocks of magnitude 4 or more, 19 of them spiking up to a magnitude of 6.0 to 6.9, nearly
the magnitude of Haiti's devastating earthquake.[1]

SHIFTING INTO HIGH GEAR

Days before the event, Claudio Seebach, who ran a think-tank at the
University of Chile, had taken his children for a vacation in Chile's Lake

District some five hundred miles south of the capital. It was an area of active volcanoes, and when the earthquake rocked his wooden house, he initially thought that it must be a nearby eruption. But the power outage implied otherwise, and he soon confirmed by car radio that it was an earthquake. Later that day he drove to a wedding nearby, and found that a third of the invited guests never arrived. The following day, Seebach set out for Santiago—normally an eight-hour drive up the nation's arterial expressway—that became a twenty-one-hour ordeal as he was repeatedly forced to maneuver around road debris and downed overpasses.

Joining the president-elect's office later that week, with responsibility for interministerial coordination, Seebach attended a two-hour briefing by the president-elect. Citing his shocking personal visit to Concepción, Sebastián Piñera vowed that his administration would first work to restore essential services, to "get people up and running," and to do so quickly. But presaging the broader agenda as well, the incoming president told Seebach and his colleagues who would soon be running Chile's White House, La Moneda, that the event should also be seen as an opportunity to make the country more resilient, more prepared for the next big one. Still, it was already evident to all that this had been a very big one itself.

A MASSIVE CALAMITY

Seismologists often sum up the power of an earthquake with a single indicator, the moment magnitude, abbreviated as Mw, representing the amount of energy released. This measure builds on the more familiar Richter scale developed in the 1930s, but scientists have found the Mw to be more indicative of an earthquake's full impact.

Other important characteristics of an earthquake are ground acceleration, specific location, and surface depth. The 1994 earthquake in Northridge, California, for instance, one of the most devastating recent earthquakes in the United States, was only a 6.7 magnitude event, but it displayed one of the highest ground accelerations ever recorded, and that accounted for much of its destructive power.

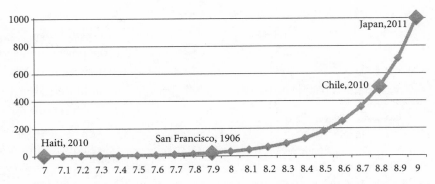

Fig. 2.1. Energy Released by Earthquakes of Varying Magnitudes (standardized at 1 for a 7.0 Mw earthquake). Data from U.S. Geological Survey, 2014.

In comparing Chile's 8.8 Mw event with Haiti's 7.0, it is important to appreciate that the moment magnitude scale is not linear. While these magnitude numbers can seem relatively close, they in fact characterize earthquakes of very different destructive powers. The factor that captures the difference in energy released is thirty-two: for every unit of increase on the magnitude scale—such as moving from 7.0 to 8.0—nearly thirty-two times more energy is released. The 8.8 earthquake in Chile in 2010 thus delivered 501 times more power than the 7.0 event in Haiti in 2010, and it emitted nearly half the energy recorded for Japan's catastrophic earthquake of 2011 (Figure 2.1).

Compared with San Francisco's terrible 7.8 earthquake of 1906, whose resulting fire destroyed 80 percent of the city, Chile's earthquake released thirty-two times more energy. It was the sixth greatest earthquake worldwide since 1950, as seen in Table 2.1.

F27 had a nationwide impact, with more than two-thirds of Chile's citizens experiencing some pulsation. "It was like we were being shaken around in a box," reported Claudia Rosario, a twenty-seven-year-old receptionist in Temuco, some 170 miles south of the epicenter. "It came in waves and lasted so long," recalled Santiago housekeeper Dolores Cuevas, 185 miles north of the epicenter. "We kept worrying that it was getting stronger, like a terrifying Hollywood movie." A driver who abandoned his car on a wrecked highway thought that he had blown a tire. "But then I saw the highway

Table 2.1. The World's Ten Most Intense Earthquakes since 1950

Rank	Location	Date	Moment Magnitude	Estimated Fatalities
1	Valdivia, Chile	May 22, 1960	9.5	5,700
2	Prince William Sound, Alaska, USA	March 28, 1964	9.2	125
3	Off the western coast of Sumatra, Indonesia	December 26, 2004	9.1	230,000+
4	Off the coast of Tōhoku, Japan	March 11, 2011	9.0	19,848
5	Kamchatka, Russia	November 4, 1952	9.0	2,300
6	Off the coast of the Maule region, Chile	February 27, 2010	8.8	533
7	Off the coast of Ecuador	January 31, 1960	8.8	1,000
8	Rat Islands, Aleutian Islands, Alaska, USA	February 4, 1965	8.7	Unknown
9	Northern Sumatra, Indonesia	March 28, 2005	8.6	1,303
10	Assam and Tibet	August 15, 1950	8.6	780

Source: Data from U.S. Geological Survey, 2013; Centre for Research on the Epidemiology of Disasters, 2014.

moving like it was a piece of paper and I realized it was something much worse." Tremors were felt as far away as Peru and Argentina. Walkways collapsed at Santiago's main airport, and domestic air services did not come back fully for four months.[2]

The ensuing tsunami damaged not only the Chilean oceanfront—waves crested at forty feet in some areas—but also caused destruction on the California coastline and across the Pacific Ocean from New Zealand to Japan. Some 420 miles off the coast of Chile, the tsunami struck the Juan Fernández Islands—also known as the "Robinson Crusoe" islands after Daniel Defoe's famous novel—with a crest of 150 feet. "Although the earthquake itself was not felt, later there was a series of waves that got bigger and bigger," recalled an eyewitness, air pilot Fernando Avaria. Although a warning sounded for the main town of San Juan Bautista, the surging sea killed three in the town and swept away four.[3]

Juan de la Cruz Moraga, a fisherman in Pelluhue Bay, 120 miles north of the epicenter, described the moment:

> When I was a young boy, my father told me that when the water looks like it is about to boil, you have to get out, because it is a tsunami, for sure. Little bubbles start to form, kind of like a school of sardines passing by.

Luckily that night a huge moon was out, lighting the way for us, just like daytime. At first the ocean looked like it was being held up by floodgates, and when they opened, a wall of water was upon us and it grew from one moment to the next, sweeping everything away. Then the wave came. From far away you could see a dark line that turned into a black cliff that advanced towards us. When the tide went back out you could see the same rock clusters where we used to fish for red conger and you could see the ocean floor.[4]

Most of Chile's electrical grid shut down within a minute of the earthquake to prevent electrical fires, affecting more than 90 percent of the public, and much of the country's telephone, mobile phone, and Internet services went dark. The earthquake and tsunami displaced 800,000 people from their homes, and 2 million experienced at least some residential damage. More than forty-five hundred schools were severely damaged, leaving more than a million children without classrooms.

The earthquake affected virtually every facet of Chile's life. During the month after the quake, for instance, the flow of visitors from abroad compared with a year earlier declined by nearly a quarter, falling from 246,000 in March 2009 to 193,000 in March 2010 just after the earthquake, and the foreign flow remained depressed for another six months. Sixty-nine percent of the municipalities suffered damage from the quake.

In the six regions closest to the event, the earthquake left more than one in twelve housing units uninhabitable. In the Maule region, the hardest hit, the shaking destroyed or severely damaged 21 percent of residents' dwellings. In all, the event affected more than 370,000 housing units, predictably hitting hardest those constructed of adobe—a soft mix of clay, sand, and straw.

Indicative of the event's brute strength, the earthquake tipped over the newly completed fifteen-story Alto Río condominium in the center of Concepción—the building that had been visited by Sebastián Piñera and Rodrigo Hinzpeter just hours after the event. The building contained 113 units, and fortunately it was only partially occupied at the moment of the earthquake. "The building started to shake about 30 seconds after the earthquake occurred," recalled one of the startled residents, Gunther Bohn.

On surviving the toppling, he dryly added, "I could see the ceiling was vertical."[5]

Opened in 2009, the Alto Rio building had adhered to Chile's tough 1996 building code, with reinforced concrete throughout designed to resist anticipated vertical and horizontal stresses. It appears that no single cause resulted in its failure, but rather that four separate structural shortcomings combined to do so. In total, the F27 event severely damaged more than fifty multistoried reinforced-concrete buildings across the country, four collapsing completely.[6]

Of the nation's 190 hospitals, the earthquake impaired 118, inflicting high damage on 40 and making 17 completely unusable. It closed 171 surgical units and more than 4,000 hospital beds—70 percent occupied at the time. In the Biobío province, one of the areas most affected by the quake, a later survey of its seven hospitals found that F27 had closed their emergency rooms on average for five days, operating facilities for six days, and dialysis services for more than two weeks—just at the moment when many of those services were most needed. These hospitals, ranging from 26 to 433 beds, had served a population of 500,000 residents (Table 2.2).[7]

The hospitals maintained stand-by electricity and water supplies, but even with such backups they were nonetheless forced to evacuate many patients. The largest of the province's seven facilities, the 433-bed Los Angeles hospital, for instance, squeezed all patients and staff from a now uninhabitable older wing into a less damaged newer one, shutting some 40 percent of the hospital's capacity. To allow for the contraction, hospitals imposed a reverse triage: administrators sent the least-ill patients to their homes with medications, instructions, and the promise of home-visits by hospital staff.

Medical teams improvised of necessity in a host of other ways. All of the hospitals had lost their telephone and Internet services, with no means for contacting off-site patients, employees, pharmacies, or other health facilities. Staff members at one asked local ambulance crews to share their two-way radios, which had remained functional. Ad hoc creative solutions were evident in other areas as well. When one hospital's water failed because of damage to a backup pump, a resourceful employee jerry-rigged a workaround with a pump from the boiler room.[8]

Table 2.2. Damage to Seven Hospitals in Biobío Province

Percentage of Medical Areas Damaged	
Elevators	75%
Radiology	57%
Inpatient area	43%
Laboratory area	43%
Outpatient area	28%
Operating rooms	25%
Average Days without Service	
Dialysis	>14
Surgery	6
Rehabilitation	5.5
Sterilization	5.3
Pediatric	5
Outpatient clinic	5
Emergency department	5
% of Hospitals without Utility Service	
Electricity	100
Telephone	100
Water	71

Source: Data from Mitrani-Reiser et al., 2012.

The national government arranged to distribute food supplies where stores and wholesalers had been knocked off line. It purchased the entire stock of local supermarkets at prevailing prices and then arranged for the army to hand out the food for free, helping to ensure that communities received essentials, that prices were held in check, and that storeowners did not suffer significant losses.

A SURPRISINGLY LOW CASUALTY COUNT

Despite the near-record intensity of the F27 quake, the government reported in January 2011 a final death toll that was not nearly as high as might have been: 533 perished and 18 missing. About half lost their lives from collapsing structures, such as the Alto Río building; the other half

Table 2.3. Major Earthquakes in Haiti, Chile, Japan, and New Zealand, 2010–11

	Haiti Jan. 12, 2010	Chile Feb. 27, 2010	Japan Mar. 11, 2011	New Zealand Feb. 22, 2011
Earthquake Event				
Magnitude (Mw)	7.0	8.8	9.0	6.3
Estimated deaths	223,000	533	15,883	181
Economic damage in $ billions	8.1	30	309	15
Economic damage as percent of GDP	117%	18%	5.6%	10.5%
Pace of incoming international aid during the first four days ($/hour)	107,812	16,297	260,417	60,417
Pre-event				
Population (millions)	9.0	17.1	128.1	4.3
GDP per Capita	$1,338	$14,340	$35,500	$28,400
Population Below Poverty Line (%)	80	18	16	15
Funding relief and reconstruction ($ millions)				
National government	950	9,000	198,000	8,500
Insurers	108	8,000	35,000	12,000
Foreign aid: cash, in-kind, and pledges	4,052	125	17,100	2,668
Governments and multinational agencies	2,941	51	12,500	971
Private individuals and organizations	1,111	74	4,600	1,697

Source: Data from Ballesteros, 2013.

were killed by the high waves. One of the greatest of the losses came on a low-lying isle in the mouth of the Maule River near the seaside resort city of Constitución. Chilean revelers camping on the island of Orrego had been enjoying an end-of-summer festival—Noche Veneciana (Venetian Night)—when the tsunami swept away more than a hundred celebrants.[9]

Whatever the immediate cause of fatalities, Chile's losses were just one six-hundredth of the casualties in Haiti despite the five hundred times greater force of Chile's earthquake. Japan's Tōhoku earthquake left more than 15,000 dead, and New Zealand's Christ Church event, far weaker in magnitude—6.3, compared with 8.8 in Chile—killed 181 (Table 2.3). For one of the largest seismic events in modern history, the number of fatalities in Chile was the lowest recorded except for a massive earthquake in 1964 in the largely uninhabited region of Alaska's Prince William Sound (Table 2.1).

Given the magnitude of F27, far more deaths and disappearances might have been expected, but several factors accounted for the unusually low casualty rate. Most important was Chile's history of severe earthquakes that translated into a well-enforced building code supported by a relatively high level of political accountability and rule of law. A legal provision, for instance, holds builders personally liable for their structures' durability for a decade—a strong incentive to meet the best seismic standards. These and a host of other on-the-ground factors elaborated on in later chapters can be traced to a set of institutional practices that have placed strategic and deliberative thinking at the forefront of public policy.

Some of these institutional practices have emerged from Chile's long history with major earthquakes, a history deriving from its anchoring in the southeast corridor of the ring of fire. Three-quarters of the world's volcanoes are situated on the horseshoe-shaped Pacific Rim extending from Chile to Alaska to Japan to the Philippines and Indonesia, an area that experiences 90 percent of the world's earthquakes. Chile itself counts some five hundred active volcanoes, and it suffered eight earthquakes of magnitude 8.0 or greater since 1900, many of them resulting in large numbers of casualties and significant property damage. However, an earthquake as high as F27's magnitude of 8.8 had not been experienced for half a century.

Another way to appreciate the devastating impact of F27 is to contrast it with the three other most destructive earthquakes during the 2010–11 period, as shown in Table 2.3. The economic damage relative to GDP was far higher in Chile than Japan or New Zealand, though far lower than in Haiti. We also note that the flow of international aid during the first days following the event was lower in Chile than in the other three countries, perhaps the result of donor fatigue after the massive flow of emergency aid into Haiti at nearly the same time. Despite the relatively greater economic damage in Chile than Japan or New Zealand, Chile found itself more on its own.[10]

A ROADMAP FOR RECOVERY

Rescue and reconstruction requires a massive and concerted effort by the national government, but F27 came at a maximally inconvenient moment. The newly elected administration was still twelve days from assuming authority. Although initially without national power, the president-elect and his cabinet nonetheless began to plan recovery informally during the few days before their inauguration on March 11.

The president-elect had concluded straightaway that relief and reconstruction would become a national primacy. From afar, that seemed obvious, but the incoming president had several additional goals. First, Sebastián Piñera insisted that his campaign promise of economic growth and job creation would not be compromised. Second, he required that his government think strategically and act deliberatively so that the nation's comeback would go well beyond its existing condition at the time of the event. Third, he insisted that all of the reconstruction be guided and constrained by the nation's traditions and values. And fourth, he declared that the restoration would have the highest national priority and that it would be completed by the end of his term on March 11, 2014.

3 FIRST ORDER OF BUSINESS

Chile's economic performance in recent years has been impressive. The rebound from the 2009 global financial crisis and the 2010 earthquake was quick and strong.
—International Monetary Fund

After focusing on the most urgent matters of the moment, the new administration set public health as an immediate priority, vaccinating nearly 4 million people in the earthquake region between March and May—winter's flu season was on its way—and reopening nineteen hospitals and eighteen surgical wards. It restored more than 90 percent of the nation's hospital beds within six months of the earthquake.

The nation's communications were restored soon as well. Within three days of F27, a major provider, Compañía General de Electricidad, had reconnected electrical service to 70 percent of its 1.5 million customers in the stricken regions, and within two weeks it had 99.6 percent of its customers back on the grid. Another energy company, Compañía Chilena de Electricidad, with 1.5 million customers in the Santiago region, had power flowing again a day after the earthquake to 85 percent of its customers, and it had restored power to all within eleven days. Landline telephone service was restored within four days to 90 percent of users in and around Santiago. Mobile service had come back within four days to 76 percent in the capital city. Internet providers had restored service to virtually all customers within twenty-four hours.[1]

Perhaps most remarkable was the fact that the government managed to reopen all of its schools—albeit some in very improvised quarters—within six weeks of the disaster. With children back in school during the day, parents found that they could return to work or even help with the recovery.

In making a public commitment to restoring everything within four years, the president asserted the importance of determination, speed, and readiness to cut through bureaucratic cobwebs: "Many people thought that it was absolutely impossible," he said, "and therefore we put together this emergency plan" with the powers of the executive "to move very fast" since "otherwise it would take a long time because in a normal period you have to go through a lot of process." The key, he said, was very quickly to establish a program, a plan: "This is what we're going to do, this is the timetable, and this is the amount of resources that we need to fund it."

The president-elect instructed his cabinet-elect to prioritize attention on the regions most affected and to do so in ways that also engaged stricken residents in the reconstruction with "dignity" and "freedom of choice." The several hundred thousand homes that had been destroyed or damaged were to be rebuilt as quickly as possible—though the rebuilding would have to be respectful of neighborhood networks and local preferences.

The minister of planning, Felipe Kast, offered instructive illustration. Upon taking office, he believed that the government should target those most in need—as judged by those in Santiago. But in time he came to rely increasingly on the judgment of local mayors whose priorities and perceptions he appreciated would vary significantly, town by town. He recognized, consequently, that "you must be willing to allow some suffering," as he learned to trust the differing judgments of local officials. They would decide which families had lost most and were thus highest in priority for relief. Some in the national government were leery that public funds might be improperly diverted for political purposes, but Kast found that mayors proved no less committed to overcoming the suffering, and granting them autonomy to engineer it had the effect of building their trust and customizing their work.

The country's restoration, the president insisted, would proceed apace but also go well beyond a return to what existed prior to the quake: better housing designs and residential arrangements as well as more effective tsunami defenses. Six months following the quake, the government set forward an ambitious multiyear plan—the Concepción Reconstruction Plan—whose goals were to supersede what the country already had in place before the moment of calamity.

NO EASY TASK

The agenda was not going to be easy to implement. Skepticism if not pessimism prevailed at the outset, as thousands were living in postdisaster camps for months until new housing could be reconstructed. Media pressed the government to reconstruct all homes immediately, even if the quality of the rushed construction would suffer. Rebuilding adobe homes would have been responsive to some owners' desires, but their inherent fragility would not be a foundation for long-term seismic resistance. The same went for allowing residents who wanted to rebuild in exactly the same spot, even if a tsunami zone.

ONEMI, the emergency agency, would require extensive overhaul, as would coordination with the navy's oceanographic service and other agencies that carried crisis responsibilities. Only the navy could actually issue a tsunami warning at the time of F27. With authority concentrated in Santiago, local use of emergency resources was slowed and their application sometimes flawed. "There was too much intervention" and "no coordination," complained a resident. Firefighters in one area would mark buildings with a cross if they were redeemable but not yet safe for occupation. But, believing that the mark actually signaled irreparable damage, local officials razed the structures.[2]

Chile depends almost entirely on a long tradition of volunteer firefighters (*bomberos*)—some thirty-eight thousand throughout the country organized into 311 fire station crews—not only for firefighting but also for search and rescue and emergency and medical response. In Concepción, the hardest hit metropolis, a muster point for crews and equipment had been designated for just such an emergency, but with roads and bridges out and looting erupting, many of the firefighters could not reach their assigned meeting point, and no backup plans had been put in place. Equipment in some firehouses could not be used, as the buildings themselves had been severely damaged. The firefighters' protocol called for them first to ensure their own family's safety and then to respond to an emergency, but no protocol had been developed for firefighters already on duty—who unsurprisingly sought to check on their families before turning to their emergency tasks.[3]

CHILE'S ECONOMIC RECOVERY

Despite the enormity of the task, Chile drew largely on its own resources to jump-start the recovery, seeking no financial support from the International Monetary Fund (IMF) or other international agencies. Just five months after the earthquake, it enacted legislation to modify tax and reserve rules over the coming four years to finance the reconstruction. The government benefited from a provision in the constitution that permitted the transfer of 2 percent of each ministerial budget for other purposes during an emergency. Since the earthquake occurred near the beginning of the fiscal year and most of the money had not yet been spent, that latitude proved substantial.

With constitutional and legislative flexibility, the government moved to increase tax revenue by $2.9 billion, reduce tax evasion by $1.3 billion, rebudget $2.9 billion, transfer $600 million from its copper reserve fund, secure $300 million in donations, and obtain $4.5 billion from increased fees and asset sales (see Chapter 7, "Financing Recovery"). The private insurance industry, which had been growing rapidly in Chile, paid out another $8.4 billion in claims for earthquake losses, primarily to businesses and residential structures, more than a quarter of the $30 billion total loss. Of this $8.4 billion, 95 percent was backed by global reinsurers, a record high by international standards (see Chapters 8 and 9).[4]

Chile's economic recovery came relatively swiftly in the view of virtually all outside appraisals. A forecast from a premier U.S. financial institution, Goldman Sachs, just days after the earthquake foresaw as much: "In all, the earthquake will impact the economy during the first half 2010," estimated Goldman Sachs economist Alberto Ramos, "but significant policy flexibility, institutional credibility and the resilience accumulated in recent years should assist Chile in overcoming this tragedy."[5]

External reviews later confirmed what Goldman Sachs had anticipated. A team from the IMF, for example, offered an approving assessment of the government's post-earthquake actions just months later: "Chile's economy had begun to recover when the February 27 earthquake hit," reported the IMF, and the "new administration took a decisive stance to use these challenges as opportunities to push for significant reforms aimed at reconstructing lost infrastructure, restoring fiscal balance and, ultimately, attaining higher potential output growth for Chile." As a result, "Chile is currently on a solid recovery path, with output growing at healthy rates and decreasing unemployment."[6]

An IMF site-visit team a year later affirmed the country's continued comeback: "Chile's economy has recovered rapidly from the global financial crisis and the February 2010 earthquake," the IMF concluded. "Its resilience was underpinned by solid policy frameworks" and "a strong policy response."[7]

The Organisation for Economic Co-operation and Development (OECD), an association of more than thirty of the developed democratic countries in the world, offered a similar favorable report card in 2011, attributing much of Chile's recovery to the government's energetic stance: "The government's approach to emergency and reconstruction was pro-active," and "Chile's management of the earthquake was successful overall."[8]

A university research team reached the same conclusion, reporting that "the national government provided a swift and clear path to recovery and reconstruction." In a comparison of the recovery from the massive earthquakes in Chile, Japan, and New Zealand in 2010–11—those countries' greatest natural disasters of modern times—the researchers found that although the three nations shared relatively stable democratic governments and functioning market economies, Chile stood out among the three for its rapid recovery.[9]

The annual GDP growth in Chile had gone negative in the wake of the financial crisis of 2008, as it had in so many nations, and the country sank

Table 3.1. Annual Growth Rate in Real GDP for Brazil, Chile, Mexico, and U.S., 1994–2012

	1994–2003	2004	2005	2006	2007	2008	2009	2010	2011	2012
Brazil	2.5	5.7	3.2	4.0	6.1	5.2	−0.3	7.5	2.7	0.9
Chile	4.6	6.8	6.3	5.8	5.2	3.1	−0.9	5.7	5.8	5.6
Mexico	2.6	4.0	3.2	5.1	3.2	1.2	−6.0	5.6	3.9	3.6
U.S.	3.3	3.5	3.1	2.7	1.9	−0.3	−3.1	2.4	1.8	2.8

Source: Data from International Monetary Fund, 2012, 2013.

even further in the immediate aftermath of the earthquake. Yet, just a year later, the country's annual growth had bounced back to the 5 to 6 percent range that it had been averaging during the earlier years of the decade and that the new administration had pledged to restore. This growth rate was all the more notable when compared with that of the three largest economies in the Western hemisphere, Brazil, Mexico, and the United States. During the year following the earthquake, Chile's annual expansion stood at 5.8 percent, well exceeding that of the three other economies, whose growth rates registered only 2.7, 3.9, and 1.8 percent, respectively, as seen in Table 3.1. And that disparity was again evident in 2012, suggesting that this was not just a short-term boost from the immediate stimulus in the months that followed the catastrophe in 2010.[10]

EMPLOYMENT, TOURISM, AND TRADE

While the country's overall economic growth was soon back on track, specific components of the economy trended in the same upward direction. Consider just three: employment, tourism, and trade.

Chile's unemployment rate, relatively high but declining at the time of the F27 earthquake, stood at 9.0 percent. Instead of rising in the earthquake's aftermath, with so much of the country's infrastructure in ruins, unemployment actually declined in the months that followed. By the end of 2010, ten months after the event, it had dropped to 7.1 percent. Unemployment a year later inched back up to 7.4 percent, but it then continued

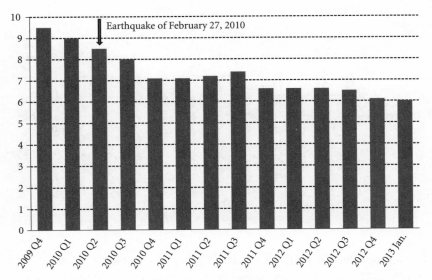

Fig. 3.1. Percentage of the Workforce Unemployed in Chile, 2009–13. Data from Government of Chile, 2013.

to decline, and by early 2013 it was only 6.0 percent (Figure 3.1). Experience from other disasters shows that there is often a surge in demand for reconstruction jobs after a disaster, and that can produce a temporary drop in unemployment. Yet job growth in Chile continued far longer than the typical short-term job stimulation observed in the aftermath of disasters elsewhere, and this held in both the affected and nonaffected regions, indicating that the decline in unemployment was more a product of general policies than a short-term stimulus from F27.[11]

Still another measure of Chile's economic comeback was the strong flow of international visitors. Foreign tourism is not a great source of Chile's income compared with the country's premier export industry, copper. In 2010, copper exports exceeded $40 billion, while tourism brought in just a little more than $2 billion. Still, travel is a significant source of foreign exchange, and inbound travelers are sensitive to perceptions of economic normalcy and political stability. The number of international tourists arriving in Chile plunged sharply in March 2010 compared with the same month in the previous year—from just over 246,000 to less than 194,000.

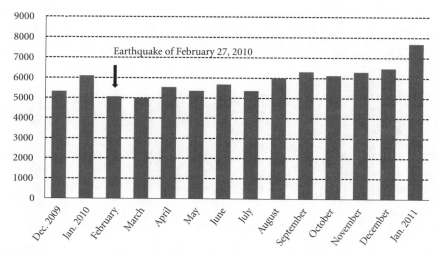

Fig. 3.2. Monthly Value of Chilean Exports, December 2009 to January 2011 ($ millions). Data from Trading Economics, 2013; Banco Central de Chile, 2010.

Yet in the latter part of 2010, the international flow snapped back to the long-term trend line. The annual total of international visitors even grew slightly, from 2.75 million in 2009 to 2.77 million in 2010, the year of the earthquake, and then in 2011 rose to 3.07 million, aided by a strengthening of economies abroad.[12]

Similar trends are evident in Chile's export revenues. The total monthly value of Chilean exports had sharply declined in the immediate wake of the F27 event, dropping from $6.1 billion in January 2010 to $5.1 billion and $5.0 billion in February and March. Yet by the end of the earthquake year, monthly exports had risen back to their pre-quake level as the country restored its trade capacity to meet international demand, as seen in Figure 3.2.

STOCK TRADING AND CREDIT RATING

With Chile's economy back on track within a year according to both external appraisals and internal metrics, company investors and credit raters took notice, and the stock market and rating agencies barely blinked.

Share prices never really dropped after the earthquake, nor did Chile's sovereign debt rating, in marked contrast to stock prices and Japan's credit ratings after its earthquake of 2011.

Compare the premier stock market index for Chile in the days after the F27 event with that of Japan after the Tōhoku earthquake. The Nikkei 225 plummeted after March 11, 2011, dropping from more than ¥10,500 to less than ¥8,600, an 18 percent decline. The Japanese index regained about half of its loss by the end of April but then fell even lower than it was immediately after the quake by the end of October. It would not recover fully until 2013. By contrast, when the F27 earthquake struck Chile, the premier stock index for the Santiago Stock Exchange—IGPA—did not budge.[13]

Looking over the four-year period from mid-2008 to mid-2012, an even broader gauge of Chile's relative resilience, Japan's Nikkei 225 declined by 10 percent and a major U.S. barometer—the S&P 500—rose by 10 percent. The Chilean index, IGPA, by contrast, went up in the same period by more than 40 percent.[14]

Similar trends are evident in the sovereign debt ratings by the three major rating agencies, Standard & Poor's, Moody's, and Fitch. We summarize in Table 3.2 the credit-rating responses to the relatively contemporaneous earthquakes in Chile, Japan, and New Zealand. The credit raters downgraded both Japan and New Zealand but made virtually no change in the ratings for Chile, singling out the latter's resilience in the wake of the F27 event.

In summary, virtually all investment banks, rating agencies, and stockholders were upbeat on the country's recovery. So, too, were international tourists to Chile. By the end of 2011, annual GDP growth had increased to 5.8 percent, and by early 2013 unemployment had dropped from 9.0 to 6.0 percent.

REBUILDING WITH MILESTONES

Focusing on the earthquake recovery itself, the government of Chile reported that it had reached at least 75 percent of its restoration goals within three years of the earthquake in each of the five major areas of education,

Table 3.2. Credit Rating Agency Response to Earthquakes in Chile, Japan, and New Zealand, 2010–11

Standard & Poor's	Moody's	Fitch Ratings
Japan Earthquake, March 11, 2011		
April 2011: Threatened to cut Japan's credit rating, saying that the cost of the earthquake will further weaken public finances unless taxes are raised. Affirmed long-term rating of AA but downgraded its outlook from stable to negative.[A]	May 2011: Warned that the earthquake makes recovery from the financial crisis more difficult. Placed Japan's Aa2 rating on review for possible downgrade.[B] August 2011: Lowered Japan's rating by one notch, warning that the earthquake, tsunami, and nuclear-reactor disasters made government debt reduction more difficult.[C]	May 2012: Lowered Japan's double-A long-term foreign-currency rating and double-A-minus local currency issuer default rating to A-plus.[D]
New Zealand Earthquake, February 22, 2011		
September 2011: Reduced rating on long-term local-currency from AAA to AA+ and foreign-currency debt from AA+ to AA. Cited concerns that government and household debt were expanding.[E]		Downgraded government debt, citing the cost of earthquake recovery.[F]
Chile Earthquake, February 27, 2010		
December 2007: Upgraded country rating from A to A+ with stable outlook, saying Chile's was "more resilient than ever." December 2010: Revised country outlook to "positive" because of "Chile's strong financial profile, growing economic stability, and good growth prospects."[G]	June 2010: Upgraded Chile's credit rating from A1 to Aa3 with positive outlook because of "the country's demonstrated economic and financial resilience even in the face of major adverse shocks, including February's historic earthquake."[H]	February 2011: Upgraded its sovereign credit rating from A to A+ because features of the economy "have allowed Chile to remain very resilient despite the two severe shocks emanating from the global credit crisis and the 2010 devastating earthquake."[I]

Standard & Poor's	Moody's	Fitch Ratings
	(Chile Earthquake, February 27, 2010–*cont.*)	
	December 2012: Further upgraded the country rating from Aa3 to A1 with stable outlook, citing the country's fiscal condition, debt profile, and earthquake recovery.[J]	

[A] http://www.reuters.com/article/2011/04/27/us-japan-economy-rating-idUSTRE73Q0J920110427.

[B] http://www.theguardian.com/business/2011/may/31/japan-unemployment-credit-rating-threat.

[C] http://www.nytimes.com/2011/08/24/business/global/japans-credit-rating-cut-by-moodys.html?_r=0.

[D] http://online.wsj.com/article/SB10001424052702303610504577419700029425564.html.

[E] http://www.businessweek.com/news/2011-09-30/new-zealand-yields-surge-as-ratings-cut-by-s-p-fitch.html.

[F] http://online.wsj.com/article/SB10001424052970204226204576601601469975690.html.

[G] http://www.hacienda.cl/english/investor-relations-office/why-chile.html.

[H] http://www.moodys.com/research/Moodys-says-Chiles-ratings-remain-stable-after-15b-bond-issuance?docid=PR_203197.

[I] http://www.hacienda.cl/english/investor-relations-office/why-chile.html.

[J] http://www.hacienda.cl/english/investor-relations-office/why-chile.html.

health, construction, transportation, and housing, as seen in Figure 3.3. Taking the five rebuilding components together, the government estimated that it had achieved 87 percent of its overall target by February 2013. And then, a year later, at the end of the Piñera administration, the government reported a 97 percent overall completion rate, not quite the 100 percent that had been promised by the president in the first days of his administration, but very close to it.

Within each of these five major areas, government ministries applied dozens of specific metrics to both track and administer their rebuilding initiatives. They followed a long-standing management prescription that calls for measuring what is to be managed. Tracking goals in detail allowed for proactive intervention when specific timetables were not being reached, focusing leadership attention on underperforming areas. The government adopted a metric-based strategy. One such component, for instance, de-

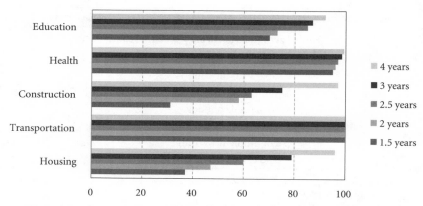

Fig. 3.3. Government of Chile's Estimated Completion of National Rebuilding by Sector by Year, 2011–14 . Data from Government of Chile, 2013, 2014.

tailed statistics on the rate of reconstruction within eight categories of public buildings. Of church buildings, 42 percent had been rebuilt within three years; prisons and justice centers, 50 percent; naval shipyards, 69 percent; and government quarters, 80 percent.[15]

Similarly, the government's numbers on housing reconstruction revealed substantial growth in the post-earthquake home units across the four years after F27, compared with the four years before the event. The total number of government-supported units averaged 178,771 per year before the earthquake, but 193,303 after the earthquake. The total expenditure also increased, from an annual rate of $1.809 billion during the three years before F27 to $2.431 billion during the three years following the quake.[16]

The government tracked restoration of its public infrastructure—roads, bridges, communications, hospitals, schools, and other facilities—with another set of metrics. The Ministry of Public Works, for example, distinguished between partially and fully operative infrastructure. It defined a public works as *partially operative* when its basic functionality had been recovered, though at a lower level of service than before the earthquake. A restored bridge, for example, was considered somewhat operative if it allowed connectivity but with more restrictions—such as the flow rate or maximum weight—than before the earthquake. It defined a public works

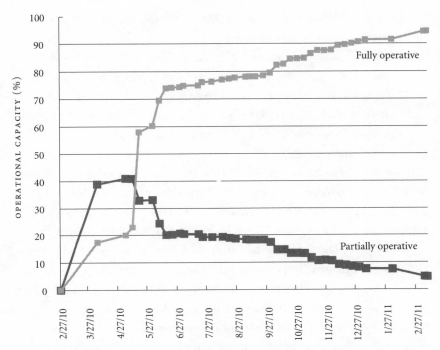

Fig. 3.4. Partial and Full Restoration of Infrastructure, February 2010 to February 2011. Data from Ministry of Public Works, 2013.

as *fully operative* if it was at least as good as or better than before the event. As seen in the month-by-month tracking for the year after F27 in Figure 3.4, more than two-fifths of the damaged or destroyed infrastructure was at least partially operative within two months, and 95 percent fully operative within twelve months.

The government compiled and released a host of other statistics and summaries on the rate of reconstruction. For instance, on the third anniversary of the F27 earthquake, it published a detailed summary of what it had achieved, ministry by ministry:

Ministry of Defense restored 105 barracks, shipyards, arsenals and other military installations, and increased the number of sea-level monitoring stations from 17 to 35.

Ministry of Economy subsidized 42,000 small and medium enterprises in the repair of assets and equipment.

Ministry of Education placed 1.25 million children in schools—some in tents—within 45 days of the earthquake—and repaired or reconstructed 3,923 schools of the 4,654 that had been damaged or destroyed.

Ministry of Finance created the National Reconstruction Fund to incentivize private donations, drew upon copper reserves, and borrowed from the international market.

Ministry of Health repaired 110 hospitals, constructed 9 replacement hospitals, and repaired or rebuilt 207 rural clinics and health centers, recovering 4,249 beds that had been destroyed by the earthquake; immunized 3.1 million residents against H1N1, including 651,000 children ages 2 to 14.

Ministry of Housing installed more than 70,400 emergency dwellings, and then gave priority to permanent housing; shortened the process of obtaining ownership certificates from 2.5 years to less than 1 year; built or repaired more than 220,000 housing units (113,570 new dwellings, 80,848 repaired dwellings); and tightened building codes for concrete. Nearly half of the government's expenditures on the post-quake recovery went into housing (another 17 percent was devoted to health, 17 percent for infrastructure, 10 percent for education, and 4 percent for public buildings).

Ministry of the Interior restored 565 public buildings, parks, theaters, and cemeteries, and repaired and reconstructed 768 historic, cultural, and sacred buildings, ranging from the Museum of Contemporary Art and Pompeii Theatre to the Church San Pedro de Alcantara and Palace La Rioja; conducted 21 drills involving 3 million people in response to earthquake, tsunami, or volcanic threats, including mobilizing 1.2 million students in 2,500 schools in the greater Santiago metropolitan region.

Ministry of Justice repaired five major prisons.

Ministry of Labor created 65,000 jobs to assist emergency reconstruction.

PREPARING FOR FUTURE DISASTERS

The government of Chile opted to go well beyond restoration, as discussed in detail in Chapters 5, 6, and 7. Premised on the oft-stated adage that crises also create opportunities, it sought to strengthen the country's resilience, to make it even more prepared for the next catastrophe by developing a new emergency telecommunications network, improving seismic monitoring and early warning systems, strengthening coastline defenses, tightening building codes, adding disaster training, and instituting large-scale drills.

The National Emergency Office (ONEMI) had been responsible since 1974 for preventing and responding to large-scale risks, operating an early warning system for everything from blizzards to tsunamis. Its mandate had been for civil protection, understood as protecting people, property, and environment in a situation of collective risk, whether naturally occurring or generated by human activity. It trained the public and mitigated hazards in collaboration with both public agencies and the private sector. It also carried responsibility for warnings of earthquakes, but it had been criticized for its poor management of F27, mainly because of the lack of funding that limited its capacity to intervene.

In the wake of F27, the government reconfigured the emergency office as an around-the-clock operation, with its own generators and satellite phones, and with its facilities moved safely out of any tsunami zone. It built a national emergency communications network, and it staged more than twenty national drills around earthquakes, tsunamis, and wildfires that drew in more than 3 million of Chile's 17 million citizens. It arranged with the navy's Hydrographic and Oceanographic Service to take joint responsibility for coastal warnings and possible evacuations in the event of future earthquakes and tsunamis.[17]

The government required that private telecommunication companies install their own backup power systems. It developed an Emergency Alert System that would dispatch text messages to those residing in a disaster-threatened region. It had installed 49 warning sirens along the coast by 2013 and planned for another 31 by early 2014. It added 18 sea-level measuring devices to 17 already in place. It doubled the number of seismographic stations to a total of 104. It installed 130 GPS-enabled stations to monitor movements in Chile's tectonic plates. It created a protocol to swiftly activate ambulance, fire, and police services and ensure communications among them.

THE SUCCESS OF THE RECOVERY

The swift restoration following the earthquake was a factor that led the OECD to invite Chile to become a full member in 2010—the two hundredth year of the country's founding—the first Latin American nation so included. It also played a role in the decision by the G20—the most affluent and powerful countries, responsible for 80 percent of the world's production and trade—to invite Chile to join the G20's summit meeting in 2012 in Mexico City, where disaster risk management was for the first time considered as a key priority on the G20 agenda.[18]

An assessment by the International Monetary Fund of Chile's economy and national policies in mid-2013 captured the essence of the country's fast and full comeback: "Chile's economic performance in recent years has been impressive. The rebound from the 2009 global financial crisis and the 2010 earthquake was quick and strong, and the economy has outpaced most of its peers over the last 2–3 years." Much of that rebound, concluded the IMF, could be attributed to the nation's leadership, characterized as "technocratic, rules-based, and transparent." In an evaluation of Chile's housing reconstruction, a team of academic investigators similarly concluded that the program's success came in part because of "strong leadership at the national and local levels" and the country's "political will."[19]

Country leadership, as we shall see, proved one of two vital drivers of Chile's recovery. Institutional practices—the deeply rooted ways that Chile operates—also proved a major driver. The country's leadership could more effectively implement decisions by virtue of the nation's emphasis on the rule of law, a primacy on follow-through, and a focus on merit over politics.

Chile's experience in the wake of one of the greatest seismic events of recent times is thus likely to suggest an array of leadership behavior and institutional arrangements for ensuring fast and enduring comeback when calamities strike. For these practices to be appreciated elsewhere, we believe that it is important to view them through the organizing lens of several conceptual frameworks, outlined in the following chapter.

Part II

HOW THEY DID IT

4 FRAMEWORKS FOR ACTION

A captain's mettle is not measured when the waters are calm. It is measured when the seas are stormy, and today, without a doubt, we are living through tempestuous times.
—President Sebastián Piñera

Anyone following global news reports is painfully aware that the world has suffered a number of catastrophic events in recent years. F27 was no outlier, but what is special about the Chilean experience was the country's swift and complete comeback. We now turn to how the nation's leadership responded to the calamity so that others can examine and learn from its strategy and experience in facilitating their own recovery should disaster strike.

Learning from the recovery of others has become more vital as more countries and organizations have found themselves in the unwanted territory of catastrophic events, whether stemming from natural or man-made sources. Extreme events by their very definition exceed what a country's leaders or institutions have come to expect or have faced in the past. For any head of state or organization, it is always better to learn from the experiences of others prior to suffering a disaster of one's own.

After noting the world's growing losses from natural catastrophes, this chapter identifies a set of principles for examining leadership decisions in the face of risk and uncertainty. It also proposes a related set of principles for making strategic choices under conditions of risk and uncertainty. Drawing on these concepts, Part II provides a more detailed look at Chile's national leadership and the institutional traditions that propelled its rapid recovery.

GROWING LOSSES FROM NATURAL CATASTROPHES

Most trend lines over the past several decades indicate growing catastrophic losses worldwide, suggesting that countries, companies, and communities are all now more likely to face extreme events than in the past. Data from the world's largest reinsurer, Munich Re, show that constant-dollar global annual losses from catastrophes rose from less than $75 billion in 1980 to more than $170 billion in 2012. Decade by decade, the average annual inflation-adjusted economic losses nearly tripled during the three decades beginning in 1980, from $54 billion in the 1980s to $131 billion in the 1990s, $151 billion in the 2000s, and $250 billion during the 2010s. The World Bank reported similar trends, noting that annual losses from disasters in the 1980s averaged around $50 billion but had reached nearly $200 billion in the 2010s.[1]

Recent years have also seen massive increases in insured payouts in the wake of natural disasters. With the exception of insured losses from the September 11, 2001 terrorist attacks in the United States, all of the twenty most costly events since 1989 have been natural disasters. The Chile earthquake of 2010 ranked seventeenth; its insurance payout of $8.4 billion stood as the fourth most costly among earthquake-driven disasters, topped only by the 2011 Japan earthquake ($35.7 billion), the 1994 California earthquake ($21.7 billion), and the 2011 New Zealand earthquake ($15.3 billion).

As a cautionary note in interpreting these losses and insured-loss trends, however, it should be kept in mind that part of the upslope results from population growth in hazard-prone areas, higher property values, and more insurance underwriting. Climate change and rising sea levels account for increased losses from hurricane flooding, but more extreme weather does not appear to have had any impact on seismic activity. Nevertheless, whatever the sources, the worldwide economic impact of catastrophes has been growing, placing greater weight on a nation's leadership and institutional values for facilitating preparedness, resilience, and recovery. Moreover, growing cross-national interdependencies in finance, trade, and supply chains are increasing the likelihood that local or regional catastrophes will have global consequences far exceeding their impacts in the past.[2]

In light of the increasing worldwide losses from natural and man-made catastrophes, a number of national and international organizations have given greater attention to issues of risk management. These include the G20, OECD, United Nations, U.S. National Academies and similar agencies around the world, World Bank, and World Economic Forum.[3]

The World Economic Forum, for instance—the organization best known for gathering the world's business and political elite every year in Davos, Switzerland—has initiated an annual *Global Risks Report* and created a Global Agenda Council on Catastrophic Risks. Launched in alliance with the Wharton School's Risk Management and Decision Processes Center and several other partners in 2005, the Forum's *Global Risks Report* surveys some one thousand experts worldwide to annually evaluate thirty to fifty global risks on their likelihood and impact over a ten-year horizon. The Forum's Catastrophic Risk Council annually convenes some twenty business, public, and civic figures to help identify policy priorities for governments and companies concerned with catastrophic risks.

Similarly, the secretary-general of the OECD established the International Network on the Financial Management of Large-Scale Catastrophes in 2006 to promote exchange of information and experiences among policy-makers, industrialists, and researchers, and it has joined with the G20 in developing policies on catastrophic risk management.[4]

LEARNING FROM LEADERSHIP DECISIONS

Much of Chile's readiness for the massive 2010 earthquake and its recovery from the event stemmed from strategic decisions taken by its country leaders before and after the disaster. Their decisions entailed choices that were neither mandated nor preordained. Others in the same offices might have behaved differently and reached very different choices.

We define *leadership decisions* to be those moments when individuals with organizational responsibility face discrete, tangible, and realistic opportunities to commit resources to one course or another on behalf of the enterprise's objectives. Making quality decisions has long been well recognized by academic investigators as a defining aspect of leadership. Gary Yukl, one of the premier academic researchers on leadership, for instance, has singled out decision-making as one of the most vital capacities required of all leaders.[5]

Timely and effective decisions are of course expected of all holders of high office. That is one of the defining functions of country or company leaders everywhere. Yet most positions of authority also grant occupants great latitude on what alternatives to consider and how to choose among them. If leaders reach decisions based on a set of declared goals and then achieve those objectives despite the uncertain choices that abound, they normally receive high praise for their actions. And, when their decisions fall short, they are as equally subject to castigation.[6]

NATIONAL LEADERSHIP AND INSTITUTIONAL PRACTICES

To appreciate the Piñera administration's behavior in the aftermath of the F27 earthquake—and for preparing for future disasters of any magnitude—we believe that it is essential to examine Chile's national leadership and institutional practices. Both factors are essential, neither sufficient without the other.

We define *national leadership* as those who hold positions of country-wide or regional authority and influence. Although the focus here is primarily on those in and around government, we also direct attention to nonprofit and business leaders who stepped forward to assist the national recovery as well. Of special interest are the tone that these individuals set, the principles they applied, and the decisions they made.

We use *institutional practices* as shorthand for a nation's long-standing and widely accepted beliefs, values, norms, and customs that serve as behavioral blueprints. Institutional practices are deeply rooted in the nation's culture, they are inherited products of decades of experience and evolving traditions, and they are sustained—and occasionally changed—by contemporary actions and events.[7]

The power of institutional practices to make a difference in disaster recovery can be seen in a far-reaching study of disaster resilience in the United States by the National Academies. Their 2012 study defined a nation's resilience as "the ability to prepare and plan for, absorb, recover from, and more successfully adapt to adverse events" and concluded that strengthening resilience must be a "national imperative." It also underscored the importance of taking charge to lead a comeback. "Creating a culture of disaster resilience for the nation is a proactive, rather than a reactive, approach to the problems caused by disasters," said the National Academies report. And a culture of disaster resilience "can provide a pathway for reducing vulnerability and the impacts of disasters before they occur, with the potential to decrease the costs of disasters at all levels."[8]

Drawing on this and a host of other studies and research, we outline four frameworks that have proven particularly instructive for our study of Chile's national leadership and institutional practices in the wake of the disaster. The first two focus on leadership principles and the last two focus on the role of institutional practices and learning from past disasters. We use principles from these four frameworks as lenses to capture and characterize what is most salient and instructive in Chile's response to F27.

STRATEGIC THINKING AND ACTING

Given the discretionary spectrum that national leaders face, we believe that the individual leadership capacities they bring to office can make a large difference in a nation's conduct during a disaster. Among the principles most important to individual leaders for taking charge to lead a comeback are eight that we have here extracted from a range of other sources and experiences. While they are all important in the exercise of leadership, we have found thinking and acting strategically to be of particular value for appreciating the Chilean experience and understanding its most valued lessons:[9]

Individual Leadership Principles

1. *Articulate a Vision.* Formulate a clear and persuasive vision for addressing catastrophic risk and resilience, and communicate it to everyone at risk.

2. *Think and Act Strategically.* Set forth a pragmatic strategy for achieving that vision both short- and long-term, delineate specific tasks and timelines, and ensure that measurable objectives are widely understood; consider all the players, values, and agendas to anticipate and confront emergent conflicts and resistance before they are manifest; help everybody appreciate the impact that the vision and strategy for catastrophic risk and resilience are likely to have on their own lives and livelihood.

3. *Take Charge.* Stimulate a widespread bias for action, of taking responsibility even if it is not formally designated, particularly among those best positioned to make a difference. At the same time, delegate authority downward except for the most strategic actions, and stay close to those most directly engaged in the work of catastrophic risk and resilience. Build a capacity for making good and timely decisions, and an ability to implement and execute around them.

4. *Motivate the Public.* Communicate messages and well-specified goals in ways that large numbers of people will not forget; simplicity and clarity of expression are of special value here. Appreciate the distinctive intentions that people bring to catastrophic risk and resilience, and then build on those diverse motives to stimulate the best actions from all. Frequently express confidence in and support for those who are working on catastrophic risk and resilience. Develop leadership throughout the ranks for addressing and responding to catastrophic risk.

5. *Convey Your Character.* Through events, accounts, and communication, ensure that national leaders are viewed as persons of character, committed and able to carry forward the national vision and strategy for catastrophic risks and resilience.

6. *Dampen Overoptimism, Combat Excessive Pessimism.* Counter the hubris of success, focus attention on latent threats and unresolved problems, and protect against unwarranted risk-taking; combat the pessimism of set-

back, focus attention on shared resolve and initial gains, and protect against needless risk avoidance.

7. *Build a Diverse Top Team.* Take final responsibility, but also lead indirectly through a diversely experienced team that is collectively capable of addressing all the key challenges in catastrophic risk and resilience.

8. *Place Common Purpose First.* In setting strategy, communicating vision, and reaching decisions, common purpose comes first, political or personal self-interest last.

DELIBERATIVE DECISION-MAKING

Thinking and acting strategically becomes especially important during a period when decisions are urgent and the stakes are high. It is then that decision-makers are confronted with a host of unanticipated choices, and it is then that careful assessment of the options and the final selection among them are likely to be particularly impactful on an organization's or a country's ability to rebound from a disaster.[10]

Fifty years of academic research had repeatedly confirmed that intuitive thinking has enormous influence on human judgments and choices. Intuitive processes work well when decision-makers have copious data on the outcomes of different decisions, and recent experience is a meaningful guide for future actions. These processes may not be fully effective, however, during low-probability, high-consequence events for which decision-makers by definition have limited or no past experience. These are events for which leadership decisions can also become especially thorny, complex, and risky, and thus more in need of deliberative thinking. Business-school professor Phil Rosenzweig characterized the two ways of approaching decisions at such moments as "left brain"—analytic thinking— and "right stuff"—bold action. Both are essential, he argues, but sometimes the analytic can be lost in the crisis of the moment, as he and others have shown.[11]

The distinction between intuitive and deliberative behavior builds on a large body of cognitive psychology and behavioral research that can be traced to the early work of William James in psychology and to Friedrich Nietzsche and Martin Heidegger in philosophy. Psychologist Daniel Kahneman, a contemporary contributor and Nobel Laureate, has usefully characterized these two decision-making styles as System-1 and System-2 thinking:[12]

Intuitive and Deliberative Decision-making

Intuitive Thinking, System 1

Operates automatically and quickly, with little or no effort and no voluntary control.

Uses simple and concrete associations, including emotional reactions or simple rules of conduct that have been acquired by personal experience with events and their consequences.

Deliberative Thinking, System 2

Initiates and executes effortful and intentional abstract cognitive operations when needed.

Cognitive operations include complex computations and formal logic.

Kahneman further develops the distinction between Systems 1 and 2 in his book, *Thinking, Fast and Slow*. It helps clarify the frequently observed tension between automatic, largely involuntary reactive processes and more deliberate proactive processes of the human mind. The first is more instinctive, less analytic, and more tactical; the second is more deliberate, less reactive, and more strategic. These two ways of making decisions often work together in shaping an individual's decisions, and their distinction can be usefully extended to leaders of organizations or countries, who typically operate with some combination of both in reaching major decisions, though not without some tension between the more involuntary processes of intuitive decision-making and the more effortful and deliberate processes of analytic decision-making.[13]

We use this distinction to clarify our understanding of the implications of Chile's actions in the wake of F27. Intuitive thinking leads to more re-active behavior; deliberative thinking is more proactive. The latter form of thinking is more in keeping with the mission-critical leadership principle of thinking and acting strategically, and it proved to be especially import-ant in enabling the government of Chile to actively take charge after the earthquake and to facilitate a full comeback.

Intuitive thinking under uncertainty often draws directly on the expe-riences, expectations, and beliefs of the parties involved in the decision. Such simplified decision rules typically require far less effort than a more detailed analysis of the trade-offs among the available choices. Taking into account the time and processing constraints facing most organizations, in-tuitively driven decisions may be the best that executives or officials can and will want to take in the immediate wake of a calamity.[14]

Intuitive decisions produce acceptable outcomes when decision-makers have good data on the options and recent experience is a meaningful guide for the future. In the aftermath of a disaster, however, an over-reliance on intuitive thinking for reaching decisions can result in inaction. The high costs of initiating new directions can be seen as outweighing any gains, causing company or political leaders to avoid any changes, referenced in the academic literature as a *status quo bias*.[15]

A second intuitive-thinking bias can also misdirect leadership decisions in the wake of a calamity. Individuals and organization tend to focus on the recent past in judging the likelihood of future events, a myopic view that researchers have termed the *availability bias*. Drawing on both personal experience and anxiety avoidance, there is a tendency to underestimate a disaster's likelihood before it occurs and then to overestimate its future likelihood immediately after it occurs.[16]

The availability bias can help explain why emergency actions are taken in the immediate wake of a disaster but interest in undertaking longer-term protective measures against future disasters wanes over time. It is not sur-prising then that those at risk from natural hazards normally purchase in-surance only after a disaster has occurred and then cancel their policies several years later, as has been found in many countries prone to earth-quakes or floods. Short-run goals, including the reduction of anxiety and prevention of future damage, assume great importance immediately after a calamity, but they are predictably displaced by other goals soon thereafter, such as avoiding up-front investments that do not yield rapid payback.[17]

The more analytic tools associated with deliberative thinking focus attention on both short- and long-term decision consequences, leading to a more comprehensive and even-handed evaluation of alternative options. This type of thinking helps decision-makers overcome the status quo and availability biases so they can respond more effectively before and after disaster strikes.[18]

It should also be kept in mind, however, that experience-informed intuitive thinking can also provide invaluable guidance during a crisis. When leaders have learned well from earlier moments of great uncertainty and risk, they build up useful decision rules and heuristics that can expeditiously guide them through new periods of great uncertainty and risk. The practical value of these courses of action will be limited if the new crisis is far outside the zone of prior experience. And since those responsible for national recovery after the F27 event were facing a more extreme event than any they had previously encountered, their prior experience could provide only a partial and imperfect guide for their decisions after the shock of this new calamity.[19]

Chile's exceptionally strong comeback was assisted in part, we believe, by the nation's traditional emphasis on a more deliberative mindset that fosters thinking and acting strategically.

TIERED LEADERSHIP

Leadership comes from many tiers in an organization, not only the top rung. Coordination across those tiers thus becomes vital. Not only must the several levels work closely together, but the strategic and deliberative thinking of the top echelon must be conveyed and enacted through those below, a kind of mission multiplier. This can be especially true when risk and uncertainty are pervasive. With many parts moving in unpredictable ways, leadership at all levels can be essential for accurately reading and then responding to a crisis moment.[20]

Building on James G. March's and Herbert A. Simon's classic work, *Organizations*, James D. Thompson has argued in his *Organizations in Action* that the more uncertain the moment, the greater an organization's dependence on vertical coordination. The value of tiered leadership in an uncertain moment can be seen in an important academic study of "extreme action" medical teams in emergency trauma centers that face complex, fast-changing, and time-sensitive tasks. Our Wharton colleague Katherine Klein and her associates found that these mission-critical teams had come to depend on a vertical system of "shared leadership" that included delegation of specific leadership roles to subordinate members of the trauma teams while retaining overall direction by the top.[21]

The impact of tiered leadership is likely to be particularly important when uncertainty, urgency, and complexity are high, as during and immediately after a disaster. It is then that leadership actions at each level are likely to be stronger if they are shaped by guidance and collaboration from the levels below and above. It is also then that resources are more likely to be rapidly mobilized and well deployed if the several leadership tiers are jointly engaged and aligned in their actions.

INSTITUTIONAL PRACTICES

A nation's institutional practices are an enormous source of stability and predictability, powerful and enduring, similar in their social power to a country's culture. A national culture can guide citizens in virtually every facet of their behavior, and the same can be said of institutional practices. Of particular interest here is the power of those practices to reinforce national purpose and shared interest over private and parochial concerns during a crisis. A nation's institutional practices are of course an inherited product of centuries of experience and tradition, but they have also evolved and are reinforced by contemporary communications and actions.[22]

While certain institutional practices are valued in some countries but not others, an academic research team led by Robert House, Mansour Javidan, and others found a set of practices utilized in virtually all countries.

The team appraised nationwide institutional practices in the early 2000s by collecting survey data from 17,000 middle managers of 825 companies in 62 countries. The countries ranged from Albania to Zimbabwe and the survey focused on three industries—financial services, food processing, and telecommunications. Managers were asked to evaluate which personal capacities enhanced or impeded management of their firm. Almost everywhere they favored dynamism, decisiveness, and honesty; an ability to motivate and negotiate with others; and a focus on performance. Conversely, most managers in most countries did not approve of autocratic, egocentric, and irritable bosses. Although Chile was not among the countries included in the study, the qualities of dynamism, decisiveness, and honesty are likely to be highly favored there as well, as is the ability to motivate, negotiate, and focus on performance.[23]

RISK-RELATED PRACTICES

A final construct highlights the importance of undertaking systematic analysis for characterizing the likelihood of future disasters and their potential consequences. Once the nature of the peril is specified, persuasively and widely communicating that risk becomes critical and requires partnerships among the public, private, and NGO sectors, and risk-management strategies that include economic incentives, private insurance, and well-enforced regulations. The following principles furnish still another lens for understanding leadership actions in the wake of a catastrophic event like F27:[24]

Risk-Related Principles

1. *Risk Forecasting.* Improvement in the precision of forecasts is important for both averting disasters and minimizing their impacts.

2. *Communicating Risk.* Since people generally dismiss low-probability, high-consequence events by assuming that they will

not personally experience such events, the compelling delivery of risk information becomes vital.

3. *Partnerships.* Since the public, private, and nonprofit sectors share in the costs and benefits of preparing for and recovering from disasters, fostering collaboration among them ahead of time can be important for building effective partnership strategies for catastrophic risk and resilience.

4. *Economic Incentives.* Both positive and negative economic incentives, subsidies and penalties, encourage individuals to take protective measures against catastrophic risks.

5. *Insurance.* In providing coverage against large-scale catastrophes, it is important that the price of insurance policies closely reflect the real risk so that premiums can provide a simple signal for the level of exposure that people and organizations face.

6. *Enforced Standards and Regulations.* To reduce future disaster losses, the public sector is wise to develop well-enforced standards (such as building codes) and regulations (such as land-use provisions) to complement private insurance.

LEARNING FROM CHILE'S CALAMITY THROUGH THESE FRAMEWORKS AND PRINCIPLES

We draw on national leadership, tiered leadership, institutional practices, and risk-related principles as we turn to Chile's national response to the earthquake of February 27. They shape what we will look for in the actions of the country's leaders. When observing those decision-makers in action we will formulate and embrace new leadership principles that complement those already underscored here. Our goal is to develop a more elaborate and more practice-informed model for national risk resilience both prior to a disaster and in its aftermath.

Chile's experience and the resulting model are likely to be especially valuable in the years ahead as calamities have become more consequen-

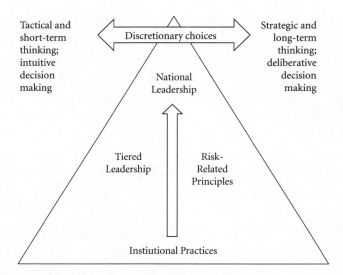

Fig. 4.1. Discretionary Choices.

tial across a variety of geographies. National leadership and institutional practices are, we will see, the essential building blocks. They guided a host of discretionary choices that President Sebastián Piñera and his cabinet ministers faced in the aftermath of the F27 calamity. They are summarized schematically in Figure 4.1, and we use them as a backbone for our account of Chile's recovery in the following chapters.

5 PRESIDENTIAL LEADERSHIP

I want to call on everyone to dry their tears and put their hands to work to rebuild our country better than we had before.
—President Sebastián Piñera

To appreciate the discretionary power of leadership and the capacities that make the greatest difference during a national calamity, we focus on the actions of the presidential administration that became responsible for Chile's full recovery from its earthquake of February 27.

Although they were several days away from taking power when the event hit, President Sebastián Piñera and his cabinet ministers would shoulder long-term responsibility for their country's recovery. By concentrating on their many decisions over their four years of incumbency, we are best able to appreciate what is required for both crisis response and long-term restoration. We briefly open with the final days of the outgoing administration of Piñera's predecessor, Michelle Bachelet, and then delve more fully into what Piñera and his lieutenants would do in the months that followed.

PRESIDENT MICHELLE BACHELET

Incumbent president Michelle Bachelet had been in the last two weeks of her four-year administration when the earthquake struck. By most accounts, and most polls, she had performed very well in La Moneda.

Bachelet had grown up in a household that had valued national service, a natural platform for a future career in politics. Her father, Alberto Bachelet, an air force officer, had served two years with the military mission at the embassy of Chile in Washington, DC, and while there, his daughter had attended junior high school in Bethesda, Maryland.

Rising to brigadier general in Chile's air force, Alberto Bachelet joined the government of President Salvador Allende as administrator for national food distribution, serving until the violent military coup in 1973 led by army general Augusto Pinochet. Eschewing exile, Alberto Bachelet was arrested and tortured by the regime, dying in detention of heart problems resulting from his physical abuse. In early 1975, the junta arrested Michelle Bachelet and her mother, and they too were tortured. The regime yielded to insider entreaties for their release, however, and they soon took exile in Australia and later East Germany.

Returning to Chile in 1979, Michelle Bachelet completed a medical degree in 1983, and after the restoration of democracy in 1990, she worked in public health, studied military strategy, and entered public service, first as national minister of health and then, two years later, as minister of defense. The latter was a first for a woman in Latin America and an ironic turn for a victim of abuse by the very institution that she now had come to head.

As defense minister, Bachelet discharged her duties with aplomb, attracting special visibility when she personally spearheaded a rescue operation in 2000 for those caught in a devastating flood in northern Chile, taking a commanding place atop an amphibious tank at one point during the rescue. Bachelet campaigned for the presidency in 2005–6 against conservative opponent Sebastián Piñera, defeating him in a runoff with 54 percent of the national vote, and taking the oath of office on March 11, 2006.

When the earthquake shook Santiago at 3:34 a.m. on February 27, 2010, the movement roused the president, and she promptly declared a state of emergency in six of the country's fifteen regions, saying, "We are facing a catastrophe of such magnitude that has caused damages that will require gigantic efforts from every sector of our country—both private and public sector. We face an emergency without precedent in the history of Chile, in which we need fast and urgent answers." She later dispatched the armed forces into areas hardest hit by the earthquake and tsunami and where shopping zones were most ravaged by looting in the aftermath. To further stem the public disorder, she declared night curfews in the most affected regions.[1]

Just days into the emergency recovery, however, Michelle Bachelet's term came to a close. She exited office on March 11, 2010, and would later become executive director of a UN agency for Gender Equality and the Empowerment of Women. Secretary-General Ban Ki-moon appointed her to the newly created entity whose charge, in his words, was to "promote gender equality, expand opportunity, and tackle discrimination around the globe."

Although Bachelet was now based in New York City, her political stock remained high in her home country, and she was widely viewed as a promising candidate for a return to the Chilean presidency in 2014. In a first-round presidential vote on November 17, 2013, Bachelet received 47 percent of the vote against childhood friend Evelyn Matthei's 25 percent, forcing a runoff on December 15. The electorate gave her a resounding 62 percent of the ballots, and she entered office for her second four-year term on March 11, 2014.

PRESIDENT SEBASTIÁN PIÑERA

Since Chile's restoration of democratic government in 1990, national leadership had been exercised through four presidential administrations by Concertación de Partidos por la Democracia—Coalition of Parties for Democracy—or an alliance of the centrist Christian Democrats and the left-leaning Socialist Party. But in the presidential election of December 13, 2009, the conservative National Renewal Party, with Sebastián Piñera as its standard-bearer, led a field of four candidates, receiving 44 percent of the vote. Without a majority of the ballots, Piñera was forced into a runoff on January 17, and he then garnered a majority—52 percent of the votes—not a landslide but nonetheless a solid democratic mandate. His election constituted an important political shift in Chile, as he became the first elected conservative leader in half a century.

After the president-elect's visit to Concepción on the day of the earthquake, he convened his shadow cabinet later that evening and publicly pledged "the full support and commitment" of the next government to President Bachelet. He met with the outgoing president, advising her to ask the armed forces to reimpose order on areas where looting had erupted. He later told his cabinet members that "we have to work with urgency because in ten days we will be in charge!" They were soon devoting fifteen-hour days to preparing to take the reins amid the crisis. "I wanted to have a very clear picture to start working on the very first day" of the presidency, he vowed, and he said that he expected the same of each of the ministers.

Sebastián Piñera had reached the presidency via a very different path than that of Michelle Bachelet. His father had served as Chile's ambassador to the United Nations, and after graduating at the top of his class from the Catholic University of Chile, he earned a doctorate in economics from Harvard University. Piñera pursued an academic career during the turbulent years of the Allende regime, teaching at Catholic University, the University of Chile, and the Valparaiso Business School. But drawn more to business than academe, he introduced credit cards to Chile; purchased Chilevisión, a national television channel; acquired a major ownership stake (26 percent) in LAN Airlines, the country's flagship carrier; and even secured a share of Colo-Colo, one of Chile's premier soccer clubs.

During his rising career in business, Piñera attained a reputation for quick and ambitious actions. He would later carry those same qualities into politics, first rising to head his political party, then serving as a senator, and finally winning the presidency in 2010. During his run for the Senate, a popular nickname referenced his ceaseless energy: "the Locomotive."

In campaigning for La Moneda, Sebastián Piñera touted his business credentials, pressed for greater government efficiency and free-market reforms, promised a million new jobs in a country whose workforce numbered 8 million, and called for boosting the country's annual growth rate by a full point and ending poverty by 2014. Industrial productivity and job creation had been languishing, and he proclaimed that he would stimulate both. He sought to move Chile into the elite ranks of the developed economies. And he pledged to continue many of the popular domestic policies of his predecessor, Michelle Bachelet, who had left office with an approval rating of more than 80 percent.

TAKING CHARGE

Consistent with his fast-acting and go-getting temperament, the president-elect immediately elevated reconstruction to the top of his agenda. His designated minister of planning, Felipe Kast, had publicly warned just days after the devastation, "We now have to rethink our entire agenda, our focus and our government goals." Indeed, "people have urgent needs that need to be met and fears that have to be calmed." The president himself declared, "We made a commitment to restore the country; we are committed 100 percent to replace within four years what was destroyed."

The president-elect asked the director of the National Emergency Office to remain in his new administration. Piñera worked to comprehend both the national scope and gritty detail of the destruction. In the few days before taking office, he devoted virtually all of his time to the immediate emergency and the subsequent reconstruction. "The urgency was key," he said. "We were pushing things very fast. We had to make a lot of decisions." The president demanded equally aggressive timetables from his cabinet. In reflecting on his first months in office, the president recalled, "one-hundred percent of ten ministers' time went into the disaster."

On March 11, the president's inauguration brought an all-too-tangible reminder of what had occasioned the country's great disaster just twelve days earlier. Attending the inauguration were a roster of Latin American presidents including Argentina's Cristina Kirchner, Bolivia's Evo Morales, Colombia's Alvaro Uribe, Ecuador's Rafael Correa, Paraguay's Fernando Lugo, and Peru's Alan Garcia. Chile's new executive was about to receive the red, white, and blue sash of the presidency from the outgoing executive when three seismic shocks of 6.9 magnitude shook the coastal city of Valparaiso where the swearing-in was underway at the National Congress. A photograph of the president of Ecuador peering anxiously up at the swaying hall captured the anxiety of the moment.

Officials rushed the presidential investiture to conclusion, evacuated the building, and canceled the formal luncheon. The president apologized: "Sorry, but there has been a very significant earthquake in the southern

President Rafael Correa of Ecuador studies the ceiling of Chile's National Congress during the presidential inauguration, March 11, 2010. AP Photo/Martin Mejia.

part of the country again, so I will have to leave. I will leave you with my wife; she will be your host."

The new president immediately held a press briefing outside the hall to declare, "Citizens who live on the coast, please follow the preventive tsunami alert." He added that he was ready to deploy the armed forces against any looting, warning, "It's better to prevent than to cure." Swift action would be essential, today and equally in the days ahead. "He had been a businessman," explained one of his cabinet ministers. "He was used to making decisions."

And it was all business, declared the president: "I want to call on everyone to dry their tears and put their hands to work to rebuild our country better than we had before." A spokeswoman for the government said that rebuilding would begin immediately: "We are going to have a president on the ground, with rapid decisions, a government with a sense of emergency." The president himself made the same point. "This government will not hesitate one instant, nor wait one second, to act." Three priorities would define his agenda: emergency needs first, then public order, and finally the longer-term rebuilding of the country. As the dignitaries gathered for the informal luncheon with his wife, the president boarded a helicopter to see the Maule region, much as he had done on February 27. On arriving in the city of Talca, he characterized F27's massive destruction: "It was like an atomic bomb had exploded because everything had collapsed."[2]

BUILDING THE TEAM

Sebastián Piñera formed a cabinet whose ministers came from business as much as politics. His leadership would be tiered, and his own stratagem was to lead the leaders and the country through them. In the summary words of the head of interministerial coordination, Claudio Seebach, "The most important lesson was to make a team with one mission and a total focus on the task."

The president had earlier decided—well before the earthquake—that his lieutenants would have to be experienced in making vexing decisions and managing their execution even if they lacked real experience in politics. Of the thirty-nine appointments he made to his cabinet during the first three years of his government, twenty-five arrived as independents without party affiliation. It was the president's way of building a top team with members whose temperaments were already given to taking charge, as many had been in leadership positions. It was a team whose members came with their own readiness to make difficult, time-driven decisions, developed from years of experience in a world that placed a premium on forceful execution and timely results. The team, the president said, would implement his intention of fully restoring the country—and more—within the four years of his presidency.[3]

By way of example, his new minister of mines, Laurence Golborne, had been an engineer, entrepreneur, and corporate executive. Golborne had served as chief executive of Cencosud S.A., a large retail firm. With plenty of business experience but no background in mining or politics, Golborne found himself in charge of an agency that regulated the mining industry, one of critical importance in the country.

Similarly, the new minister of public works, Hernán de Solminihac, who would later replace Laurence Golborne as the minister of mines, had also been trained as an engineer with a degree from Catholic University of Chile and then a doctorate in civil engineering from the University of Texas at Austin. At the moment of his first cabinet appointment in 2010, he had been serving as dean of the Engineering School at Catholic University.

Felipe Kast, the new minister of planning, obtained his Ph.D. in economics at Harvard and was a consultant who had worked in academe and a nongovernmental organization. He was called to service not from an abiding interest in politics—though his father had served an earlier president— but because he and others in the cabinet, he said, "wanted to give back" to a nation that had given them so much.

"We had the resources," Piñera explained. "We passed the laws, we allocated responsibilities to the ministers, and we coordinated it all at the presidential level." He had run on a platform of revitalizing the economy, increasing wages, and combating poverty. But now, he declared, "We are not the government of the economy—we are the government of reconstruction," and his top team was ready and had the experience to do so.

RECOVERY AND RECONSTRUCTION

President Piñera formed an Emergency Committee to drive the government's response and recovery. His specific mandate: (1) deliver food, power, sanitation, and other basic needs to all who needed them within one month; (2) ensure housing of some kind for everybody affected by the earthquake no later than June 1; and (3) work to remove wreckage and restore public services as soon as possible. The priorities spoke to the special value of setting goals with measurable objectives.

The committee initially directed the armed services to aid local police in quelling civic disorders, but beginning on March 31, five weeks after the disaster, the committee expanded the military mandate to include removing earthquake debris, erecting temporary housing, creating field hospitals, and distributing food and water.

The president himself remained late in his office at La Moneda on many evenings. "This is worse than a war," he privately mused. People ached for the most basic of necessities, with water, food, and security now at the forefront of their Maslow hierarchy of needs. The president sought to mobilize private enterprise too, reaching out to companies to assist the reconstruction: "We put the whole country to work."

In early April the president announced a plan to secure more than $8 billion to finance the country's reconstruction, leaving an estimated $22 billion more in losses to private sources. And it would be done, he averred, without increasing the country's deficit. The government would secure the $8 billion through a combination of cash accumulated in a copper-revenue fund, selling state assets, and tightening the fiscal belt. Relying on many sources of funding would not deplete any of them, finance minister Felipe Larraín reasoned. The president thus announced, "We need a formula to distribute the cost of the earthquake among all these sources of financing." Moreover, as the finance minister explained, the reconstruction projects would also serve as an economic stimulus and productivity enhancement as old infrastructure and equipment were replaced with new.[4]

Although focused on digging out of the ruins, the president also faced the simultaneous task of taking the reins of power. He had more than one thousand senior offices to fill, and after two decades of rule by left or centrist coalitions, his house cleaning was likely to be more extensive than in past transitions. He believed that ONEMI's present capacities fell short of what was required to confront such a massive setback in the future, but under the circumstance he also worried that creating a new agency would require too much time and political capital given the urgency of the moment.

Accordingly, Sebastián Piñera took two immediate steps to jump-start the recovery at several tiers of the hierarchy over which he presided. First, he pressed his regional and local representatives to take an aggressive leadership role in their local area's response and recovery. And second, he brought his cabinet ministries to work together through two temporary entities, the Committee of Emergency and the Committee of Reconstruction.[5]

The president charged the Emergency Committee with providing support to families with lost or injured kin, locating missing persons, restoring public order, reestablishing basic services, creating temporary housing, recovering infrastructure, and preparing for the cold winter months that lay just ahead. On March 22, the committee sent twelve thousand army troops into the most devastated region to search for the missing and dead, recapture escaped prisoners, and halt looting and disorder. The committee worked to construct more than eighty thousand emergency shelters, in active collaboration with nonprofit organizations such as Un Techo para Chile—A Roof for Chile—and private companies such as Compañía General de Electricidad (General Electricity Company). For those forced into temporary clusters of housing, the committee created the Aldeas—Villages—Program, in which a community worked collectively on shared needs and securing more permanent housing.

The Emergency Committee created the Fuerza de Apoyo Humanitario—Humanitarian Support Force—to mobilize civil servants, private personnel, and army conscripts to construct emergency housing, restore roads, and remove debris. Each region would be the responsibility of an army brigadier general. At its peak, the Humanitarian Support Force drew upon the services of some twenty thousand individuals.

By working through the Emergency Committee, the president pressed for all school children to be in classrooms as soon as possible. Improvisation proved essential but providential: by April 26, 2010, all of the nation's students were back in school, whether in tents, shacks, churches, police stations, modular prefabrications, or even buses.

The Committee of Reconstruction was responsible for determining the most pressing needs for each region, and it created the Plan for Reconstruction, announced by President Piñera on April 16, 2010—just six weeks after the disaster. It called for a complete restoration of the country within four years, with a focus on rehabilitating infrastructure, creating jobs, and strengthening both disaster management and national resilience. The national agenda would have to fix 1,700 points of damaged infrastructure, more than 965 miles of roads, 211 bridges, 9 airports, 6,168 educational facilities, and 133 medical facilities (more than 70 percent of the medical capacity in the affected areas). The plan noted that every sector of the Chilean economy had been affected and that the country suffered a total loss of capital of some 11 percent, most concentrated in manufacturing, fisheries, tourism, housing, and education.

President Piñera viewed the catastrophe as a turning point in the country's history, with rebuilding going far beyond repair. "Reconstruction is not limited to the replacement of assets lost in the disaster," he argued. "It is aimed at restoring livelihoods, habitat, social integration, governance, and sustainability." And given the magnitude, recovery would require active participation of all sectors.

THREE STRATEGIC PRINCIPLES

President Sebastián Piñera directed his ministries to take active part and play specific roles in the national recovery, and he insisted that they each set and achieve dozens of measurable goals on specific timetables. He also required that they adhere to three strategic principles intended to align their initiatives around common purpose, achieving more than just the sum of their individual parts. He stressed as well that the success would only come if everybody saw it as a national effort that did not leave space for those with private agendas.

The president's first strategic principle, *preserving the dignity and freedom of the population*, was to be achieved by taking into account the local concerns of residents and neighborhoods most affected by the measures. In protecting "social heritage" in neighborhood housing, for instance, the Ministry of Housing was to give families optimal opportunity to rebuild homes on their original sites in ways that could preserve their community and protect their traditions. Housing measures would require "respecting the will of those affected, by their active participation in the choice of the solution," said the president, and reconstruction more generally would entail "valuing our culture and history, and preserving the architectural image of the traditional villages." Although noble in purpose, this first principle would make projects more complex and more prolonged, since it proscribed cookie-cutter solutions.[6]

The second strategic principle was to *reconstruct in a way that would make for better communities*. The president viewed F27 as "an opportunity to build better neighborhoods and cities," and for that purpose he insisted on a master plan for urban reconstruction and regeneration that would reach well beyond a return to the status quo.[7]

The third strategic principle was to *use the moment to better protect against future calamity.* "We know that we cannot control nature," the government acknowledged. The F27 event "showed us that no earthquake" could be "fully prepared for." And "although it may be decades before an event of this magnitude affects the country" again, the nation should nonetheless be bolstered in its defenses and readiness to face whatever calamities may lie ahead. A "central axis of the reconstruction," said the government, "was to leave the country better prepared in the event of future natural disasters" and to ensure that citizens had improved protection.[8]

For instance, to make Chile's National Emergency Office and the National System of Civil Protection and Emergency immediately more effective, the government hired the strategy consulting firm, McKinsey & Co., to identify measures for strengthening the country's disaster response. Its consultants recommended, among other things, that the detection time for a tsunami should be reduced by 90 percent—to just two minutes—and evacuation time should be similarly cut from forty to just four minutes.

Part of the problem was an insidious complacency that had emerged in the many years since Chile's 9.5 earthquake of 1960 in Valdivia. Emergency officials reported that the failure of communications in the wake of the F27 earthquake, including the absence of a timely warning about the resulting tsunami, could be attributed in part to an overly sanguine mindset resulting from several decades without a massive natural disaster. The Valdivia calamity had resulted in the loss of fifty-seven hundred lives and caused widespread destruction, but nothing close to its scale had been experienced in the fifty years that separated these two earthquakes. Sebastián Piñera himself was only eleven when the 1960 catastrophe hit.

A CHECKLIST FOR COMING BACK

The president had earlier decided that much of his own leadership would have to be exercised through his second echelon, the nearly two dozen cabinet members who could take his words from meetings at La Moneda and transform them into reality in the countryside. To achieve that, the president had appointed largely nonpolitical managers to his cabinet. It was his way of extending his own abiding preference for timely execution and tangible results, and now with a new imperative upon him, he had in place a leadership tier upon which he knew he could depend in the days ahead.

Returning to the eight individual leadership principles identified in Chapter 4, we see the president embracing many of them. He set forth a vision, acted strategically, took charge, and placed country interest first. On the other hand, as we will see in Chapter 9, he did not fully embrace the principle of dampening overoptimism and combating excessive pessimism.

The president explicitly directed his cabinet members to execute three guiding principles, reflecting the need for deliberative decision-making and strategic thinking rather than tactical or short-term fixes. They would be more costly in time and resources than near-term actions for immediate restoration of the most essential functions would have required. The principles would also necessitate incorporating grass-roots preferences into neighborhood reconstruction, and they would require the rebuilding to result in stronger communities and greater resilience than before.

At the same time, the president drew upon his own intuitive thinking, which had been shaped and informed by his earlier years as a successful businessman, where making decisions and implementing actions were the currency of the realm. His experience-informed heuristics facilitated an ability to reach quick decisions and to transcend any analysis-paralysis that might afflict a less experienced denizen of the office when faced with the kinds of extreme uncertainties and high-stakes decisions that confronted this president upon entering office.

Above all, Sebastián Piñera had swiftly taken charge of a comeback agenda, and that caught the public somewhat unexpectedly, he recalled. "I think that people were very surprised because they realized that we had a very clear plan, that we were very committed to performing that plan, and that we were extremely active."

The president refused to back off his campaign commitments to revive the economy and create jobs, and his uncompromising pursuit of two expensive agendas placed a special burden on the new minister of finance, Felipe Larraín. The minister's job was to fund both agendas without taking the country deeply into debt, a path that the president had already said was not an option.

Drawing on the experience of Chile's president and his lieutenants in the wake of the F27 event, we see several implications for leaders elsewhere confronting their own disaster and crisis. Below we identify principles for action in the form of a leadership checklist, a template for decision-making composed of a limited number of mission-critical behavioral concepts. They are extrapolated from Chile's experience but expressed in a form that can inform action in a range of other contexts:

A Leadership Checklist for Coming Back from a Catastrophe

1. While recovery from the disaster is an immediate priority, remaining focused on pre-existing long-term goals is also essential.

2. If possible, build a team *in advance* of a disaster composed of diverse and complementary individuals who are experienced in and capable of making difficult decisions and seeing them implemented, and who trust one another.

3. Press for active engagement and rapid decisions by both oneself and one's lieutenants.

4. Set immediate goals, priorities, and actions not only for restoring essential services but also for long-term recovery.

5. Convey the overarching mission for the recovery by specifying its underlying strategic principles.

6. Make it clear that this is not about a personal agenda but rather about the common goal of a national comeback.

---

6 TIERED LEADERSHIP

The President "has the memory of an elephant and he's very strict with numbers, so he puts a lot of pressure on his team to deliver."
—Rodrigo Pérez, Minister of Housing

Having articulated his clear vision and decisive actions, President Sebastián Piñera's knew that he required the leadership of the next tier—his cabinet—to implement them. Here, the president was a taskmaster, requiring detailed reconstruction plans from his ministers and insisting that all targets be achieved on schedule.

A parallel with the exercise of leadership in the American armed services comes to mind. The armed services have long advocated that their officers exercise leadership through clear-minded instructions to others and the enforcement of "the commander's intent." Because officers often face uncertain, changing, and complex terrains, they are called upon to unequivocally instruct their subordinates in an operation's mission, objectives, and strategy—and then let trained and disciplined subordinates execute the strategy to achieve those objectives, with adjustments and redirections as required but without detailed guidance from above.

The U.S. armed services later expanded the emphasis on commander's intent to include "mission command," that they defined as "the exercise of authority and direction by the commander using mission orders to enable disciplined initiative within the commander's intent to empower agile and adaptive leaders in the conduct" of their duties. In the words of the chairman of the Joint Chiefs of Staff, the nation's highest ranking officer, a commander "must understand the problem, envision the end state, and visualize the nature and design of the operation"—but then delegate its execution to others.[1]

By parallel, President Piñera envisioned the end state and then pressed the cabinet ministers to achieve that state. That had not been his first thought at the outset. The president was to be the "CEO of reconstruction" in one his early formulations, but he soon appreciated that if he were to lead as chief executive, he would have to achieve the reconstruction through his ministers, and that a primary task was thus to make his intent clear, unequivocal, and tangible for them. He would serve as the leader of a team that would have to execute the reconstruction in detail.

Because of the massive amount of detail, because of the moment's urgency, and because of the tactical thinking that can prevail in an emergency unless pressed to be more deliberative, the president's effective exercise of leadership through his second tier would depend much upon clear mission intent, a strong personal drive, and an exacting focus on results.

TARGETS AND RESULTS

"The president is obsessed with targets and results," observed Claudio Seebach, responsible for interministerial coordination at the presidential office, La Moneda. "He wants to know where we are, what is missing, and where do we have to advance." The abiding focus stemmed from a personal readiness to learn and to act, and it came with steely personal discipline. The president prided himself on having never missed a day of work in the past thirty years.

Sebastián Piñera consulted extensively, reaching out to a wide range of associates. In Seebach's characterization, it was a network of friends and people that the president would frequently contact for advice, especially an inner circle of former business colleagues.

The president required evidence-based options and decisions from his lieutenants. He carried such an array of facts and figures in his head that those who worked with him conjectured that he must have a secret "third floor" at the presidential palace where he kept a hidden brain-trust. "The president is a person that asks a lot of questions that are always targeted, and he demands a lot of data and a lot of evidence before taking a decision," observed one of his senior advisors. "The best questions always come from him," said the advisor, and they "make people think out of the box." One often wondered, "Why didn't we think of that question first?"

When the president flew on one occasion to Chile's southern-most city of Punta Arenas, for example, arriving at 1 a.m., he turned to one of his accompanying ministers to explain why taxes on natural gas there differed so much from those in Santiago. He expected all of his lieutenants to be well informed. One official who had worked with the president from the outset explained that the president was "very hands-on" and "demanding," and "hates it" when a minister "does not have a good answer."

In the experience of another La Moneda staffer, the president had never failed to read any document or report that he had received, and he was a stickler for detail, even to the point of format. He expected briefing papers to be titled, dated, numbered, and authored, and only then would he digest their contents.[2]

The president absorbed and used raw data like few others, offering advice to the housing minister on everything from waterproofing temporary homes to the design of play areas. "In the area of decision making," observed Ernesto Ayala, a professional writer who worked in La Moneda, "he's extremely concrete. He goes straight to the point" and rarely strayed into personal matters.

The president was also unrelentingly demanding, sometimes to the point of intimidation. Ministers came to La Moneda very well prepared, if not overprepared. The president typically arrived for a meeting with a minister's presubmitted document marked up with red pen, and then it was all business. In the words of one of his speechwriters, the president pressed for facts, not "poetry."

Sebastián Piñera placed value on content over rank, seeking counsel from midlevel public servants when he believed they knew more than their boss, or could better solve a problem. When one official was called to explain a briefing paper he had not authored, he learned that the president cared far more about the issue than who wrote about it. Acknowledging that he was not the author, the official delved into the paper's issues to help resolve the president's concerns.

"We want to be held accountable," the president explained, "and I want to be measured not by intention but by results." To that end, he established a unit to track and chronicle his administration's progress. On the premise that more transparency is always better than less, he regularly made results available to the public. He required his ministers to openly describe and report on the government website not only what each had accomplished in the past six months but also what they had failed to accomplish, and what they promised to accomplish in the next six months. The point was to ensure that the nation was aware of each of his ministries' plans and results so that the public could judge the cabinet and the president against those benchmarks.

A demanding follow-up was part of the president's formula as well. "I meet with every cabinet member at least three or four times a month for close to two hours," he reported. In those meetings, he explained, "we establish the goals and details, the commitments, the timetables. And we even rate what has been accomplished, what has to be accomplished, and I take notes of everything." Then, when we meet again, "they are fully aware that I know exactly what they said in the previous meeting."

TIMELY DECISION-MAKING

The president was less reflective than some and more unruffled than most. With people living in the streets, no water, no lights, and distress widespread, the president nevertheless remained "cool and calm, a person who could make good decisions in very uncertain scenarios," reported Ernesto Ayala.

Sebastián Piñera also had a way of helping others reach their own timely decisions. As the enormity of the housing crisis became evident, for instance, his officials balked at the prospect of having to reconstruct more than 200,000 homes as winter fast approached. Meeting his emergency committee six weeks after the earthquake, the president suggested that half of the displaced families could move in with relatives or friends, and others could repair enough of their homes at least to get through the winter. The president wrote out these back-of-the-envelope estimates. Whether accurate or not, they helped cut a seemingly insurmountable challenge by three-quarters, making the officials' task seem far more achievable.

If two cabinet members were at loggerheads, Piñera invoked what he termed a "sudden death" session to resolve the conflict on the spot. The two ministers each presented an argument for five minutes, and then the president made the final call. To minimize such conflicts in the first place, the president adopted an open door, open phone policy, pressing ministers to walk in or telephone him for quick resolution before conflict emerged.

LEADERSHIP THROUGH OTHERS

It would be a battle not only to restore the country but also to move it forward. The president repeatedly affirmed that he would rebuild the country "stone by stone and brick by brick"—and at the same time, "We are going to achieve something much bigger and build a better country."

In one tangible example: the Pan-American Highway had lost a span across the Claro River, and although the highway had four lanes at that point, the government would rebuild the bridge with six lanes, anticipating the day when the highway would have to expand. Similarly, many schools had been built with minimal facilities in the 1960s and 1970s, and the government would now configure the new schools with larger classrooms and new libraries. Also, while it was far simpler to build a thousand new homes in a single development, the government opted to rebuild them in a thousand separate locations, if that was what their occupants wanted.

But the president also came to appreciate that his vision and personal crusade had to be executed through the country's key agencies. To see how the president's decisions and actions were accepted and executed through his top tier, we first turn to the actions of Rodrigo Pérez, who had initially served as the governor of the O'Higgins region, one of the hardest-hit areas, and then as minister of housing and urban development, one of the agencies most centrally involved in the country's reconstruction. We then consider the actions of Hernán de Solminihac, the minister of public works, and of Jaime José Mañalich, the minister of health.

After recruiting these and other ministers who brought considerable management experience, the president specified an array of objectives and followed up to ensure that they were met in detail. The ministers in turn conveyed their strategic intent within their own ranks and worked to ensure implementation in the field. The president and his ministers then actively backed the front-line managers, who were most directly responsible for delivering the government's assistance to, and drawing guidance from, those most affected.

A REGIONAL GOVERNOR

Like many of his fellow ministers, Rodrigo Pérez had long pursued a private-sector career and had never expected to enter public service. His banking associates would have scarcely anticipated that one day he would be appointed as governor—intendente—of one of Chile's fifteen regions and later to the national cabinet. But there he was, initially responsible for recovery in one of the most devastated regions and later for housing in all regions—the nation's most massive and most costly reconstruction initiative and one that would require a full four years.

Pérez had studied civil engineering at Catholic University of Chile in Santiago and earned his MBA from the University of Navarra, Spain. He had served as an investment manager at AFP Provida in Santiago, Chile's largest pension fund manager, and then Bankers Trust. He eventually rose to group executive for Deutsche Bank in Mexico and then country head for Deutsche Bank in Chile.

Pérez and his family had been vacationing near the town of Santo Domingo in the Valparaíso region, west of Santiago when the earthquake hit. They drove to Santiago and then to their family farm near Santa Cruz in the O'Higgins region (named after one of Chile's founding figures, Bernardo O'Higgins), some one hundred miles south of Santiago. They were stunned by the breadth of the destruction, with homes in ruin, power lines down, and bridges in collapse. And they would soon find that their own farmhouse had been so badly damaged by the event that they would later have to tear it down and build anew. As they motored across the shattered landscape, Pérez's secretary telephoned to say that president-elect Sebastián Piñera had just called Pérez's office.

Banking, investing, and finance had largely defined Pérez's career, and he had come to know fellow businessman Sebastián Piñera through their business dealings. Now on the phone, Piñera said that he needed Pérez to become governor of the O'Higgins region, the area's top administrative post and one filled by presidential appointment. It was still a dozen days until the inauguration, but Piñera reported that he wanted to name Pérez a regional governor now and also appoint him as a member of the area emergency committee. The president asked for Pérez's quick acceptance.

The O'Higgins region lies between the Santiago metropolis and the Maule region, the most affected region; O'Higgins had been nearly as hard hit as Maule itself. The president described many features of the devastation and their likely costs. His specific estimates were already within 5 to 10 percent of many of the final figures tallied months later, and he even forecast a total cost of some $20 billion to the government and private sector, a figure that would prove close to the final amount. The new governor's responsibilities, said the president, would be sizable and his actions urgent. The president declared that his new administration would "start full speed from day one," and he needed to know now if Pérez was ready to roll up his sleeves.

Rodrigo Pérez had been working for the family office of Eduardo Fernández, a wealthy Chilean entrepreneur. Pérez asked how soon the president required a definitive response, hoping for time to reflect on the critical career change acceptance would entail, but the president allowed no slack: "Right away!" The president-elect had decided that he wanted to take office with the governors of the six most affected region already named, a presidential designation that by convention had normally come only after the inauguration. This would allow the designated governors to become directly engaged in the emergency committees being set up in the regions, and also to name their own deputies in the most vital recovery areas including health, public works, housing, and planning.

Pérez explained to the president that he would need to consult with his family—his wife and three of his six children were in the car at the moment—but also vowed that he would let the president know by the following morning. Pérez concluded overnight that he would have to accept. When called by the country's newly elected leader at a moment of national crisis, he explained, it would be unconscionable to do otherwise. He telephoned the president to say yes, and he hastily returned to Santiago to begin assembling his own top team.

Eleven days later, on March 11, the day that the president was to be inaugurated in the national legislative chambers in Valparaiso, the regional governors including Pérez were to be sworn in by the new president at a ceremony in Santiago at 7 p.m. that same evening. When the after-tremors hit the midday presidential inauguration in Valparaiso, however, Pérez decided to forgo his own formal investiture and drove, he recalled, at breakneck speed to his region's capital city, Rancagua.

When Pérez arrived in the regional capital, flushed with the urgency of the moment, he rushed to the outgoing governor's office. Pérez asked the governor to work with him on the spot to make "a precise diagnosis of what's going on," and within half an hour they had assembled the directors of police and fire services and other members of a regional emergency committee. That was fortunate, Pérez recalled, because just then—still the same day as the president's inauguration—the newly sworn in president's office called to say that the president himself would be arriving momentarily by helicopter in Rancagua to learn what was happening in the O'Higgins region. There, the president took his first official action, declaring a state of disaster for the O'Higgins region, to "protect and ensure public order and provide basic services," and appointing a brigadier general, Antonio Yakcich Furche, to head the region's restoration of security.

Later that same day, Sebastián Piñera returned to Santiago to enter the presidential palace for the first time as president, ordinarily a potent symbolic moment. A band played as Piñera arrived at 9 p.m., the new president delivered a short speech, and then he, first lady Cecilia Morel, and several ministers walked onto a plaza adjacent to the La Moneda to observe a moment of silence. They joined hundreds of people standing with candles to honor the earthquake's many victims.

Yet in minutes Piñera called his new ministers of health, interior, and other portfolios, his army generals, and his new governors of the three most affected regions—including Pérez—into a late-night work meeting on their first day in office. They focused on what they had learned about the devastation of the earthquake and its aftershock, and what they should tackle most immediately.

The president had set his administration's revised direction during the truncated inauguration earlier that day: "Today as President of Chile, I summon you all, the generation of the bicentennial, two great and noble missions. First, rebuild on rock and not on sand what has been destroyed and, [second], raise again our homes, lift our schools, our hospitals, and raise, above all, our spirits, our courage and our will to fight."[3]

A MINISTER OF PUBLIC WORKS

A parallel leadership experience came in Hernán de Solminihac, a civil engineer, academic, and consultant who entered the president's first cabinet as minister of public works, a post that gave him national responsibility for public infrastructure and water resources. Like Rodrigo Pérez, he had no political background, nor had he personally known Sebastián Piñera when the president-elect called him for public service. He had served primarily as a research and then university administrator, first as head of the Direction of Technological and Scientific Research at Catholic University and then as dean of its School of Engineering.

On the night of February 27, 2010, de Solminihac was driving to pick up one of his daughters at a discotheque in the coastal city of San Antonio, the busiest port on the west coast of South America, to take her back to their beach home—it was still summer vacation—when he experienced a strange movement of his car. Stopping to check, he realized that the engine was not the problem. The roadway itself had been shaking, and as the tremors finally subsided, de Solminihac tried to contact his vacation home by mobile phone. No call would go through, as millions of others were also discovering. He then sought to find a second daughter in another location, also waiting for his pickup, and spotted her at 5 a.m. as she walked in complete darkness across a badly damaged bridge that he had driven across just two hours earlier. It was, he recalled, a "very, very emotional situation."

Returning home and with just a few hours of sleep, de Solminihac received a call from the president-elect's office at 9 a.m., asking that he meet in emergency with the president and other incoming ministers at 8 p.m. that evening in Santiago. As they assembled, Piñera reported the widespread damage he had surveyed from his fly-over of the most devastated areas earlier that day. The cabinet appointees each added their own distressing appraisals.

The president-elect instructed his cabinet members to gather more complete data and to work together with their outgoing cabinet counterparts. De Solminihac in turn asked his own staff, barely in place itself, to learn what it could of the devastation, and he himself contacted the outgoing minister of public works to initiate the handover. Despite the minister-designate's efforts to acquire more comprehensive data, he soon found that the "situational awareness" still remained incomplete among his incumbent counterparts.[4]

The earthquake brought an abrupt redirection of de Solminihac's plans for his ministry, as would be the case for other ministries that were soon to be on the front lines. "The most difficult decision in those days before taking office," he recalled, "was to change our priorities and concentrate on the emergency." It also proved a frustrating moment because he was not yet in charge. All that he could do was to advise the incumbent minister on decisions that de Solminihac would only be able to make himself after his oath on March 11. Still, he was not shy about rendering advice, first on the nation's severed arterial roadway, and then on its downed bridges.

Chile's geography is unique. Averaging just 110 miles in width but extending more than 2,600 miles from north to south, the country is served vertically by just a single main highway—Route 5—running from Peru in the north to Patagonia in the south, the famed Pan-American Highway. One advantage of a single thoroughfare is that it is virtually impossible to become lost, but now the earthquake had severed the highway near the artery's southern entry into Santiago.

De Solminihac knew that construction of a second major highway into Santiago—where 6.5 million of Chile's 17 million people reside—was nearing completion, and he pressed the incumbent minister of public works for its accelerated opening. The collapse of hundreds of bridges in the Maule region had made road travel there nearly impossible, and de Solminihac pressed for temporary ferry crossings at a host of choke-points, insisting that the water transports be capable of carrying not only automobiles but also trucks and buses.

Once in power, the minister of public works became a member of the National Reconstruction Committee that took on long-term planning to guide the rebuilding efforts and also advise on their budgetary impact.

Although well constituted in principle, the reconstruction committee did not in practice function well at the outset. Its first director did not have ministerial authority, and when committee decisions were reached, the director did not have the power to implement them. The president soon replaced the director of the reconstruction committee with the minister of public works, giving the committee the authoritative leadership required to ensure interministerial coordination in the country's rebuilding, even if it still lacked unfettered influence over all the factious forces.

"The most difficult and surprising" revelation, recalled the minister of public works, was that "we didn't have all the support from everybody to solve the problems." His own lieutenants and fellow ministers were on board, but outside players seemed less so, a few even opposing almost every reconstruction decision he would make. Resistance was especially vociferous among opposition political leaders from the most affected regions, who even turned to the courts to block the government's measures when their vocal criticism failed to do so.

It seemed that "in politics you work for yourself not the country," complained the president. As a result, Piñera later reflected, "we should have brought the opposition more into the process." In retrospect, de Solminihac observed, it would have been important to "put people in the same direction to work together to find the solution" from the outset.

It was that surprising lack of natural alignment around what seemed like obvious reconstruction goals that proved one of the more vexing discoveries for the public works minister. Despite the unexpected resistance, de Solminihac opted nonetheless to try to work with even the most vociferous political opponents. It was a matter, he said, "of talking to them and showing them that we were doing the right things because we have only a short time to solve the problems—and that it was important to solve the problem in a good way in as short a time as possible." The "cost to take more time," he repeatedly reasoned with them, would be "more expensive than the solutions we were suggesting." The public works minister came to distinguish between opponents who seemed persuadable from those who appeared intractable. "You work with the people that want to work with the government," de Solminihac said, and then "you try to avoid the ones that don't want to work with you."

In reflecting on the reconstruction experience—the first time through for the public works minister as for virtually all officials in the throes of a disaster—de Solminihac had come to appreciate several canons for leading through calamity. First, readiness to face a catastrophic risk is facilitated by at least some prior groundwork for reacting to it: "To be prepared, to know what to do in advance, to have a protocol on how to do it" was vital, de Solminihac observed in retrospect. With a protocol in place, it becomes easier to pinpoint what needs to be restored—or even upgraded in the process—rather than resorting to a series of ad hoc decisions.

Second, a working national communication system is vital for country recovery, a conclusion far more appreciated after the absence of a workable system in the wake of the F27 disaster. Creating redundant and disaster-proof risk communication systems was now seen as an imperative—especially when an early-warning system might well have proved lifesaving for many in advance of the tsunami that had so massively washed over the coastline.

One study reported that those who heeded Japan's tsunami warning after the Tōhoku earthquake that was issued some fifteen minutes ahead of the surge were far more likely to survive than those who did not hear or respond to the warning. Among those who sought higher ground, only 5 percent were struck by the tsunami, but among those who did not flee, 49 percent were hit. If coastal residents in Chile could have been trained to flee—and did evacuate—in the case of a warning, or were prepared to move on their own even without a warning system after they felt the shocks from a quake, casualty rates in Chile might well have been far lower.[5]

A MINISTER OF HEALTH

The F27 challenges would be severe as well for Chile's health minister-to-be, Jaime José Mañalich. A physician who had specialized in kidney disease, he had been at the ready to serve as health minister when Sebastián Piñera had run unsuccessfully for La Moneda in 2006. Now, just ten days from coming to serve as the new minister of health after Piñera's successful second run, the violence of the F27 event wiped out much of the public hospital capacity in the hardest hit areas. It was soon to be his nightmare, but since he was still directing a private clinic, his first concern in the early hours was to ready his own facility for casualties. Within three hours he and his staff had managed to discharge half their existing patients to make room for an anticipated onslaught of the injured.

Like the regional governor and public works minister, Mañalich came with no political history but plenty of passion for responsible spending and a desire to end corruption. He, like de Solminihac, also reported that he had little choice but to say yes when the president-elect called him to take the public role. Although Mañalich would be part of a conservative administration that had campaigned for less government, he believed that the powers of the state would be fairly but forcefully applied by the new president.

Jaime Mañalich joined Sebastián Piñera and Rodrigo Hinzpeter near the epicenter on their first-day fact-finding in Concepción. He then checked in on his own with the region's public hospitals during the next three days. These hospitals were part of a vast agency he was soon to head, with 28,000 beds, 150,000 employees, 16,000 physicians—more than half the country's 30,000 doctors—and an annual budget of $6 billion, making his the largest of the cabinet agencies. Of the nation's 186 hospitals he was soon to oversee, he learned that half had been damaged by the quake and a quarter were partially closed or completely destroyed. In the major cities of the most affected regions, including Concepción, all of their facilities had been shut down. "The challenges we faced during those months," he said, "were terrible."

The world's most intense 9.5 Mw earthquake, near the Chilean city of Valdivia of May 22, 1960, had stunned a region some 350 miles south of Santiago. Its impact was enormous. By one estimate, a quarter of the seismic energy of all the world's earthquakes taken together from 1906 to 2005 had been released by that one event alone. Although of weaker magnitude, the 8.8 event on F27 hit closer to the capital and rocked a larger zone. Despite a long tremor history in Chile, the new health minister found that the health system had been unprepared for such widespread destruction.

The president-elect turned to his incoming health minister: "What should we do?" Mañalich responded with assurance: "We will take control of the situation." Restoring emergency services would be at the top of the list. The president urged fast action but delegated its execution: "Let's get something done and tell me about it if you've got a problem." To that end, the health minister designate worked with his outgoing counterpart to arrange for international donors to bring field hospitals to the area via airlift. They came from Argentina, Bolivia, Germany, Peru, even Russia. Working with the Chilean Army, the U.S. Air Force constructed overnight a field hospital in the fifty-thousand-person town of Angol on March 12 that would serve its townspeople through the end of 2010.

Many of the arriving personnel had been trained for combat wounds—a surfeit of traumatologists and vascular surgeons had arrived. Whatever their specialties, these doctors attended to thousands of victims through the end of the year in hospitals for civilians as well as military hospitals that the new health minister had managed to commandeer for public use. By March 15, 2010, his ministry had reestablished a working hospital in almost every major city.

To make way for the injured, some 60 percent of the ministry's patients nationwide were discharged. Even patients in the country's north—far from the epicenter—were cleared via reverse triage to make space for casualties from the south. In one case, for example, the ministry transferred earthquake victims from Temuco, a city of a quarter-million 415 miles south of Santiago, to a relatively undamaged hospital 125 miles north of the capital.

Mañalich discovered that the crisis had unleashed a psychological force nearly as debilitating at the physical force itself. With families and facilities traumatized and stressed, depression took a toll on the victims as well as those committed to aiding them. "When you go to a city where every building, every house, and the hospital are destroyed, people have no water, no light, the kind of depression people suffer, even medical personnel, was very, very profound," he recalled. Some had lost relatives, others their life's possessions. "It was very difficult."

Although the minister could have presided from his well-supported office in a high-rise headquarters not far from La Moneda in the center of Santiago, he opted instead to reside for the next month in the country's most devastated regions to provide personal direction and counsel. He set up an office in a van with little more than a satellite telephone. "I spent almost the whole first month in the field," he recalled, "going from one city to another city, trying to make people confident about the kind of care they could deliver." He deployed himself at the center of the trauma, and in so doing added still another level to MBWA—*management by walking around*—popularized by the 1982 best-seller by Thomas J. Peters and Robert H. Waterman, *In Search of Excellence: Lessons from America's Best-Run Companies*. Mañalich practiced MBLA—*management by living around*—which enabled him to console and inspire others personally: "We have to recover hope. We have to work. We have to survive. We have to help."[6]

Beyond the compelling dynamic of urgent care, the health minister pressed for rapid restoration before the onset of winter, a harsh season with widespread respiratory infections expected in the weeks ahead. By way of comparison, the cities of Temuco, Chile, and Washington, DC, are at nearly equivalent latitudes—39 degrees south and north, respectively. It would be unthinkable to have no health care facilities during a Washington, DC, winter, yet that was the situation facing many southern cities in Chile as their winter approached.

To expedite reconstruction, the health minister utilized prefabricated materials, and within a year Chile had managed to restore all twenty-eight thousand hospital beds. Bringing the destroyed facilities back to functioning condition also required completely replenishing everything from sheets and blankets to ventilators and x-ray machines. The rebuilding was not without its unexpected delays. In one instance, the ministry had inadvertently sought to reconstruct a hospital on a sacred, native burial site.

The Ministry of Health built some facilities it knew would last just a year—a temporary measure—but it targeted others for fifteen years, and still others for fifty years. Operating rooms in older hospitals had often been sized at 325 square feet, but now 540 square feet had become conventional, and all the new facilities would have to meet that standard.

With the benefit of looking back on the trauma of F27, the health minister urged greater health service readiness for low-probability, high-consequence events in the future. "Hospitals always should be designed for the worst possible scenario—because they have to stay in place whatever happens. If you have a big fire, earthquake, tsunami, or whatever, you need hospitals not to fail." But as the F27 event faded in active memory, he feared, this point would be lost. He also worried that the country was still not training enough for the unthinkable: the human element—the "people behind the scenes"—have to be ready to face the unthinkable, he said. "You need to commit people to solidarity," he offered, "to work very hard. It's not just a matter of an institution." It is a "very personal business."

A DEMANDING AGENDA

As recounted by these three ministers, the president imposed an arduous agenda on his top team. Piñera insisted on facts and actions, required in-depth reporting, and demanded that detailed action plans and timetables be specified and deadlines be met. Setting tangible goals and holding his team—twenty-two cabinet ministers and fifteen regional governors who were all in charge, too—to explicit timetables, the president defined the reconstruction targets in graphic and timely ways.

"He likes to be involved in all the important decisions," said Housing Minister Rodrigo Pérez, "a commander-in-chief on the ground from day one." In Pérez's characterization, the president "has the memory of an elephant and he's very strict with numbers, so he puts a lot of pressure on his team to deliver." As a result, the housing minister observed, "you feel the pressure, you cannot bluff. If you say something that proves incorrect, he will catch it and you will hear about it," he warned. "You cannot say vague things. You have to be precise, and you have to be consistent, and you have to have backup numbers because you are going to be asked." And the essence of the president's message, he said, was to "rebuild faster" *and* "rebuild better."[7]

The president's pressure on his subordinates was unrelenting as he followed a habit of regular multihour monthly meetings with each of the cabinet ministers and regional governors required to review in detail what they had individually achieved. The president sought graphic particulars and reams of numbers, and questioned or challenged almost everything, probing to see that options, decisions, and actions were supported by compelling logics and strategic rationales. Ministers would introduce problems and solutions, ideas and policies, and the president would delve into each. "It's not micromanagement," said Housing Minister Rodrigo Pérez, but "he's a very hands-on president."

Despite a feeling of being dragged over the coals, the "value-added" was evident to those on the receiving end. The president looked for ways to incentivize each of the affected parties to have a personal stake in a government initiative. Decisions coming out of the bilateral meetings were often modified or refined during the meeting to reflect this.

By way of one example, the housing minister proposed to modify a policy for public parks in the most damaged towns, many of them with residents of modest means. By prior stipulation, the national government could fund construction of a park but not the costs of maintenance, which could be as high as 20 percent of the original building costs, an amount beyond the budget of many poor settlements. To reinvigorate areas wiped out by the earthquake or tsunami, the minister asked the president for approval also to cover their operating costs, but the president insisted that the local municipalities pay half. It would be less costly to the national government yet affordable by many town governments, but, most importantly, it would incorporate an incentive for local officials to support a new park, since they would have some skin in the game.

The president also proved a financial stickler: "He's very strict in spending money, and he behaves like it was his own money," said the housing minister. "He doesn't accept money going down the drain." To guard against waste, Piñera required that a representative of the Ministry of Finance attend all ministerial meetings to ensure that whatever was planned by the president's lieutenants had adequate funding—otherwise the president would block the initiative.

The president retained the ministers' presentations from the bilateral meetings, made notes, recorded decisions, and returned to their next encounter with detailed comments on the previous meeting. "If there's a topic that is coming back again," said Rodrigo Pérez, "he will know what he has said before." Disciplined in the art of general management through others, it seemed like Sebastián Piñera was right out of the pages of Larry Bossidy's and Ram Charan's classic account, *Execution*, whose subtitle was aptly descriptive, *The Discipline of Getting Things Done*. "He extracts from his people the most, the best they have," said the housing minister. "Sometimes it hurts, but he's able to do it." The president frequently telephoned his ministers with specific questions or instructions, calls that sometimes came well into the night. In the summary words of the housing minister, "He's very strict, very, very, very demanding."[8]

As noted previously, the president also demanded that all the reconstruction be completed by the time he left office on March 11, 2014. And to back that up, Piñera created a special unit to track and enforce all of the specific commitments and goals promised by his cabinet ministers and regional governors. In the case of the O'Higgins region, for instance, the president sought detailed data on the pace of recovery within health, education, agriculture, and tourism. In the case of health, the president demanded particulars about the pace and cost of constructing replacement hospitals in the three cities of Rancagua, Santa Cruz, and San Fernando. He repeatedly checked their actual restoration against their governors' promised timelines.

The president was criticized by some for acting too much like a chief operating officer and too little like a chairman of the board: too engaged in operational detail, with too little broad oversight. And some governmental officials did not take well to the tough grilling and unrelenting demands of the president. But for ministers and governors with prior management experience in the private sector, it was a disciplined leadership style with which many were already well familiar.

A LONGER-TERM STRATEGIC AGENDA

Another important element of the strategy was that Sebastián Piñera pressed his ministers and governors for longer-term solutions for national reconstruction—even when they proved more costly than more immediate fixes.

For example, one city in the O'Higgins region had some two thousand public housing units that had been poorly designed when they were originally built in the 1990s. Now, three-fifths stood badly damaged by the earthquake. Rather than simply repairing what had been far from optimal in the first place, Piñera instead pressed for a more far reaching step—but also a far more costly and time-consuming step—of tearing down the damaged units and rebuilding from scratch. Critics would later suggest that the resulting demolition was sometimes too massive, as some buildings might have been salvaged. They claimed that efficiency had too often yielded to expediency.[9]

If two families had been crowded together in one of the destroyed dwellings, for instance, the president insisted that his government provide two new homes rather than trying to squeeze them back into one new dwelling. More generally, the president pressed for "customer" contact, asking those most dislocated by the earthquake what steps seemed most responsive to their family needs and neighborhood networks.

The president, reported Housing Minister Rodrigo Pérez, "was very tough on us, he wanted wise decisions, he wanted us not to do stupid things." He pressed his ministers to take the harder road when it appeared the better road. "A normal guy," said Pérez, "would try to make his life easier," but he "always made life tougher."

As still another illustration, the president decided that the rebuilding should restore the traditional colonial look of village and town centers, many of which were of adobe materials. For that purpose, the Ministry of Housing issued grants for architectural preservation, but found that this was not enough. Little expertise still existed in Chile for adobe structures, since they were no longer built in the country. But Peru was another story. The government pitched in, importing architects and builders from Peru to help restore town centers with adobe—or at least an adobelike look. Here, cultural preservation trumped efficiency and expediency.

The president encouraged families to reconstruct their domiciles in locations of their own choosing, even if the place proved more costly for the government. If they had resided in a small rural community, for example, they should not be required to rebuild in a nearby town where services and construction would be less expensive but where the family would be less contented.

The volume of customized requests proved vast, with more than fifty thousand appeals requiring a special vetting by the ministry. But the president's edict—family roots should take precedence over public efficiency—became a dominant principle, albeit an expensive one. From a longer-term perspective the final siting also had its costs, as restored homes could be in locations that were still vulnerable to natural disasters.

The same principle guided residential reconstruction along the coast where the tsunami had caused such ruin. Most residents sought to return to their original homestead, but that required expensive rebuilding on pylons. Their design required site-specific forecasts of future wave heights and speeds, and the installation of tsunami-mitigation barriers in some areas.

The president asked each region to prepare a strategic plan for restoration of its health services, education, agriculture, and tourism. The central government's ministries each would have to formulate their own master plan, and the regional governors soon found themselves working within a classic matrix, having to lead all of their own operating agencies and at the same time collaborate with an array of central agencies.

TANGIBLE GOALS AND SPECIFIC TIMETABLES

The president's style at the top was replicated down through the ranks, as ministers and governors in turn pressed their own subordinates for detailed goals and supporting data that they could use both to manage work and to report to the president. Cabinet ministers would occasionally even ask that their own direct reports accompany them to meetings in La Moneda with the president[1] so that the next tier down could appreciate firsthand the hard-hitting demands from the top. The president's actions had a cascading effect down the government organizational chart.

The president embraced an unrelenting data-driven emphasis on aggressive but achievable targets, and in so doing might well have qualified for portrayal in Jim Collins' and Morton Hansen's account, *Great by Choice,* as to what makes companies change from determined to sustained performers. To illustrate this concept, Collins and Hansen contrast the expedition of Norwegian explorer Roald Amundsen to reach the South Pole for the first time in 1911 with the simultaneous but ill-fated effort by British explorer Robert Scott. Amundsen had methodically tested his equipment and transport—snow skis and sledge dogs—and consistently marched some ten to twenty miles a day, regardless of the weather; Scott had relied more on intuition and less on planning—adding another explorer to the crew at the last minute and bringing horses yet untested in Antarctic conditions. He pressed far forward when conditions were good but paused for the day when they were not. Amundsen reached the South Pole first and his expedition returned unscathed to report their conquest; Scott arrived at the pole a month later and his expedition perished during its return journey.[10]

In setting aggressive but achievable targets, the president followed a proven tradition of motivating subordinates by methodically setting tangible goals and specific timetables, and then holding himself and his team to them, as Amundsen had done in the race to the South Pole. Stretch goals were a part of the formulation as well. Steve Jobs was the master of that art, going well beyond what most others thought feasible, as he took Apple from a $2 billion value when he returned in 1997 to a valuation of more than $500 billion fifteen years later. He became known for his "reality distortion field" in which he would push his engineers to do what all thought unimaginable. "You did the impossible," recalled one of the original Mac computer designers, "because you didn't realize it was impossible."[11]

One of the clearest examples of this behavior in Chile was the government's decision to have all students back in school within just weeks. Without fully consulting his education minister, the president declared on national television on March 11 that the 1.2 million public school students whose schools had been destroyed or severely damaged (out of a total of 3.5 million) would be back in the classroom by the time their summer recess was over. The president asserted that all schools would reopen within forty-five days. The minister of education—Joaquín Lavín—grimaced. He privately believed it would take more than a year—probably eighteen months—to fully rebuild the damaged or destroyed schools.

The president had set a stretch objective for his team, but then of course could achieve it only by mobilizing those who had direct responsibility for ensuring those goals would be met. With the government having publicly declared that the early reopening would be reached, the education minister mobilized his agency to meet the commitment.

The government decided that any place that could be used as a classroom should be considered, including churches, police stations, even temporary shelters. "In times of emergency, we have to be creative," explained Joaquín Lavín. The creative edge could be seen in an initiative of a Chilean bus maker, Industrias Metalúrgicas Paredes S.A., known as Metalpar. It refitted buses of Transantiago, the capital's rapid-transport system, to serve as classrooms by insulating their floors, sides, and roofs, adding desks, turning the engine cavity into a storage area, and then removing the wheels once the vehicles had been driven to a neighborhood location. It installed five such "bus-schools," in Constitución, for instance, providing classroom spaces for 140 students.[12]

Private homes became classrooms as well. The Ministry of Education surveyed neighborhoods to identify residents who would lend their home for part of the day for such a purpose, and some students soon found themselves moving from subject to subject by walking from home to home. Whatever the venues, all Chilean students were again in school by the president's deadline of April 26.

The government learned fortunately that its initial estimate of sixty-five hundred damaged schools was too high, as many schools had been unnecessarily evacuated. By July 2010, the Ministry of Education was estimating that only forty-five hundred schools required rebuilding or replacement. As the ministry's assessment further sharpened with better data, the initial price tag of $2.5 billion for the repair and reconstruction was reduced to $500 million.

The earlier $2.5 billion estimate had come from a bottom-up flow of requests. With little specific guidance from the central government other than building standards and consolidating locations, each region had been allowed to develop its own plan for rebuilding its schools. Mayors thus often proposed that their schools be rebuilt in a better location or substantially improved. In the face of those predictable upward pressures—encouraged by the principled premise of asking those on the front line what they believed they needed—the government reevaluated, moved away from yielding to local preferences, and capped its spending per school at $60,000.

Some unanticipated temporary distortions resulted, since Chile supports not only a public system but also private schools through a voucher program. Since private schools receive state subsidies on a per capita formula, they were incentivized to reopen as soon as possible. And as a result, the families of a number of public school students transferred their children temporarily into private schools.

Virtually all of the nation's students were indeed back in school with a teacher at the front of a classroom and a roof over their heads by the start of the school term. The government then pressed for changes in legal requirements to facilitate more permanent school construction. This included new legislation to finance the construction and encourage private donations to school rebuilding.

The Ministry of Education itself—some eight thousand employees—required restaffing in the view of its officials. Some long-standing employees were not given to sufficiently rapid-fire decisions and actions. For every thirty long-serving employees, five were relatively new when Education Minister Joaquín Lavín first arrived, and he managed to change that ratio to about 50:50. Though ready to move with more tempo, some of the newer civil servants knew too little about how to manage their portfolios. The education minister created a small working group to build a new culture of urgency within the ministry to meet the tough demands for new and better schools on a breakneck schedule.

When the president promoted Rodrigo Pérez from governor of O'Higgins region to Minister of Housing and Urban Development after the president's first housing minister was forced to resign barely a year in office, the president doubled down by insisting that Pérez reconstruct more than 200,000 dwelling units and at the same time modernize the government's housing policies. During his first meeting with the president in his new role, Pérez was told by the president, "Minister, I have some bad news for you. You're not only going to have to take care of the reconstruction but also you have to implement" a host of improvements in housing policies. "So you'll have to do both things at the same time. Don't forget the housing policies. We have to do both!" The housing minister embraced both.

The president and his ministers and governors carried their guiding concepts to medium and small towns, creating a host of urban regeneration plans that would guide the rebuilding in ways that maintained the character and identify of the towns and even neighborhoods within them. Habitable zones were to be protected and made safe from future disasters. They directed grants to homeowners who in rebuilding would commit to preserving the architectural image of the traditional villages. The Ministry of Housing focused national efforts on low- to middle-income families, those in the lowest three earnings quintiles, primarily families with incomes below $12,000—personal income averaged about $12,000 in 2010—and whose home value was less than $88,000.[13]

Because the damage to some towns near the coastline had been so massive, initial proposals called for the settlements to be reconstructed elsewhere. Yet people along the coastline "lived from the sea," observed the housing minister. In deference to the sensitive but more costly alternative of keeping families where they had long lived, the government opted to make as many communities as tsunami-proof as could be reasonably achieved.

The coastal towns would have to survive a wave front of up to fifty feet in height. They would have to create public parks and other features that would help deflect a tsunami. Buildings in the "invasion zone" would have to follow new codes of survivability. Evaluation protocols and dress rehearsals would have to be part of the formula as well.

Homes would also have to be better than before, replacement-plus.

All this added a third or more to the total costs—a tsunami-proof home could cost twice the alternative—though even then some areas were simply deemed uninhabitable, and the government expropriated the property.

BOTTOM-UP HOUSING

The president and his cabinet pursued a simultaneous top-down and bottom-up initiative. While they set ambitious goals and executed them, they at the same time drew local sentiment into the equation, allowing the grassroots to shape many of the key decisions.

The Ministry of Housing, for example, gave families substantial discretion in the type of building and their contractor. Owners could apply for several forms of support, including funds for repair or for rebuilding, and the latter could be either on the existing tract or in a new location. To ensure appropriate family use of the public subsidies, the ministry released them in increments of 30 percent, then 40 percent, and then the remaining 30 percent, after a final inspection confirmed compliance. In the end, given the choice, more than 70 percent of the families chose to repair or rebuild homes at the same location where the family had traditionally lived.

Those rebuilding their house from scratch had a choice of several preset models from certified local builders, or they could design a new house themselves or buy an existing home. Available designs allowed for private additions or later modifications. The typical single-family subsidy ranged from $18,000 to $20,000. The ministry also supported the building of new condos for organized groups of families.

For identifying those in need of housing, the government delegated the task to town mayors, who were asked to create a registry of disaster victims within six months. It was from this roster that the government finally subsidized 220,000 homes—half repaired, half new. Some families had been doubled up or were renting from one another when F27 struck. In Talca, the capital of the Maule region, for instance, the mayor's disaster registry identified 1,200 owning families and another 1,800 renters. The Ministry of Housing allowed them to go their separate ways if they so wanted. In all, the government supporting the building of some 30,000 additional units to accommodate displaced families that had been renting or sharing a home.

For more than 4,000 families who could not be resheltered in their original location, many because they had lived in the tsunami zone, the government created 107 emergency camps complete with clinics and schools. The Ministry of Housing asked groups of such families to organize and plan their new dwellings in concert, good for sustaining networks but less good for timely reconstruction. Since that delay would take displaced residents through a second winter, the Ministry of Housing offered temporary dwellers the option of a subsidized housing rental, and 17 to 55 percent of the 107 camps' occupants opted for a temporary roof rather than canvas over their head. In the end, it required some two years to find and build homes for all on entirely new sites. Such delays were frequently cited by opposition politicians and skeptical journalists as a sign of inefficiency in the recovery strategy.[14]

Housing of course is only one component of urban reconstruction, and since fifty towns of at least 5,000 residents had been hit by the F27 event, the national government, municipal authorities, private companies, and nongovernmental organizations invested in new plans for seismic and tsunami protection, better land use, and effective zoning. The national government backed the plans, but also asked that town councils approve them. Protecting the country's architectural traditions was important as well, and the Ministry of Housing created a heritage subsidy to support classic exteriors and covered sidewalks at some 5,000 units.

In one town whose adobe homes dated back four hundred years, for example, the residents were ready to replace them, but the mayor secured the involvement of a local enterprise that added $3,000 to $30,000 for restoration of historic buildings on top of $11,000 from the government for the repair itself. But other communities opted to forgo heritage preservation, since it was far more costly and time consuming than plain-vanilla repair or replacement.

To expedite what otherwise could be become a drawn out process with tens of thousands of homeowners seeking to rebuild or start over, a division of the Ministry of Housing—the Housing and Urban Development Service—arranged for groups of local owners to meet with several builders who would pitch their products—and then the groups would vote on the preferred offering, making that the choice for the entire community. The precertified options included prefab vs. site-built, wood vs. masonry, and sometimes extras like solar heating or bay windows. The choices reflected the government's principle of not only rapid reconstruction but also grassroots guidance.

In a study conducted in collaboration with the Ministry of Housing, University of California-Berkeley, architecture faculty member Mary C. Comerio reported on three divergent paths that groups of residents in one area pursued in light of the locally driven outcomes. Dichato is a town of 4,000 residents near Concepción, and the F27 event destroyed more than 1,300 of their units. One group, which had lived in a 91-unit housing project that could not be reinhabited, opted to start over on the same site, and two years later its families moved into a newly built project. A second group of some 450 families divided, half wanting to rebuild nearby, the other half preferring to move into the town center, and by early 2013 both subgroups had secured their separate housing. Residents of a third project, near the sea, were less organized, and a new set of 128 units were constructed for them on the same spot to withstand a future tsunami, though in the end only 15 of the families opted to move into those homes. The remaining units were placed on the open market.[15]

Coordination among government ministries was well illustrated here as Dichato sought to rebuild itself for greater earthquake resilience. The Ministry of Education funded the move of a school out of the tsunami hazard zone, the Ministry of Public Works supported the reinforcement of a river channel, and the Ministry of Housing arranged for the rebuilding of homes. Their efforts together were intended to make the town more resilient to seismic risk.

Often the government went well beyond basic reconstruction. When townspeople in Dichato complained about one aspect or another of the reconstruction, a vocal critic argued that what the town really needed was jobs. In response, Felipe Kast, who had been minister of social development and later presidential delegate to villages and camps, helped to organize a local music and arts festival that became an annual affair that brought some thirty-five thousand visitors in Dichato by 2012—and had created local jobs along the way.[16]

Several key principles guided the top-down, bottom-up reconstruction of housing. First, the government set forward what it sought, but then let residents select their own builders and models from among a "diversity of solutions for a diversity or problems." The government would define boundary conditions such as size and quality while leaving open creativity and competition. Residents then had a choice of models within those boundaries; some seven hundred government-licensed advisors and brokers worked with families to find the right builder. Private companies and nonprofit organizations would then construct with a government-subsidized credit card held by the residents.

This three-way partnership had the advantage of allowing the government to leverage pre-existing private and NGO builders and avoid creating its own reconstruction capacity, the latter requiring legislative action and time that the housing minister and president felt they did not have. None of the 220,000 families that required a housing solution were forced to accept any particular solution, and none of the 750 companies working on the reconstruction were assured of any work, forcing them to compete for family choice.

Second, individual solutions were sometimes aggregated into collective decisions in remote areas where it would be impractical to attract builders for single homes. In one case, for instance, in the village of San Vicente in the O'Higgins region, 150 families dispersed across the rural landscape gathered in a theater in the town plaza to decide among five house designs, each by a different builder. Sentiment converged on one of the five, and it received three-quarters of the votes by the end of the meeting. In a summary observation by the housing minister, Rodrigo Pérez, "The government facilitated a private solution" by articulating a model but not defining its details. For the government, it was a more expensive model, a more complex model, a slower model, but for the residents it was a better model. And it came with plenty of headaches. In the end, some of the local builders did not have the financial or management strength to complete the building, abandoning the work.

Third, the rebuilding was to allow families to reconstruct where they had always lived, what the ministry termed "reconstruction in their own place." This required proof of ownership, and proof of damage or destruction. Without formal deeds, the former could be proven with electricity bills and the like, and the latter could be confirmed by the local municipality that had been empowered to decide if a house was repairable or completely destroyed; about 100,000 homes qualified by the first criterion, and 120,000 by the second.

Fourth, the government opened the building process to some 50,000 families that did not even own the property that had been devastated. Many had been leasing, but whatever their legal status, they no longer had a home. They received support for the construction of a new home—and once completed, they moved from renting to owning. The president himself had authorized this policy that reached well beyond a return to the status quo.

PRINCIPLES FOR TIERED LEADERSHIP

President Sebastián Piñera brought the art of executive intent and mission command to La Moneda. With a top team that had been assembled for its ability to follow through, the president made his intent crystal clear, laid on a host of implementing directives, and then kept his ministers' feet to the fire.

The president embraced the fundamental principles of tiered leadership, delegating responsibilities to layers below. He insisted that his lieutenants in turn take charge, think strategically, execute effectively within their own domains, and be held fully accountable. All of his ministers would have to set forward and achieve aggressive timetables through the exercise of their own leadership, and that depended upon their embracing many if not most of the principles of individual leadership identified in Chapter 4.

Vital elements of this directive formula could be seen in the experience of the regional governor and housing minister, Rodrigo Pérez; the public works minister, Hernán de Solminihac; and the health minister, Jaime Mañalich. They each learned that they would have to rebuild their respective area rapidly and wholly, and do so in ways that went beyond mere re-placement and in ways that brought in the voice of those directly affected. The most critical elements of the process can be summarized in a checklist for tiered leadership in the wake of a disaster:

Tiered Leadership Checklist

1. Recruit lieutenants who bring management experience with large-scale organizations and are capable of executing a strategy.

2. Set forward strategic goals with stretch objectives, establish specific timetables, and follow up regularly to ensure rapid, detailed, and complete implementation. Hold lieutenants accountable.

3. For the lieutenants the formula is much the same, preparing the next tier to rapidly execute their plans through their own subordinates.

4. Strive to meet long-term goals and press for fast action by actively supporting the next tier.

5. Bring the voice of those most affected by the reconstruction decisions into the formulation of plans and strategies.

6. Devote personal time and tangible presence to counsel and support front-line managers who have been called to rebuild the country.

---

7 FINANCING RECOVERY

How much will it cost us? How are we going to finance this?
—President Sebastián Piñera

In the wake of the F27 earthquake, Chile's president and finance minister worked to create a financing strategy for reconstruction. The finance minister took the lead, though he regularly consulted with the president to develop a strategy to pay for the recovery, grow the economy, and at the same time keep the fiscal house in order.

The president and finance minister quickly found that the cost of the restoration would be massive and the choices would be daunting. The estimated $30 billion loss, 18 percent of Chile's 2009 GDP, would be the equivalent of a $1 trillion loss in Japan, more than three times the cost of the 2011 Tōhoku earthquake, or $2.7 trillion in the United States, over twenty times the cost of the 2005 Hurricane Katrina. By way of another comparison: China's five-year development plan for 2011–15 called for a ceiling of acceptable losses from a disaster at 1.5 percent of the GDP. Chile's loss from F27 was twelve times the upper limit of what China is willing to tolerate.[1]

Many countries would simply not be able to mobilize the necessary cash to recover from such a staggering setback without deep indebtedness or long-term adverse impacts on the economy. Yet just a year later, Chile's losses were covered with little debt, and the economy was on track to grow at an annual rate of 6 percent. What made this possible?

While the politically expedient way might have been to tap Chile's Sovereign Wealth Fund, with $11.3 billion in the bank (a rainy-day reserve that had been created in 2007 by President Michelle Bachelet), Finance Minister Felipe Larraín opted not to do so. Instead he drew on a portfolio of other actions, ranging from temporarily increasing taxes on large businesses and reducing them on small firms; drawing on funds from a copper reserve under the Reserved Copper Law; pushing for economic growth that would in turn enhance government revenues; reducing tax evasion; and dipping into the international debt market.

Chile's public financing of the recovery was complemented by a thriving private insurance industry. Prior to the event, insurance had achieved the greatest penetration rate of any Latin American country, which meant that much of the cost of recovery could be borne through claims payments to businesses and residences suffering damage. A number of companies voluntarily stepped in as well. Financing the recovery could thus rely upon a de facto public-private partnership. This chapter focuses on the financial policy established by Finance Minister Larraín, and Chapters 8 and 9 focus on insurance payouts and private donations as complements.

HOW MUCH WILL IT COST?

The first priority for any head of state after a large-scale calamity like F27 is to concentrate public resources on saving lives and rescuing victims. No government can shirk this responsibility, though its timeliness and thoroughness has varied greatly in practice, and there are significant political costs associated with delay or incompleteness. From the crisis-management debacle in the wake of Hurricane Katrina in 2005, we know that media-amplified perceptions of tardiness or unresponsiveness can tarnish a sovereign's credibility and even its legacy.[2]

Following the emergency phase, however, significant longer-term financing decisions come to the fore as the full recovery typically far exceeds available reserves. And here discretionary decision-making is even greater than in the emergency phase, with many alternatives facing those most responsible for the country's future. The large financial decisions will of necessity stretch over months or years, depending on the scale of the catastrophe and the resiliency of the country.

Whatever the time frame, two fundamental questions are inevitably on the desk of those most responsible for the nation's longer-term recovery from a calamity: (1) How much will it cost? and (2) who will pay?

Answering the questions is normally the prerogative of the country's finance minister in consultation with the president. So consequential are the answers that a preassessment of their prospective impact can be vital. Stress-testing a nation at the start of a new administration can prove an essential precautionary measure for any leadership team coming to power. In this case, stress-testing entails quantifying how the economy would be affected by a set of specific shocks and then identifying the policies that would be best suited to reduce their impacts. The not-yet-installed Piñera administration, however, had had no time even to consider, let alone apply, any such stress-testing when the earthquake hit.

The individual in the hot seat for developing a financial recovery plan from scratch was the president's new finance minister, Felipe Larraín. He was coming to government as a U.S.-educated economist and a noted scholar in the field of development economics, a discipline he had taught at the Catholic University of Chile in Santiago for the previous twenty years. Although he had advised many governments and international organizations over the years, he had never held line responsibility before. And now, eleven days before he was to take the oath, the president-elect pressed these same two key recovery questions on him: "How much will it cost us?" And then, "How are we going to finance this?"

The answers were neither obvious nor even calculable at the moment, but Larraín knew he would quickly have to produce a response to at least the first question, though a definitive answer proved elusive, as he recalled:

> Our first task was to estimate the damage of the earthquake as accurately as possible. What is the cost? How much have we lost? We devoted probably a month, two months, working closely with all the ministries, centralizing all the estimates, then the revised estimates. Numbers kept changing for several weeks as more information was coming in here in the Finance Ministry.

Within two months of the event, Felipe Larraín concluded that the total cost to restore and improve infrastructure, reverse private sector damage, and cover production losses and emergency expenditures was close to $30 billion. This was a prodigious number for a country the size of Chile. About

Table 7.1. Estimated Economic Costs of F27

Sector	Expected Economic Impact ($ Millions)			
	Public	Private	Total	%
Manufacture, fisheries, and tourism		5,340	5,340	18.0
Housing	3,258	685	3,943	13.3
Education	1,536	1,479	3,015	10.2
Health	2,720		2,720	9.2
Energy		1,601	1,601	5.4
Public works	1,458		1,458	4.9
National assets	805		805	2.7
Agriculture	9	592	601	2.0
Armed forces and public order	571		571	1.9
Transportation and tele-communications		523	523	1.8
Other infrastructure	130	137	267	0.9
Municipalities	96		96	0.3
Total estimated public and private loss	10,583	10,357	20,940	70.6
Expected production loss			7,606	25.6
Other			1,117	3.8
Total			29,663	100.0

Source: Data from Government of Chile, 2010; Ministry of Finance, 2010; Pan American Health Organization, 2010.

Note: Estimates were compiled in 2010, and some modestly vary from later figures reported elsewhere in this book.

a third came from damage to the public sector, including schools, hospitals, infrastructure and housing, a third from private-sector damage, and a third in lost production and emergency spending. The estimated costs are displayed in Table 7.1.[3]

The public sector costs included $2.7 billion for rebuilding 130 hospitals, and $3.2 billion for subsidizing reconstruction of 220,000 homes.

Emergency costs included $200 million for the National Office of Emergency and a range of other government agencies.[4]

The private sector, a pillar of Piñera's support and the putative engine for growth, had been hard hit by the F27 event as well. Many companies were themselves staggering, their own facilities devastated by the earthquake. Combining all industries, the destruction of their physical assets resulted in an estimated 3 percent decline in the gross domestic product during the first quarter of 2010.[5]

One example is the setback suffered by a staple of Chile's export-driven economy, the country's extensive network of vineyards. With bottles and barrels shattered and a near-term harvest thrown into doubt, the wine industry had lost more than $400 million overnight. Chile is the world's fifth largest exporter of wine, and the heart of Chile's wine country, west and south of Santiago near the earthquake's epicenter, experienced widespread damage to its stock and equipment. One winery in the Santa Cruz region 110 miles south of the capital, for example, lost more than five thousand gallons of wine when one of its stainless steel storage tanks collapsed. Damaged homes, roads, and communications impaired the grape harvesting that had been slated at many vineyards for just weeks after the earthquake.

Vinos de Chile, the industry association of Chilean winemakers, estimated that approximately 33 million gallons of wine worth up to $250 million were lost from the collapse or overturning of storage tanks and the breaking of oak barrels and wine bottles. It also estimated that damage in the industry's infrastructure ranging from irrigation canals to wine cellars totaled some $180 million. Fortunately, close to 90 percent of the wine industry's total loss of $430 million would be covered by private earthquake insurance.[6]

Hurricane Katrina—the most expensive natural disaster in recent American history—cost about $125 billion, representing nearly 1 percent of the U.S. GDP in 2005. The $235 billion cost of the 2011 Tōhoku earthquake in Japan was the most expensive natural disaster in world history, represented 4 percent of Japan's GDP. The $30 billion estimated cost of the F27 earthquake represented 18 percent of Chile's GDP.

Chile's recovery would be complicated by another factor. The presidential administration was coming to power from the center-right of the political spectrum after two decades of center-left rule. The newly elected team had run its campaign with an ambitious agenda of kick-starting growth. Over the four years leading up to 2009, the annual GDP growth had averaged around 3 percent, and the new administration had run on a platform of doubling that rate. The goal could be achieved, the new team had originally believed, only by lower growth in state spending and lowered taxes. The massive cost of recovery now seemingly negated any prospect for cutting budgets or reducing taxes.

Despite the high cost of recovery, the president and finance minister sought to devise a financial strategy that would not compromise their longer-term macroeconomic goals. They also concluded that they could rely on private insurance for covering much of the property and commercial losses in the private sector. This allowed the presidential cabinet to focus attention on the uninsured portion of the losses to schools, hospitals, and infrastructure, and on much of the uninsured portion of the losses to houses.

HOW IT WILL BE FINANCED

By May 2010, three months after the event, the Ministry of Finance concluded that $8.4 billion in *public* funding would be needed for its part of the reconstruction efforts. But now the finance minister and president faced a situation that all administrations of high-income countries encounter in the wake of an unanticipated disaster. While low-income countries often turn to international donors for financing reconstruction, but Chile's relative affluence—it had one of the highest incomes per capita in Latin America—led the president and finance minister to opt to rely almost entirely on the country's own resources.[7]

In the wake of hurricanes Katrina in 2005 and Sandy in 2012, the United States had also pursued a course of self-reliance, but the two countries pursued very different paths in financing their recovery plan. The U.S. opted simply to enlarge the national deficit by more than $140 billion: $90 billion for federal relief and special appropriations in 2005, and another $50 billion in 2012. That of course meant that the ultimate cost of recovery would be even greater because of the interest on the additional indebtedness. It also meant that the incumbent administration would not have to undertake politically unpopular measures: the burden of the cost of recovery would be imposed on future taxpayers.

Some inside and outside the presidential palace had been arguing for debt financing as had been done in the United States. "Chile is in such good shape that there is really no need to do any increase in taxes because you can go into debt for the full amount," Larraín characterized one stream of advice he was receiving at the time. "But," he said by contrast, "we strongly thought that we had to honor our responsibility towards long-term fiscal goals." Despite having campaigned on a promise of tax reductions, Chile's president and top tier embraced a strategy very different from that of the United States: taxes would have to be increased on most payers, at least temporarily, and enough so that tax relief could be provided to the most hardhit. The "responsible thing to do," Larraín concluded, "was to send a bill that would raise a few taxes for those who could pay and also reduce taxes for those who are in trouble."

Even that path, however, faced a headwind from still another source. Chile had accumulated $11.3 billion in a sovereign wealth account, the Economic and Social Stabilization Fund, created as a buffer against financial crises and similar emergencies. Many in the administration now called for drawing down that account in the wake of the natural disaster rather than raising taxes and cutting spending.

But the president and finance minister worried that any use of their sovereign reserves would further impair the country if it faced another financial cyclone like that in the wake of Lehman's failure in 2008. They decided to leave this sovereign wealth fund untouched. As Larraín explained: "If we were to use this fund for an earthquake, then what would have happened if we would really need this money to offset the economic impact of an international financial crisis in subsequent years? The fund would be empty at a time it would be hard for us, and anyone else, to borrow money on international markets at a reasonable price."[8]

With large-scale debt financing, international assistance, and a raid

on the sovereign fund ruled out, the president and finance minister resolved within months of the disaster to finance the nation's reconstruction through a four-pronged strategy: (1) increase taxes and reduce tax
evasion, (2) reallocate existing budget lines, (3) draw resources from the
state-owned copper producer via the Reserved Copper Law, and (4) issue
a limited amount of international debt. By combining several sources but
depending on no one, they reasoned in deliberative fashion that the economic impact on each would be manageable and the country's growth and
reputation would be preserved and sustained for the years ahead.

With the larger financial parameters resolved, the president and finance
minister turned to specific facets of the four prongs. The largest single feature was the tax increase, with 40 percent of the required $8.4 billion to
come from that source. The president repeatedly reassured business leaders
that it would be only a temporary measure for up to two years, and that
the measure should not adversely affect small and midsize enterprises in
any case, since it specifically exempted smaller firms. But his arguments
fell largely on deaf ears within the business community, even though it had
been a mainstay of the president's political base. Still, Congress approved a
measure on July 31, 2010, to ramp up national taxes on corporate profits
from 17 percent in 2010 to 20 percent in 2011. In 2012 the rate would drop
back to 18.5 percent, and in 2013 it would finally return to 17 percent.

Higher copper and tobacco taxes would add still more to the coffers.
Since 2005, the government had received a fixed 5 percent of the profits
from its mines, and now that was generating more cash since international
copper prices were on the rise. The price of copper had risen from a low of
$2.35 per pound in February 2010 to a high of $4.50 a year later, a more
than 90 percent increment. Even the 5 percent tax on profits was increased
in some cases as high as 9 percent (or decreased in some cases to 4 percent, depending on a firm's operating margins), a change that would apply
from 2010 to 2012. Smokers would also have to pay more for their addictive
habit, as taxes on tobacco were permanently increased.

The higher taxes and tougher enforcement yielded $3.6 billion, funds
from the Reserved Copper Law chipped in another $1.2 billion, and budget

Table 7.2. Public Funding Sources and Targets for Reconstruction in Chile, 2010–13

Funding	$ Billions
Funding Sources	
Tax receipts	3.625
Budget reallocations	2.920
Reserved Copper Law	1.200
National Reconstruction Fund	0.308
Other sources	0.378
Total public financing	8.431
Funding Targets	
Emergency costs	0.433
Housing	2.310
Health	2.142
Education	1.206
Public infrastructure	1.170
Other	1.160
Total public spending	8.431

Source: Data from Caldera-Sanchez, 2012, with data from Ministry of Finance.

Note: Higher tax receipts include temporary increases in corporate and property taxes, a change in the mining tax, increase in tobacco taxes, and reduced tax advantages. Codelco transfers 10 percent of its copper export sales to the Armed Forces.

reshuffling, made easier by the earthquake's occurrence early in the fiscal year, produced an additional $2.9 billion. The government also stimulated private giving through the creation in May 2010 of the National Reconstruction Fund to tax-incentivize individual and corporate donations and to assure givers that their gifts would be wisely applied. The several major sources of public funding and targets of public spending are summarized in Table 7.2.[9]

Even then, Larraín's projections came up short of what he believed the recovery would ultimately require. And to close that gap, he calculated that a growing economy could generate $600 million in extra government revenue for every additional percentage point increase of GDP. Thus, if the government could coax national annual growth to rise from 3 to 6 percent—one of their campaign promises in the first place—the three additional points should also add another $1.8 billion in annual revenue. The premise invited general skepticism. "Would it come from additional growth?" he was often asked. "We thought it would," he affirmed, "but nobody believed us when we said that the country will grow at 6 percent per year." He patiently explained that every extra point in growth would generate close to an additional $600 million in government revenue. "It is a simplified calculation," he confessed, but one that he embraced.

For a final source of funding, the president and finance minister turned to the international debt market. They decided to borrow $1 billion in dollar-denominated bonds, and another $500 million in peso-denominated bonds. The latter would break new ground, since it constituted the first global peso-denominated bond in the country's history. And it would be consistent with another of the finance minister's agendas—to internationalize Chile's currency.

The global market proved receptive, a sign that Chile's strategy for financing reconstruction was viewed favorably by international standards. Helped by low international market rates and a strong fiscal position, its ten-year dollar-denominated bonds obtained a yield of 3.89 percent, Chile's lowest borrowing rate ever since its separation from Spain in 1818. Similarly, the peso-denominated bonds obtained a yield of 5.50 percent, nearly 60 basis points below the yield for similar bonds in the domestic Chilean market, a sign of international investor confidence in the country. A year later, Chile borrowed another $1 billion in ten-year bonds at a new record low of 3.30 percent, just 130 basis points higher than U.S. Treasury bonds at the time, an indication of how confident the international investors and central banks that bought these bonds were in Chile's capacity to pay them back.

Indeed, the government's financing strategy proved crucial in prompting an upgrade in the country's sovereign-risk rating. In elevating Chile from A1 to Aa3 (credit-rater nomenclature for high marks), Moody's explained, "Fiscal saving by themselves would be enough to cover the government's estimated $8.4 billion in post-earthquake financing needs, but the new center-right administration has chosen to rely mainly on a combination of taxation and new debt issuance, and keep most of the fiscal savings for future use."[10]

As pointed out above, the president's and finance minister's strategy was partly made feasible by the high degree of insurance penetration and international reinsurance. Much of the recovery would thus be financed by the private sector, radically limiting the direct burden on the state. Large companies, international organizations, and other enterprises stepped forward with large donations as well. We see here again that leadership and institutions proved to be two key pillars of the comeback. Government decisions within a broad discretionary framework proved critical, and so too did the pre-existing tradition of private insurance and private giving. Each required the other in creating a viable short- and long-term pathway ahead, as we will see in the following chapters.

LEADERSHIP IMPLICATIONS

The president and finance minister had opted for far-reaching—if less immediately appealing—steps for financing the recovery. They might have tapped into the sovereign wealth fund, or they might have borrowed heavily from abroad. But they instead chose the less expedient path of combining four sources in a balanced way. They financed the restoration without deep indebtedness, and at the same time they managed to stimulate growth. And they did so without also creating a state-backed earthquake insurance agency.

Chile did indeed achieve an annual GDP growth rate of 6 percent during each of the three years after the earthquake. The unemployment rate dropped to 6 percent two years later, down from more than 10 percent three years earlier. *Emerging Markets* named Felipe Larraín "Finance Minister of the Year for Latin America" in 2010, saying that the honor "unequivocally signals the confidence you have inspired by virtue of your wise strategy to finance the country's reconstruction efforts."[11]

Good decisions always look easier and more obvious in retrospect than in prospect, and that was evident among those who led the country through the aftermath of the F27 calamity. The discretionary options in front of the president and finance minister had come with much handwringing as they were successively confronted, but in hindsight they proved prescient. In reaching the critical decisions in the early weeks and then many months after the disaster, the president and the finance minister had been guided by two strategic imperatives that could have been mutually exclusive but in fact they had managed to reconcile: (1) restore the country to where it was before the earthquake—and to go beyond, and (2) do so in a way that was fiscally responsible for the longer run.

In politics with great short-term demands, the president and finance minister had managed to transcend intuitive reactions that can some-times prevent prudent decisions. "I'm not a politician," said Felipe Larraín, though he had frequently consulted with central bank officials, cabinet ministers, elected legislators, and business leaders. "I came to office for four years to do a job: foster Chilean economic growth so all Chileans can benefit from it. It's just that with F27 the test came much sooner than I thought it would."

The president and finance minister followed a strategy that soon restored water, electricity, homes, hospitals, roads, companies, and schools across the country's most affected regions—and they did so without massive indebtedness. Their playbook called for working with banks, insurers, and adjusters to inject cash back into the economy quickly—and with just about everybody else who might make a difference in line with a working dictum that "No one can be subtracted from the reconstruction of Chile."

Nor did the president force a contraction in state spending. He and his finance minister moved funds across major budget lines—$730 million in all—and postponed some projects, such as a roof for the National Stadium in Santiago, but they increased public outlays by far more than they reallocated or postponed. And they did so without touching their sovereign funds or borrowing much against the future.

In 2010, Chile became the only Latin American country highly rated Aa3 after an upgrade by Moody's Investors Service. The international rating agency cited the country's fiscal savings and "financial resilience" in the wake of the February earthquake as a key element supporting its decision. Sebastián Piñera and Felipe Larraín had managed to lead their national economic policy through what could have been a fiscal disaster on top of the natural disaster. From their experience we suggest several additional principles for country leaders facing a national disaster:

Leadership Checklist for Financing Recovery after Disaster

1. Quickly evaluate the total cost from the disaster to the economy and its impact on specific communities and segments of the economy.

2. Work closely with the insurance industry to identify the losses it will cover and ensure that it expedites claim payments so that you can focus elsewhere, and draw upon the private sector's services and contributions where feasible.

3. Consider a portfolio of financing options rather than a single solution.

4. Bring the long-term future into the present to identify what is required even if politically risky.

5. Publicly announce and explain major decisions and new policies.

6. Monitor progress regularly against the financing's specific goals.

7. Do not wait for a calamity to hit; conduct stress-tests of the economy now under major disaster scenarios, and prepare the foundations ahead of time for financing recovery from each.

8 INSURANCE PAYOUTS FOR RECOVERY

Ninety-five percent of Chile's insured losses were paid from outside the country, providing a strong influx of international capital.
— Chilean Superintendent of Securities and Insurance

The president's strategy for recovery was partly made feasible by another feature of the economy over which he and his cabinet had little control. Chile had an exceptionally high degree of private insurance coverage. A significant portion of the recovery would thus be financed by the private sector, radically limiting the direct burden on the state.

We see here again the dual interplay of national leadership and private institutions. Government decisions within a broad discretionary framework proved critical, and so too did the pre-existing tradition of private insurance. Each depended on the other for creating both short-term and long-term pathways ahead.

A FAST-GROWING INSURANCE INFRASTRUCTURE

As a risk-transfer mechanism, insurance allows individuals and organizations to pay a small premium on a regular basis in exchange for financial protection against the major losses from a low-probability event such as an earthquake. The feasibility of insurance depends on two fundamental features: risk pooling and large numbers. Insurers cover major losses of a few policyholders by combining the small premiums from a large group of customers facing independent risks. Insurance faces a problem, however, when providing coverage against disasters, since thousands of customers can be simultaneously stung by the same event and their risks become interdependent. To guard against such correlated setbacks, insurers often resell packages of their insurance policies to international reinsurers who then take on this residual risk.

International reinsurers help protect national insurers in much the same way that insurers help their individual customers. International re-insurers charge a premium to indemnify a domestic insurance firm against catastrophic losses that the local insurer would otherwise have to cover. Reinsurers in turn are also concerned about their own concentration of correlated risks, and they, too, predictably limit their exposure in specific catastrophe-prone regions. Large reinsurers that operate worldwide can diversify their geographic risks far more readily across the globe than those that operate locally.

Chile's preparedness against earthquake damage in early 2010 is evident in the country's insurance penetration. Insurance penetration is defined as a country's total insurance premiums divided by its GDP. In 2006, Chile's penetration stood at 3.57 percent. While this was substantially below the average of 9 percent among OECD countries at that time, it stood well above that of Mexico and other countries similar to Chile in their level of economic development.

During the several years prior to the F27 earthquake, insurance penetration had been rapidly expanding in Chile. Insurance penetration corrected for inflation increased by 22 percent in 2006–9, as displayed in Table 8.1, three times more rapidly than the country's GDP growth. We also note that Chile's insurance penetration predictably accelerated in the immediate aftermath of F27, growing by 18 percent in 2010 alone.

Table 8.1. Growth of Insurance Penetration in Chile, 2004–12 (Indexed: 2003=100)

Year	Annual Change	Cumulative Index	Year	Annual Change	Cumulative Index
2003		100.0	2008	8.8%	141.0
2004	8.2%	108.2	2009	−1.7%	138.6
2005	−0.7%	107.4	2010	18.2%	163.8
2006	6.1%	114.0	2011	14.4%	187.4
2007	13.7%	129.6	2012	6.2%	199.1

Source: Data from Asociación de Aseguradores de Chile.

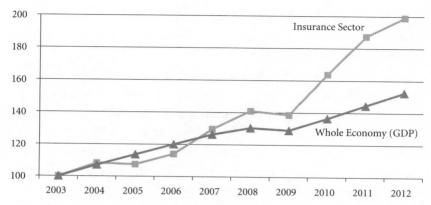

Fig. 8.1. Comparative Growth of the Insurance Market and GDP in Chile, 2003–12 (Indexed: 2003 = 100). Data from Asociación de Aseguradores de Chile.

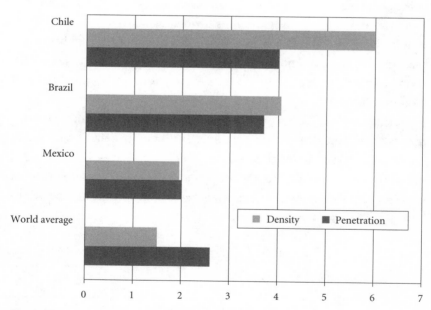

Fig. 8.2. Insurance Density and Penetration in Chile, Brazil, and Mexico, 2012 (Density = \$ premiums per capita/100; Penetration = Premiums as % of GDP). Data from Swiss Re, 2013; Sigma, 2013.

Chile's insurance preparedness was also evident in the country's insurance *density*, defined as premiums per capita. Displayed in Figure 8.1, we see that this measure of the insurance market had been increasing more rapidly than the economy during the years from 2003 to the time of the earthquake. With both density and GDP indexed at 100 in 2003, the GDP index had risen to 129 by 2010 but insurance had climbed to 139. And during the two years after the earthquake, the GDP had grown to 152 while insurance had soared to 199. In 2006 insurance per capita had stood at $350, but by 2012 it had climbed to nearly $600. The number of insurers operating in the country also grew, from 53 in 2003—with 23 property-casualty insurers and 30 life insurers—to 60 in 2012—with 28 property-casualty and 32 life insurance companies.

By 2012, Chile had emerged as the top-ranked Latin American country in both insurance density and penetration, as displayed in Figure 8.2.

INSURING EARTHQUAKES

Our analysis of the world's twenty most costly *insured* catastrophes over the period 1970–2013 introduced in Chapter 4 reveals that F27 ranked fourth among earthquake-driven disasters, after the 2011 Japan earthquake, the 1994 California earthquake, and the 2011 New Zealand earthquake.

California does not require that residents in seismic areas of the state purchase earthquake insurance, and banks do not require it as a condition for a mortgage. As a result, it is estimated that only some 10 percent of Californians exposed to earthquake risk actually have insurance today. Since 1996, this insurance has been primarily provided by a state agency, the California Earthquake Authority, rather than private insurers.

Chile's practices by contrast have been far more aggressive. Residential mortgage holders—about a quarter of all of Chile's 4 million homes—are strongly advised to purchase earthquake insurance, and as a result, 96 percent of the mortgaged residential properties in Chile were insured to some extent against earthquakes in 2010. Among homeowners *without* a mortgage, however, the take-up rate for fire insurance in 2010 was estimated to be 17 percent, and only 3 percent held coverage against fire and earthquake damage.[1]

Looking specifically at those who suffered losses from F27, the Ministry of Housing reported that the earthquake had damaged more than 370,000 houses, with a large fraction concentrated among the country's least affluent, where insurance is less prevalent. Among those, 147,500 homeowners (with and without a mortgage) or their banks filed a claim, and 125,000 received payment from their insurers. The other 22,500 claims were not fulfilled, however, because the estimated loss fell below the deductible limit, typically 1 percent of the insured value, or $1,000. Some 86 percent of the F27 claims came from residential coverage, representing almost 20 percent of the total insured homes in the most affected areas.

According to one independent assessment at the end of 2010, insurance companies had provided $2.78 billion to homeowners or their banks for their earthquake or tsunami coverage. Since the government had provided $2.5 billion in housing reconstruction subsidies, the private sector had in effect covered more than half of the $5.28 billion required for housing reconstruction. It is estimated than another $1.75 billion in losses were simply absorbed by the homeowners themselves.[2]

Private earthquake insurance was fortunately more widespread among businesses. Of small business owners, 30 percent held a policy, and of large companies, 75 percent did so. It is estimated that private insurers paid out a total of nearly $5.25 billion to business enterprises. Among industrial firms, about half the payouts came from business-interruption policies that cover forgone income when production facilities are damaged.[3]

The pace of disaster recovery depends much upon the rate of claims settlement. Insurers responded relatively quickly in Chile, in part because the government required that insurance claims be filed within two months of the earthquake. The Chilean Insurance Association reported that within twelve months, 80 percent of commercial claims and 95 percent of personal claims had been settled. Despite the number of claims, more than 93 percent of residential insurance claims totaling over $1 billion had been paid within eight months, and 69 percent of commercial and industrial claims,

Table 8.2. Percentage of Earthquake Losses Covered by Insurance by Country (nominal dollars)

	Date	Insurance Industry Percent of Total loss	Insured Losses ($ Billion)	Economic Losses ($ Billion)	Economic Losses as % of GDP	Insured Losses ($ Billion)
New Zealand	9/4/2010	81	5	6	5%	5
New Zealand	2/22/2011	80	15	19	13%	15
Chile	2/27/2010	27	8	30	18%	8
USA/ California	1/17/1994	24–27	14	52–57	0.7%	14
Mexico	4/4/2010	21	0.2	1	0%	0.2
Japan	3/11/2011	17	35	210	4%	35
Italy	4/6/2009	14	0.5	4	0.2%	0.5
Turkey	10/23/2011	4	0.03	0.75	0.1%	0.03
Haiti	1/12/2010	1.3	0.1	8	121%	0.1
China	5/12/2008	0.35	0.3	85	1.80%	0.3

nearly $2 billion, had been closed as well. Virtually all claims were settled by the end of 2011.[4]

Aon, a large insurance broker with a significant presence in Chile, applauded a requirement that hastened the company's ability to settle. "This proved to be a very positive step for the insurance industry," Aon wrote in an assessment one year after F27, "particularly in contrast to the very drawn out claim settlement process" after the 1994 Northridge earthquake in California.[5]

It is estimated that insurers ultimately covered 27 percent of Chile's total loss. This is far lower than in New Zealand, as seen in Table 8.2, where insurers covered 80 percent of the overall cost of the 2011 earthquake. Some 90 percent of its homeowners were covered by earthquake insurance through the government-run Earthquake Commission. But Chile's 27 percent insurance payout compared well with other recent earthquakes. For California's Northridge event, the private payout was some 24 to 27 percent of losses, and after the Tōhoku event in Japan, private insurers contributed 17 percent. And even lower payout ratios had prevailed after earthquakes in Italy, Turkey, and Haiti.

Given the unprecedented scale of the losses in Chile, it would not have been surprising if some insurers declared bankruptcy and others opted to end earthquake coverage. The accumulated premiums from earthquake insurance in Chile over the prior thirty years totaled just $3.4 billion, less than half of the $8 billion that the insurance companies paid out after F27.

Yet no insurers went bankrupt—unusual in the aftermath of a large-scale disaster—and most continued providing coverage after the earthquake. Much of the insurers' resilience can be traced to their extensive reliance on reinsurance; 95 percent or more of the insured losses in Chile were reinsured, compared with 40 percent in the case of U.S. disaster insurance. The Chilean Superintendent of Securities and Insurance estimated that purely local insurers ultimately covered less than 3 percent of the F27 claims. F27 was really an international event for the insurance industry.[6]

The relatively quick and complete closure of insurance claims could also be traced to the absence of any insolvency among the insurers. That was partly a product of Superintendent of Securities and Insurance's authority to suspend firms that had not held sufficient reserves to meet their financial obligations. The superintendent had also required that the country's insurance firms contract only with solvent international reinsurers. In 2011, every reinsurer with a contract in the Chilean market had a relatively high rating of A- or better, even though the regulation required only that insurers contract with reinsurance companies having a risk rating of at least BBB.[7]

Still other institutional practices facilitated the F27 claims process. Chile had implemented a procedure in 1989 in accordance with the best-practice criterion of the OECD for administering insurance claims rapidly and fairly. Insured parties are encouraged to express their views on contractual and numerical aspects of the indemnification amount, and that resulted in a relatively low level of insurance litigation: less than 1.4 percent of the F27 claims ended up in the courts.[8]

Given the massive payouts, it came as no surprise that earthquake reinsurance rates for Chile jumped sharply in the event's wake. The country does not regulate prices, and from the price level in January 2010 (two months before the catastrophe) to a year later, premium rates soared by 50 percent. Two insurers, BCI Seguros Generales and Mapfre Seguros Generales, for instance, more than doubled their premiums between December 2009, just before the earthquake, and December 2011.

The behavior of the insurance market after the quake followed a combination of both immediate intuitive reactions and long-term deliberative thinking. The availability bias (a focus on an event that recently happened) increased public demand for earthquake insurance following the disaster, and insurers increased their rates significantly, mainly driven by reinsurance prices that increased 50 percent even though there was no scientific evidence of any increase in the actual risk of seismic events in the near future. If anything, one would anticipate a lower likelihood of a major earthquake in the immediate future following F27, since the fault line had released so much of the built-up stress that had caused the event. Insurers may have raised their premiums simply because they anticipated that the earthquake's recency would increase customer willingness to pay, and increase reinsurers' premiums because of a greater cost of capital. Despite the price hikes, domestic demand rose strongly as well, increasing by 30 percent within two years of the event.[9]

CONCLUSION

Private insurance played a vital role in providing many victims of the catastrophe with the means for recovery. Fundamental to Chile's comeback alongside the public financing was the private financing by domestic insurers backed by international reinsurers. Their high market penetration and rapid payout provided a swift influx of capital to pay for recovery.

Prior to the Talca earthquake of 1928, Chile had no insurance coverage for damage from earthquakes and accompanying tsunamis and fires. Following that and subsequent seismic events, the private sector began issuing coverage for earthquake-related damage to residential and commercial structures, and over the years such coverage has spread widely. By the time of the F27 event, the penetration of earthquake insurance was on a par with that of Japan and higher than in California today.[10]

Despite sharp price hikes for private insurance after F27 because of the predictable market reaction, domestic demand for insurance actually increased during the months following the event. Both insurers and reinsurers remained in the market, and by 2013 earthquake insurance in Chile had become twice as prevalent as in California, America's earthquake epicenter. The earthquake not only tested the country's political leadership, but it also strengthened the private institutions that worked alongside the nation's leaders on the recovery.

Private Insurance Leadership Checklist

1. Expand national insurance penetration and density to protect against catastrophic risks and ensure a rapid economic recovery.

2. Foster international reinsurance for domestic insurers, and facilitate rapid payout by both insurers and reinsurers in the wake of a disaster so that individuals and businesses can get back on their feet more quickly, lessening the need for government assistance.

---

9 PRIVATE GIVING FOR RECOVERY

> Our role in disaster recovery came directly from Anglo American's strategic goal of being the preferred partner for the country.
> —Vice President Felipe Purcell, Anglo American plc

Chile's recovery was also aided by commercial enterprise. Some companies stepped forward with cash, and others with time. Whatever the form of the contributions, the restorative work of the public sector was complemented by the recovery commitment of the private sector.

PRIVATE DONATIONS

Many businesses sought to contribute in kind and financially to facilitate the recovery process. And given the business-friendly character of a government with company leaders in the cabinet, some business executives were drawn to donating through public channels. They personally knew the president and other business figures who had joined the government.

Still, businesses faced administrative red tape that slowed the delivery of funds, including a requirement that the president personally approve each private donation. One later policy change to stimulate more private giving was to allow the donor to name the recipient, yet that measure actually compounded the bureaucratic thicket. A company would propose a recipient, but then a national ministry would have to embrace the project, the finance ministry would have to vet the project, and then a third office would have to attest that there was public value for the project. Finally, the president would still have to approve the initiative, and he brought independent judgment to the table, turning down, for instance, two donations from a developer that wanted its donation to go to new shopping malls in the affected areas.

With private donations through public channels falling short of expectations, in part for these reasons, the government created an office in the Ministry of Finance to expedite donations, strengthened tax incentives—it formed the National Reconstruction Fund in May 2010, with a tax incentive to speed donations—and thinned the bureaucracy. But even then the inflow remained modest.

The National Reconstruction Fund opened for business in July 2010. The government forecast that the fund would pull in more than $300 million, but through June 2013 it attracted just a fraction of that, somewhere between $39 million and $100 million, according to public estimates. That was not insubstantial for the donors: the average donation was $142,000, and one totaled $6.6 million. But the total flow fell disappointingly short of expectations, and many of the gifts came from just a handful of companies. One report estimated that more than half, 51 percent, had been contributed by just three firms: Anglo American, the mining company, at 27 percent; Grupo Enersis, an electrical power firm, at 19 percent; and the Cámara Chilena de la Construcción—the Chilean Association of Construction—at 5 percent. Still, the donor-designated projects were significant for the recipients, ranging from the rebuilding of a hospital and university in Talca to constructing navigational inlets and cultural centers in Maule.[1]

A set of large companies donated through other channels—and often gave in-kind contributions rather than cash. Airbus, the large European aircraft manufacturer, for instance, contributed an aircraft to fly emergency supplies in Chile; Sprint and AT&T, large U.S. telecommunication companies, gave free airtime; BHP Billiton, one of the largest mining companies in the world, headquartered in Australia, furnished water purification plants.

Private giving was supplemented by international giving from multi-

Table 9.1. Cash Contributions of at Least $1.5 Million for Recovery
from the F27 Earthquake

Business Corporations

Company	$ Million	Recipient
Anglo American PLC	10.0	Affected communities; emergency relief and reconstruction
Antofagasta PLC	10.0	Affected communities; emergency relief and reconstruction
Enersis	10.0	Government of Chile; Red Cross
Wal-Mart	4.0	Affected communities and emergency relief
Barrick Gold Corporation	3.8	Government of Chile; reconstruction
American Airlines	1.6	UNICEF; emergency relief

Foreign Governments, International Agencies, and NGOs

Donor	$ Million	Recipient
United Nations	10.3	Government of Chile; emergency supplies and services
United States	9.9	Government of Chile, Red Cross; emergency supplies and services
Japan	5.5	Government of Chile; Red Cross; shelter and health
European Commission	5.4	Government of Chile; humanitarian aid, telecommunications, shelter
Australia	4.4	Government of Chile; reconstruction
Church of Jesus Christ of Latter-Day Saints	3.5	Affected communities; emergency relief
China	2.0	Government of Chile; chartered aircraft with relief supplies

Source: Data from Ballesteros, 2013.

lateral agencies, foreign governments, and nongovernmental organizations, including the United Nations, United States, and the Church of Jesus Christ of Latter-Day Saints. Their gifts along with company donations are detailed in Table 9.1.

A MINING COMPANY STEPS FORWARD

As a case in point, consider the actions of Anglo American, a London-based multinational mining company with 100,000 employees, $30 billion in annual revenues, and major copper operations in Chile. The company's country vice president for corporate affairs, Felipe Purcell, instantly appreciated that the F27 devastation had hit Chile without recent precedent. Although Anglo American had no operations in the afflicted regions, the company pledged $10 million after the earthquake, the largest gift it had ever made in Chile.

Company management sought to avoid the appearance of self-interested generosity. We did "not want to play the reputational and image game," explained Purcell. The pledge stemmed instead from the company's ongoing commitment to a sustained relationship. The firm had already been giving as much as $8 million annually to education and microenterprise in Chile, and Purcell viewed the new gift as a logical expansion of the ongoing engagement. "Our role in disaster recovery," he explained, "came directly from Anglo American's strategic goal of being the preferred partner for the country."

Purcell received quick backing from London for his pledge, and by March 3, just a few days after the event, he was ready to act. He and his associates met with representatives of the stricken regions to identify the most urgent needs, and a day later the company dispatched a fleet of heavy equipment to gather street debris, thwart rockslides, and erect emergency housing. When the crisis later subsided, Purcell turned to the mining ministry for further guidance, and it asked the company to support the emergent priority of reopening the nation's schools within six weeks.

Purcell and his team traveled from Santiago to the Biobío and Maule regions to pinpoint where their help could best be leveraged. To avoid bureaucratic delays, the government urged the company to move through its own channels, and Purcell concurred. "There was no time for sitting and making big plans, strategies, and budgets," he said. "We needed to act in urgency." Though the company had no special history with building schools, it did have plenty of large-scale construction know-how. Mobile buildings and new camps were its life-blood.

Purcell and his team contacted the makers of mobile structures with which his company had long contracted, and they were soon delivering state-of-the-art structures that might have rimmed a copper mine—but now were redirected to towns without a schoolhouse. The company specified materials and designs for the new schools: they were to be resistant to seismic shocks, waterproof, and temperature resistant for at least a decade.

Like the Ministry of Housing's rebuilding strategy, discussed in Chapter 6, this initiative would require a simultaneous bottom-up and top-down initiative by the company. Schools would have to be situated where towns wanted them—but also where nature would tolerate them. And this would require a working dialogue with local officials. "For a reason associated with human nature, people commonly wanted to have their homes and schools where they were located before the tsunami," recalled Purcell, "which meant flood-prone areas. Therefore, in some cases, our role involved a negotiation with community members."

With local guidance, Anglo American built six schools for more than 4,500 students in the communities of Caleta Tumbes, Constitución, Quirihue, Yungay, and Cocholgüe, including one massive 80,000-square-foot building for 2,000 students. And it did so by the president's deadline of having all of Chile's children back in school by April 26. The buildings were far more than skeletal, coming with computer labs, food services, and curricular materials. The minister of education or the president personally joined the inauguration of each school.

Anglo American also opted to further invest in two other areas where it had already been active—and that now were urgent government priorities as well. In collaboration with a nongovernmental enterprise—Fondo Esperanza (Hope Fund)—the company distributed emergency loans to microentrepreneurs to get them back on their feet, and it partnered with another NGO to rebuild 450 homes in poor communities.[2]

DRIVING RECONSTRUCTION

Companies also stepped forward after the disaster with their own resources if they were in a critical area and they were in a position to do so. Many firms were of course as much the victims of the disaster as were cities, schools, and hospitals, but some were nonetheless able to assist.

We turn by way of example to Pedro Pablo Errázuriz, who was at home in the city of Rancagua, in the O'Higgins region, when the earthquake struck. As he ventured tentatively outside, his first reaction was that a window in a nearby building seemed much larger than he remembered, but in the faint light he finally realized that an entire wall had given way. As executive chair of Essbio (a privatized water company that served O'Higgins and four other of Chile's fifteen regions), he knew that he would have to reach the O'Higgins operations center as soon as he could.

Arriving at his company hub at 7 a.m., Errázuriz found it already filled with managers discussing what to do first, since outage reports were pouring in from everywhere. They estimated that well more than half of the residents in the region had no running water. Dispatching crews to repair the greatest water breaks seemed obvious, but the infrastructure that they would normally take for granted had been shattered. Food, housing, and even cash and communications for sustaining work crews in the field for several days at a time were simply unavailable.

Although the homes of many of the water-company employees were as much in ruins as any, workers came streaming into the nerve center, appreciating that they were responsible for one of the region's most vital lifelines. With no comprehensive data at the outset to prioritize the repairs, however, company managers found that their only choice was to dispatch work crews to address outages as they came across the transom.

Still, little water was flowing in more than half the region, and in emergency response, Essbio began trucking tanks of water into town centers. Urban disorder and looting made even that challenging, but fire, police, and militia gave priority to the trucks' safe passage. As a result, work crews were able to place water tanks across towns and to refill them several times a day, providing cooking if not potable water.

Sebastián Piñera imposed a nearly impossible time demand for restoring full water flow, just as he had set for school reopenings, though in this case the target of his directive was a private firm rather than a public entity. The president had declared during a radio interview in Concepción that the local water company would have the flow restored within several days. Errázuriz knew that his counterparts in Japan after the Tōhoku earthquake had required nearly three months in some areas to restore the water supply.

Stunned by the "within several days" assertion, Errázuriz called the president's personal mobile phone number that he had retained from earlier business dealings. Both had worked with LAN, the national airline. Expecting to leave an unhappy voicemail message, Errázuriz actually reached Piñera. "President, you are saying that we have to have the problem solved by Friday? There is no way we will have that done!" Concepción's water system had been almost completely destroyed, he explained, and it will require at least a month. When the president replied that his understanding of the situation was less dire, Errázuriz became even more distressed and resistant. "Who is going to solve the problems?" he shot back. Unfazed by the caller's antagonistic tone, the president accepted the pushback. At the end of the phone call, Piñera even asked Errázuriz if he might be available at some point for public service.

Finding where the region's water pipes had been fractured proved daunting. The standard procedure for tracing a leak back to a cracked pipe would not work, since the pipes were for the moment without any water pressure. The company thus of necessity initiated a trial-and-error method: dig up pipes that might have been fractured to discover if they really were. Work crews were able to find and repair the biggest leaks by the president's deadline, but it required another three weeks to bring the whole system back on line, and even then some forty thousand homes remained without supply.

Despite the crewmembers' own private misfortunes—some had lost their homes—virtually all remained on the job around the clock. Then, as water finally began to flow again through most of the network, the crews faced the equivalent of starting over. Sewage drains had also been extensively fractured, but it was only with the water flowing again that the sewage breaks became evident. That required still another month of nonstop emergency work.

Throughout the repair, Errázuriz noted that securing support from the police or the public proved unproblematic. "The key things that I learned from this experience," he reflected, is "how strongly people were committed to the task and how relevant water is, because everyone would help the water company. They wouldn't care about the gas company. They wouldn't care about electricity. But for the water company, everyone was helping."

Because the stress of the moment was sure to affect those most responsible for recovery, Errázuriz found that his personal engagement with the emergency responders proved vital. After several weeks of around-the-clock work, he appreciated that the repair crews were displaying symptoms of distress and even depression. As the company's top manager, he turned to the nontechnical but equally vital task of shoring up morale, reminding crew members of the great strides they had made and how vital their work was for the families of the region. "Although I'm a civil engineer," he said, "I spent most of my time in keeping people up."

The following January 16, the president called Errázuriz and, as he had done just after the earthquake, asked him again if he might be available for public service. The president grilled him for an hour on any conflicts of interest, and then informed Errázuriz that he was one of three finalists for the Ministry of Transport and Telecommunication. The president called the next day to tell Errázuriz that his appointment was 90 percent likely. "Go and iron your suit," said the president.

Although missing the president's impossible four-day deadline, Errázuriz had impressed him with his nonstop efforts to restore the water supply. His management credentials had been proven by the crisis, the leadership characteristic that the president wanted in the cabinet. A day later Errázuriz moved from the private to the public sector. In his new position he found himself reporting to a fast-acting and always demanding personality, much like his own.

CONCLUSION

A set of large private companies, foreign governments, international agencies, and nongovernmental organizations stepped forward with significant cash or in-kind contributions. Though less than $1 billion in total value, and though relatively modest against the $30 billion damage to the country, these sources nonetheless proved to be important, plugging gaps or facilitating aid where public agencies could not.

Private Giving Leadership Checklist

1. Stimulate private-sector support for reconstruction with a state-sponsored fund open to company donations that minimizes administrative burdens and provides tax incentives.

2. Encourage companies to donate not only cash and equipment but also time and know-how, as illustrated by Anglo American's construction of public schools.

3. Anticipate that company employees and managers in the hardest hit zones will mobilize above and beyond the normal call of duty to urgently restore essential services, as seen in the work of the private water company in the O'Higgins region and its executive chair, Pedro Pablo Errázuriz.

4. During the immediate aftermath of a disaster, given the urgency, stress, and complexity of the moment, private-sector leaders will want to become visibly engaged with front-line workers involved in the recovery.

With both public and private entities massively mobilized for the recovery, the nation's leaders' most urgent task had been achieved. Yet unless the nation's mission and goals were articulated and explained with qualifying nuance, they could generate excessive expectations. Rallying national commitment is essential given the despair present in the immediate aftermath of a disaster. If the resulting hopes are not well modulated, however, a leader's capacity to stay the course can be impaired—not fatally, but enough to cause heartburn or worse. Sebastián Piñera and his cabinet ministers stumbled into this gap, not entirely surprisingly, since many came with extensive management experience on their resumes but scant political experience in managing public expectations for the millions of Chileans who had just gone through one of the most traumatizing experiences of their life.

By way of a parallel, when a business manager becomes a top company executive, he or she is confronted with a wholly new task, and that is managing investor expectations. It is a leadership challenge that the executive had not previously been required to master but now is required to do so of necessity. The same is true with public expectations for elected and appointed officials in government, as we will see in the next chapter.

10 EXECUTION AND EXPECTATIONS

> People wanted everything *now*. We created so much in
> the way of expectations that people took it for granted.
> —Minister of Housing Rodrigo Pérez

The take-charge attitude of the management-experienced president and cabinet cascaded through the president's ranks, an effective exercise in multitiered leadership. It had worked for the president and many of the cabinet members while in business, and now it worked for them in government.

Yet one of the leader's callings whatever the level is also to dampen overoptimism and combat excessive pessimism, to find the middle path between false hopes and undue skepticism. The first part calls for countering the hubris of success by focusing attention on latent threats and unresolved problems, and warning against unwarranted risk-taking. The second part calls for combating the pessimism of setback, focusing attention on shared resolve and initial gains, and also taking steps to protect against excessive risk avoidance. Sebastián Piñera and his cabinet members arguably had worked the second part of the equation well, but were less successful with respect to the first.[1]

INFLATED EXPECTATIONS

The president's and ministers' aggressive goals produced a large and mostly unanticipated emergent tension between the government and the general public. In the words of O'Higgins governor (and later cabinet minister) Rodrigo Pérez, "People wanted everything now," and that was admittedly the government's doing. "We created so much in the way of expectations," he said, "that people took it for granted."

The public's anticipation of a speedy recovery far outstripped the time-table by which the government could deliver. "We should have been more convincing of how huge the problem was," Pérez reported with hindsight. He and his largely nonpolitical fellow cabinet members came with little track record that might have alerted them to the separate but equally salient task of modulating civic hopes.

Public expectations were predictably high for the new administration just before Sebastián Piñera took office. In a national survey in February 2010, only days before the earthquake, a strong majority—58 percent—reported that, regardless of their personal preference in the election, they expected the new government of the incoming president to do well, while just 10 percent expected it to fare badly. In a poll of March 3–6, a week after the F27 earthquake, 59 percent expected it to do well and now only 3 percent badly. Similarly, when asked how they expected the new administration to handle "housing and public works" and "security and public order," 63 and 73 percent, respectively, of the public expected it to do well, and only 2 and 3 percent thought badly.[2]

Yet without careful modulation to guard against unrealistic aspirations that can emerge when caveats are not forcefully attached to an aura of confidence and optimism, when nuances and contingencies are not sufficiently communicated, a take-charge posture can have the unintended effect of overly bolstering hopes. And it did. The business-skewed composition of the top team, with a platform for taking charge, proved less adept at managing public expectations.

The president, for instance, referenced aggressive goals for the restoration and then cited his early achievements in the immediate aftermath of F27. Comparing the government's swift work on housing, schools, hospitals, and bridges with that of earlier regimes, for instance, the president said, "In 20 days, I feel I have made more progress than others, perhaps in 20 years." True or not—and many doubted it was—claiming such great accomplishments in the first three weeks had the effect of raising benchmarks and public expectations very high for the next three years.[3]

The government's successful reopening of schools on a draconian time-line gave some authority to its early assertions of moving faster than others—but it also had the effect of excessively strengthening public confidence that aggressive targets in other areas would soon be met as well. Yet many of those other targets proved more intractable than school reopenings, and housing in particular—the largest single public reconstruction program—proved a nagging challenge without easy resolution.

The president had vowed, for instance, that all homeless residents from destroyed or severely damaged houses would soon have a roof over their head. But once the rebuilding process got underway, the actual time and cost of constructing new homes to new standards proved more daunting than had been initially anticipated, as we chronicled in Chapter 6. Establishing the legal ownership of many homes slated for rebuilding, for example, proved more of a complex time-sink than had been foreseen.

Unsurprisingly, the public benchmarked Chile's rate of recovery not against the pace of recovery in other countries or against Chile's past earthquake comebacks, but instead against its national leaders' own publicly avowed targets, and expectations here had inadvertently been allowed to soar too high, forcing later revision and personal contrition. The president, for instance, promised in his State of the Union address in May 2012 that all those still in temporary housing would find permanent quarters by mid-2013, but he also confessed not yet having provided what he had earlier promised: "Honestly, reconstruction has been very difficult and demanding," and, "I know we've made mistakes and apologize for them."[4]

Political opponents soon capitalized on the emerging public perception that the nation's housing rehabilitation should have come more quickly. Opposition figures, for instance, began to question virtually everything that the Ministry of Housing was doing to expedite the reconstruction. Some homeowners had not been able to produce their ownership papers, for instance, raising a legitimate question of whether they should receive government assistance to rebuild a home for which they lacked proper documentation. Still, for them, waiving a perfunctory requirement to expedite the home's rebuilding appeared to ministry officials a reasonable and expeditious administrative action.

Still, as rational as a waiver on requiring proof of ownership may have seemed for streamlining the process, authorizing the waiver ran the danger of appearing to opposition politicians and the public at large as an improper bending of state rules. Outward appearances are often more salient in public life than in private business, and political opponents soon succeeded in sowing doubt about the waivers and other measures intended to help achieve what the president had pressed his ministers to accomplish in record time.

MODULATING EXPECTATIONS

Symptomatic of the emergent self-inflicted problems, the National Congress, at the prompting of the largest opposition party, forced the president's first minister of housing—Magdalena Matte—to resign after barely a year in office. The triggering factor had been a scandal in her ministry over the issue of a planned payment to one of the private construction companies. The ministry had intended to issue the payment through an irregular procedure, and the minister herself had put a stop to it when she learned of it. The flap had nonetheless made her vulnerable, and it became one of the opponents' ostensible rationales for her ouster. But her credibility had already been weakened by reconstruction timetables for housing that were lagging behind public expectations.

When the housing minister was finally forced out on April 11, 2011, President Piñera asked O'Higgins governor Rodrigo Pérez to replace her. Despite Pérez's evident absence of a housing background or connections with the building industry, the president insisted that Pérez would bring the requisite management talent to the ministry, again indicative of the president's management emphasis on getting things done whatever the political experience or consequence. "Look," the president bluntly told Pérez, "the minister has resigned. I want you to take over." Pérez appreciated that he would face serious challenges ahead. It would be "very, very tough" sledding, he thought.

Appreciating that the government had raised expectations too high and had allowed an aura of rule-breaking to emerge in its rush to act, which ran against the country's institutional tradition of consistency and fairness, Pérez as housing minister worked to bring public anticipations back into line with reconstruction realities. The enormous scope of the rebuilding, he cautioned repeatedly, was going to require time. Thousands upon thousands of homes were in ruins, and entire cities like Concepción were going to have to be rebuilt largely from scratch.

The hard reality was that reconstruction would require both herculean effort and public patience, Pérez warned. He cautioned against a miracle response, but he also plunged headlong into the effort. He spent the first days in his ministry taking stock and meeting with construction companies, housing developers, and displaced families. He asked for fresh ideas and new ways for expediting reconstruction that would be above reproach.

One idea that Pérez embraced was to speed the rebuilding pace in remote areas where construction companies had been reluctant to go. A "home kit" could be created, he believed, complete with specified materials, detailed instructions, and technical advice. The housing ministry already had seven such models on the shelf, and the minister decided to provide rural residents with what amounted to a dedicated credit card to purchase the kit's designated materials and to hire additional labor to assist in the building of their own home from the kit. Those whose homes were repairable could apply for $800 to buy tools and materials (some fifty thousand homeowners took advantage); those whose homes were beyond repair could receive up to $30,000 in vouchers to rebuild a home within governmental guidelines.

Although first focused on expediting solutions, the housing minister also began to work on tamping down expectations. Unlike schools, roads, and hospitals, he warned, it would take several years to restore the country's housing stock fully. Planning Minister Felipe Kast had also belatedly come to appreciate the same point. "We did not manage expectations well," he confessed: "People in the field are very sensitive about dates."

PERSUASIVE COMMUNICATION

Against an emergent national mood of skepticism, the president belatedly confronted the second side of the leader's bipolar dilemma of dampening overoptimism *and* combating excessive pessimism. He sought to focus greater public attention on what had been achieved, not just what was yet to be done.

In the early days of the presidency, Sebastián Piñera had declared that *he* would restore the country. This of course accurately captured his personal resolve. Yet the phrasing also introduced a formula that he did not intend. If *he* would be restoring the country, by literal misinterpretation this could be taken to imply that others would therefore have to bear less responsibility. It was a courageous decision to express it that way—taking complete charge—but it was also, in the view of one official, the wrong nuance, since he would not want to come across as a "superhero."

As coping with the immediate crisis gave way to long-term reconstruction, the president increasingly referenced shared cause over individual leadership. One of us personally witnessed such an effort on August 28, 2012. The president and his entourage had flown from Santiago to the earthquake region. The short flight had included the usual safety instructions and in-flight meal service, and then the president summoned the housing minister and his American guest to join him in his private cabin for a discussion of his national leadership in the wake of F27. Among his still vexing concerns: how to ensure that public perceptions of the rebuilding project were more factually informed and less driven by either excess hope or underappreciation.

The minister of housing had visited Santa Bárbara just two months earlier, but it was the president's first visit there—and it was one of the occasional moments that Sebastián Piñera had learned were essential for communicating the country's comeback without generating unrealistic expectations. If MBWA had become code for getting out of the executive suite for "management by walking around," and if Health Minister Jaime Mañalich had helped redefine it as MBLA, management by living around, the president was now given to MBTA, management by traveling around.

Upon landing, a police escort led a procession of presidential vehicles toward Santa Bárbara—a town of some sixteen thousand inhabitants in the Biobío region, one of the three hardest hit by the earthquake and home to more than 2 million residents. The region's capital city of Concepción, a hundred miles to the southeast, was where a horrified president-elect had stood with his interior minister-designate on the afternoon of February 27,

2010, when they had heard residents trapped in the toppled Alto Río building crying for help.

The president's convoy this day, two and a half years later, passed a billboard that seemed to anticipate the very message that he was determined to deliver in person at one of the new housing neighborhoods that the national government helped build: "We're Reconstructing Chile" (though the important caveat of its taking time had been omitted). A van just ahead held the region's governor, Victor Lobos, and the press corps. The president's van also held the minister of housing, a security detail, staff members, and several photographers who let few moments go unrecorded. None of the entourage seemed to give the billboard much notice, though the housing minister affirmed in passing that the purpose of our trip was indeed to "put the spotlight on the reconstruction" that had already been completed.

Now, approaching the new housing project, it was evident that this visit had been well anticipated by those in the town, as dozens of local officials in red jackets with titles embroidered on their backs lined the street and several hundred residents gathered to welcome the president. Beaming, the president boldly waded into the crowd. Wearing his own red jacket with upraised collar and "Presidente" on his back, he clasped as many hands as he could while a festive band added to the moment. He paused to embrace several residents in wheelchairs near the front of the assemblage.

At 11:45 a.m., the band sounded the national anthem and the local mayor stepped forward to tell the throng, including several dozen reporters, that Chile had now completed rebuilding more than 90 percent of the homes in this community—238 units in all. The new units with fresh paint and bright facades rose all around us, and the mayor invited one of the project's new residents to take the stage with him—and with the president.

Microphone in hand, the resident began reading from a prepared text, saying that 8 percent of the Santa Bárbara community now lived in the new housing. But then she choked up, momentarily unable to continue. In the silence, the faint clicks of cameras punctuated the wordless tension. Gathering herself, she soon resumed, reminding the listeners that they were at the heart of the earthquake zone. All the homes had been destroyed, 264 residents of the area had been killed, but the mayor had helped find temporary housing for the survivors and then his leadership had led the way to "the construction of the homes around us today." The housing minister explained in a whisper to the American observer, "Homes are very important in Chile, a great source of pride."

Then the president took the microphone, and without notes or teleprompter, he referenced families by name who had already moved into new homes, even noting that one was expecting a fourth child. While other families, he said, had opted to rebuild on their own land, many had chosen to start anew here. Either way, said the president, "we understand the value of having a house." And here they were, two and a half years after the sixth largest earthquake ever recorded had shaken their part of the planet, with new homes fully ready for occupancy.

"On February 27, I was not even yet the president," Piñera reminded the residents, "and we had our first cabinet meeting even though we were not in power." He recounted learning that a third of all the schools had been wiped out, and a third of the hospitals, and 220,000 homes had been destroyed. The Pan-American Highway was severed, 220 bridges were down, and even the governor's home had been fractured. "The night of February 27 was awful," he said, and "the whole country cried"—but despite the horror, we had to start the reconstruction, he said, and we did.

And now, as the European economy was slowing and the American economy remained stagnant, Chile was prospering, adding jobs, and rebuilding. "Witness what we have done," urged the president: "1.2 million kids did not have school buildings, but schools opened just weeks later: 3,861 schools have been built, 220 bridges, 556 public buildings, and 856 justice centers. Rebuilding homes takes more time, but today we have 130,000 new homes in the hands of the people, and 70,000 more are being readied. And by this time next year, all the homes across the country will be completed."

Sebastián Piñera stressed the many contributions of the many parties who had helped place residents back under a roof of their own. Although himself at the visual and psychic center of the Santa Bárbara celebration, and ultimately responsible for the event, he was lavish in his praise of others, making up for earlier limitations in his take-charge attitude that had initially stressed what the government would do more than what local communities could do.

President Sebastián Piñera visits a new housing project in Santa Bárbara, August 28, 2012. Photo: Michael Useem.

The president concluded: "It has been very emotional to see this country down," but we "know the soul of Chile in the face of adversity, and we always come back." We want the nation to be a "developed country by the end of the decade, with an end to poverty," and through "our people's efforts we will reduce inequality and grow the country." Our "permanent values of justice, peace, solidarity will keep our nation free."

Applause, and then a gathering of the president, mayor, and residents for the president to cut a red, white, and blue ribbon, formally opening the new housing units. Offering thanks and congratulations to the local committee that had guided the building of the homes, he then strolled along a lane between two rows of the sparkling new buildings, national flags in ample display. Scores of adults and children pushed forward to have a word, shake a hand, or even take a photo with the president.

Here in the Biobío region the president had come to embrace the plural over the singular, reminding the new housing community that country leadership comes not only from the top but also from many tiers—including many local parties. The effort also spoke to another leadership principle encountered in Chapter 4, motivating the public. Both practical experience and academic research suggest that followers' trust in their leader depends in part on the latter's willingness to personally visit the places where disasters have had their greatest human impact. That is why national leaders so often travel to the front lines of a catastrophe, rendering intangible support to those most affected, graphically demonstrating that they are willing to shoulder the costs and sometimes even the personal risks of such an appearance. Reducing social distance, conveying heart-felt sympathy, and declaring personal resolve—public trust depends on whether a leader has been willing to do so close-in, not remotely, and the president was taking a page from that playbook.[5]

PUBLIC REPUTATION FOR NATIONAL LEADERSHIP

Chile's president and his cabinet had initially gravitated toward the take-charge and act-fast end of the discretionary decision-making range; it came with a significant political cost that would never be fully reversed by altered rhetoric and site visits. The price of the government's inadequate tempering of public expectations around the pace of rebuilding became evident in public polling in the months ahead—though not at first—as thwarted hopes gradually took their toll.

The president's forceful execution of the earthquake recovery—and later the rescue of thirty-three miners in August–October 2010 (see Chapter 14)—had initially brought public acclaim for his ability to take energetic action, face crises, and exercise authority. Majorities also approved his overall leadership and capacity to solve problems, and respected him for that. This was evident in periodic surveys of the Chilean public that asked respondents

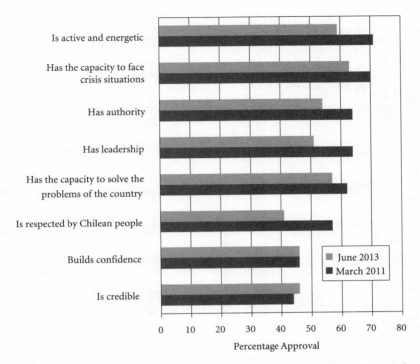

Fig. 10.1. Public Assessment of President Piñera's Leadership Capacities, 2011 and 2013. Data from Adimark GfK, March 2011, and June 2013. Survey question: "¿Cuánto cumple el Presidente Sebastián Piñera con las siguientes características?" ("How does President Sebastián Piñera meet the following characteristics?") Percentage approval = percentage responding some or much; other choices are little or nothing.

to assess the president's reputation in eight areas of leadership. As shown in Figure 10.1, majorities saw these six qualities in him in March 2011—half a year after the miners' rescue and a full year after the earthquake.

By June, 2013, however, the president's respect among the Chilean public dropped from 57 percent to 41 percent. A majority of the public still approved of the president's energy, ability to face crises, authority, leadership, and capacity to solve problems, but his ratings in other areas had dropped substantially.

The declining public perception of the president's abilities evidently took a long-term toll on his overall standing, as seen in Figure 10.2. Public

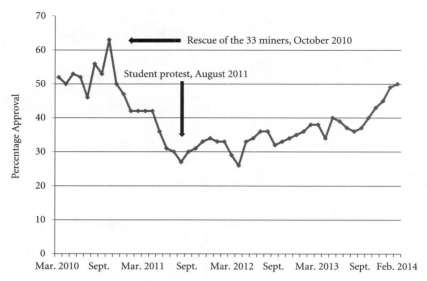

Fig. 10.2. Public Approval of President Piñera's Leadership of the Government of Chile, March 2010 to February 2014. Data from Adimark GfK, September 2014. Survey question: "Regardless of your political position, do you approve or disapprove Sebastián Piñera's government?" ("Independiente de su posición política, ¿Usted aprueba o desaprueba la forma como Sebastián Piñera está conduciendo su gobierno?").

approval of Sebastián Piñera had started with 52 percent approval during his first month in office, and it had soared to 63 percent after the rescue of the thirty-three trapped miners seven months later. But it then plunged over the next ten months, reaching a low of 27 percent during a bout of student protests in August 2011 over a government proposal to increase education fees. Public approval rose modestly in the several months following but again hit a new low of 26 percent in the spring of 2012.

Public approval of the president inched back up to 40 percent by May 2013, improving but not resoundingly, and then slipped to 37 percent in September. By his last month in office, however, public approval had returned to a three-year high of 50 percent. Although the specifics varied somewhat, the trend lines were consistent with those reported by another major polling organization, Centro de Estudios Públicos.[6]

The decline of public approval of the president's leadership served again as a reminder that leadership depends much upon the simultaneous incorporation of all of its elements identified in Chapter 4. Articulating a vision is essential, and here the president certainly performed well, as he did in taking charge and acting decisively. But without also dampening overoptimism, Sebastián Piñera's leadership credibility with the general public had been compromised.

NAVIGATING BETWEEN OVEROPTIMISM AND EXCESSIVE PESSIMISM

The polling data point to no single factor to explain the midterm decline of the public's approval of the president's leadership. His perceived ability to "face crisis situations" remained a strong suit—some two-thirds of the public still gave him solid backing in this area two years after the earthquake, the highest rated capacity of the eight surveyed in 2013. But his public approval in six of the eight polled areas had declined, and he never drew a high-marks majority for his credibility or confidence building. All this likely signified a more general disaffection with his leadership than a singling out of any particular shortcoming.

Whatever the drivers of the president's declining public approval, he and his cabinet members attributed a significant fraction of it to the mistakes they had made in the early months of their regime. They had taken too much of a savior role and had allowed popular expectations to soar unrealistically high. In then working to pull the public opinion pendulum back, the government's rubric shifted from focusing on its own role to its role in collaboration with others. The president and his ministers positioned themselves more as catalysts for restoration, less as the tip of a spear, morphing their rhetoric from can-do to let's-do-it-together. The president's early declaration that he would personally lead the recovery gave way to calls for all parties to join in national leadership of the recovery. And the president increasingly stressed the dogged challenges of restoring the nation's housing, working to tamp down expectations that he had inadvertently caused to soar.

All this was evident in the president's state visit to Santa Bárbara. Sebastián Piñera repeatedly emphasized how severe and widespread was the earthquake's damage. The implicit message was that the comeback was taking longer than the public had come to expect in part because the electorate had failed to appreciate fully how vast the damage was. The president recited the cold facts of the devastation: thousands of homes and schools destroyed. The public might have forgotten as well that their head of state was not in charge at the moment of disaster. "I was not even yet the president," he reminded the housing project residents one more time. Nevertheless, he had plunged into the vast reconstruction undertaking, hesitating not a moment before taking formal charge twelve days later. And at Santa Bárbara, the tangible results were clear to all.

In other words, remember how extreme the impact, how immediately the president-elect and then head-of-state had mobilized the nation, and how far the country had come—rather than how prolonged reconstruction had been or how far it still had to go. Public expectations should be anchored in a glass that was now far more than half full after being turned upside down on February 27.

Drawing on Chile's experience, a leadership checklist for navigating a middle way between effective execution and excessive expectation would include:

Leadership Checklist for Navigating between Overoptimism and Excessive Pessimism

1. Confidence and optimism about the prospects for recovery are essential for all who carry responsibility for recovery.

2. Pragmatism and realism are equally necessary components, helping leaders to steer a middle path between overoptimism and excessive pessimism.

3. While expressions of confidence and optimism are vital in the early days after a catastrophe, unless properly moderated, they can generate unrealistic expectations that in the longer run can work against public confidence in national leadership.

4. If expectations of timetables and tangible results have soared too high, active intervention by the top can be essential for their adjustment.

5. Since recovery from a catastrophic event requires heavy lifting by many parties, articulating a collective calling, on top of the leader's own calling, is vital, evolving a personal can-do first response into an enduring rubric of let's-do-it-together.

Active expression of a take-charge leadership style for comeback from a calamity has been a hallmark of Chile's recovery from the F27 event, but we have also found that its full impact depended much upon another factor. The country's institutional traditions place a primacy on effectiveness and efficiency, as we will see in the chapter that follows. With that foundation, Sebastián Piñera and his cabinet could better ensure that their national intentions would be translated into grassroots results. Taken together, a take-charge leadership and a pragmatic institutional mindset offer a powerful formula that others with responsibility will want to consider.

11 VULNERABILITY AND READINESS

How would you rate the ability of politicians to govern effectively?
To what extent are government reforms implemented efficiently?
—National Competitiveness Survey, World Economic Forum

The twentieth century had not been kind to Poland. Nazi Germany occupied Poland from 1939 to 1945, and the Soviet Union dominated until the lifting of the Iron Curtain in 1989. Historians estimate that 6 million Polish citizens perished during World War II, including almost its entire prewar Jewish population of 3 million. By those standards, Denmark fared far better, suffering through German occupation from 1940 to 1945 but losing fewer than eight thousand citizens.

In the decades since the end of the Cold War and the Iron Curtain, Poland has prospered with a democratic state and a vibrant economy. Denmark also emerged as one of the world's most prosperous democracies, its GDP per capita of $46,699 in 2012 one of the highest and its social safety nets among the most extensive.

Poland and Denmark are also among the nations *least* vulnerable to natural disasters according to a rating in 2012 by a U.N. agency and The Nature Conservancy. Assuming no return of the political and military disasters that defined so much of the twentieth century in Europe, Poland and Denmark can thus expect a far more benign twenty-first century.

By contrast, Chile ranked among the dozen countries worldwide most vulnerable to natural disasters, in an unhappy league with Bangladesh, Cambodia, and Japan. At the same time, Chile by still other criteria is rated among the best in the world for its readiness to face natural disasters, and here its special league includes Canada, Switzerland, and the United Kingdom. Though more vulnerable than most nations, Chile was also more ready than most to respond. And that readiness, independent of any specific set of political players, came down to the nation's core values, and institutions.

VULNERABILITY TO NATURAL HAZARDS

The UN University Institute for Environment and Human Security and The Nature Conservancy joined forces in 2012 to assess the fraction of a nation's population that was exposed to natural hazards, including earthquakes, hurricanes, flooding, drought, and rising sea level. By this criterion, Chile stood among the fifteen countries deemed most subject to natural calamities, as displayed in Table 11.1.[1]

Table 11.1. National Exposure to Risk of Natural Disaster, 2012

Rank	Country	Risk %	Rank	Country	Risk %
1	Vanuatu	64	11	Chile	31
2	Tonga	55	12	Netherlands	31
3	Philippines	53	13	Solomon Islands	30
4	Japan	46	14	Fiji	28
5	Costa Rica	43	15	Cambodia	28
6	Brunei Darussalam	41	...		
7	Mauritius	37	127	United States	12
8	Guatemala	36	...		
9	El Salvador	33	172	Malta	1.7
10	Bangladesh	32	173	Qatar	0.3

Source: Data from United Nations University Institute for Environment and Human Security and The Nature Conservancy, 2012.
Note: Risk exposure percentage is defined by the fraction of the population that is exposed to natural hazards, including earthquakes, cyclones, flooding, drought, or rising sea levels.

READINESS

Whatever the relative likelihood that Chile faces the risk of natural disaster—and it is high, according to virtually any country ranking—independent appraisals classified Chile as far more ready than most to respond

Table 11.2. Readiness to Respond to Climate-Change
Hazards, 2011

Rank	Country	Income Group	Score
1	New Zealand	Upper	0.839
2	Australia	Upper	0.837
3	Singapore	Upper	0.814
4	Switzerland	Upper	0.813
5	Denmark	Upper	0.809
6	Finland	Upper	0.797
7	Canada	Upper	0.795
8	Ireland	Upper	0.788
9	Sweden	Upper	0.788
10	Netherlands	Upper	0.780
11	Norway	Upper	0.776
12	United States	Upper	0.775
13	Chile	Upper middle	0.773
14	Iceland	Upper	0.772
15	United Kingdom	Upper	0.760
…	…	…	…
177	Iraq	Lower	0.233
178	North Korea	Lower	0.113

Source: Data from Global Adaptation Institute, Readiness Index, 2012.
Note: Readiness is defined as economic, governmental, and social indicators that enhance the speed and efficiency of absorption and adaptation;
scale ranges from 0 (low) to 1 (high).

to disasters, whether natural or human-caused. For instance, it ranked thir-
teenth of 183 countries in its readiness to respond to climate-change hazards, as seen in Table 11.2. No other highly vulnerable country, as ranked in
Table 11.1, except for the Netherlands, was rated anywhere near Chile (the
Netherlands was twelfth in vulnerability and tenth in readiness), and Chile
stood just behind the United States and ahead of the U.K. in national preparedness. Moreover, Chile was the highest ranked upper-middle-income
country in readiness; the other top fifteen countries without exception were
high-income nations.

Chile also stood highly ranked compared with other countries in its abil-

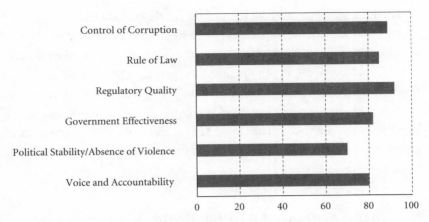

Fig. 11.1. Country Percentile Rank for Chile in World Bank Governance Indicators, 2010. Data from World Bank, Worldwide Governance Indicators, 2013.

ity to withstand and come back from economic and political risk. Monty G. Marshall and Benjamin R. Cole of the Center for Systemic Peace, for example, rated countries on their political effectiveness and legitimacy. They defined effectiveness as a combination of a range of security indicators, such as vulnerability to domestic violence; they based legitimacy on a range of political, economic, and social indicators, such as likelihood of state repression. The effectiveness metric ranged from 0 (highest) to 13 (lowest), and legitimacy from 0 (highest) to 12 (lowest). Chile rated 0 on effectiveness and 2 on legitimacy in 2010, among the best in the world and on par with the ratings accorded Norway and Singapore.[2]

Drawing on more than two dozen other sources, the World Bank annually ranks national governance in six areas, including regulatory quality, rule of law, and control of corruption. As seen in Figure 11.1, Chile stood in the upper half for all of the six governance indicators, upper quartile for three, and upper decile for two of these indicators.

Similarly, the Inter-American Development Bank compiled 137 measures of a nation's public management; compared with its Latin American and Caribbean neighbors, Chile ranked ahead of its regional average in 2008 on virtually every indicator. For instance, on "meritocratic practices in the civil service," Chile received a score of 62 compared with 36 for the regional average. For "average trust in the local government," Chile scored 59, its neighbors 50; for "capacities of external oversight institutions," Chile stood at 48, while its neighbors averaged 29; for "efficiency in the civil service," Chile scored 59, yet the region averaged 32; for "leadership consistency in the civil service," Chile stood at 53, but other regional countries averaged 28; and for "responsibilities among governmental levels," Chile came in at 49, other countries at 25. These elements help define a set of institutional practices that are an important foundation for national resilience when disaster strikes.[3]

NATIONAL AND LOCAL RESILIENCE

While one of the world's countries more exposed to natural calamities, Chile had also built a set of institutional practices in recent years that facilitate recovery from disasters whatever the source. These practices had not necessarily evolved for that reason, but they would prove invaluable for that purpose. These findings are consistent with the observation of political scientists who have contrasted the varying political traditions of Latin America. In a comprehensive study of the region, *Modern Latin America*, Thomas Skidmore, Peter Smith, and James Green, for instance, reported that compared with Argentina, Brazil, and other Latin American countries, Chile had managed to move in the direction of "pragmatism."[4]

By way of example, consider the country's housing code. It was not only formally stringent but it was also enforced; corruption was considered minimal, and builders were held liable for damage long after construction—even when they no longer owned the structure—if losses from an earthquake came from inadequate application of building codes during construction. Chile's General Urbanism and Construction Law required that the original construction company compensate those who suffer any loss as the result of even the partial destruction of a building if building codes were not followed. Article 18 specifically held the original owner of a building responsible for damage to the building for a full decade, and that a court can sentence the owner to prison (yes, prison!). This element alone accounts for much of F27's relatively modest death toll.

While the state played a significant role in enforcing the codes, thousands of builders had also understood and accepted that they should follow the codes to ensure limited casualty. Little connected with one another, like companies in most free markets, they nonetheless shared the sinews of their country's institutional practice, a mindset that stressed the legitimacy of the state, the subordination of political gain to public purpose, the rule of law, and public policies that are fairly and effectively implemented.[5]

This helped to explain why decisions for reducing the risk of additional fatalities and property damage after F27 were quickly made at the local level even without state intervention or guidance. Power company managers throughout the country had shut down most of the nation's electrical grid in the immediate wake of the earthquake, radically reducing the outbreak of urban fires. By contrast, more than half of the fires in the aftermath of recent California earthquakes were ignited by still live electrical sources.

In many areas of the affected regions in Chile, local emergency responses had been taken on their own initiative rather than from capital directives, according to an assessment by the U.S. Geological Survey and Red Cross. In the immediate wake of the earthquake, in two hospitals in the most affected region, for instance, medical directors rushed to their facilities, arriving in both cases within half an hour of the event. One hospital had 140 patients at the time; another held 275 patients spread across seven floors including a critical-care facility. Because of debris in the corridors of both hospitals, wheelchairs or movable beds could not be used to transport many of the patients from the damaged areas. Yet by the time their medical directors arrived at their respective facilities, the directors both found their hospitals completely evacuated by on-duty personnel and by many of the patients themselves.[6]

Similarly, many coastal communities in the Maule region affected by the disaster had practiced evacuations in bimonthly drills, and ONEMI officials believed that that had facilitated much of the exodus that occurred spontaneously. Public knowledge about earthquakes and tsunamis, and the aftermaths of both, had already been widely distributed, enabling many residents to take action after the event with no government directives at all.[7]

CHILE'S RISK READINESS

To appraise Chile's cultural and institutional risk readiness, we turn to an annual assessment of national competitiveness conducted by the World Economic Forum. Dating back thirty years, the Forum has annually asked panels of local experts and executives to appraise their home country, and in 2012 those national panels ranged from several dozen to several hundred respondents, totaling more than fourteen thousand observers in 144 countries. In 2012, the Forum added a question on national government risk-readiness in its survey:

> How would you assess your national government's overall risk management effectiveness of monitoring, preparing for, responding to and mitigating against major global risks (e.g., financial crisis, natural disasters, climate change, pandemics, etc.)?

Country respondents appraised their own nation's effectiveness on a seven-point scale ranging from 1 for "not effective" to 7 for "effective." As displayed in Table 11.3, Chile ranked 10th overall, well above the United States at 29th, and far higher than the most natural-disaster-risk-exposed countries identified in Tables 11.1 and 11.2.

These data points are consistent with the impressions acquired by a multidisciplinary study team of twenty experts organized by the U.S. Geological Survey and Red Cross to assess the implication of Chile's F27 experience for elsewhere. From nine days of interviews throughout the affected region, the study team reported the existence of an "earthquake culture" that had emerged over the years from prior experiences, especially the Valdivia 9.5 earthquake of 1960. Though a half-century earlier, that event had promoted, for example, the enduring folk wisdom that if a seismic event is strong enough to make one's walking difficult, it is time to exit a building as soon as the shaking stops, and also to abandon a coast line for higher ground.[8]

The survey data from the World Economic Forum implies that Chile is more generally resilient in the face of most if not all global risks. As a cautionary note, while Chile's familiarity with high-magnitude seismic

Table 11.3. Chile's Risk Management Effectiveness Compared with Other Top Ten Countries and Other Major Economies, 2012

Rank	Country	Expert Sample	Risk Management Question Score	Margin of Error
1	Singapore	171	6.08	0.11
2	Qatar	113	6.01	0.18
3	Oman	75	5.55	0.26
4	United Arab Emirates	163	5.47	0.17
5	Canada	101	5.41	0.20
6	Sweden	76	5.41	0.28
7	Saudi Arabia	94	5.41	0.29
8	New Zealand	52	5.40	0.24
9	Finland	36	5.32	0.43
10	Chile	78	5.20	0.29
...	...	...	...	...
17	Germany	127	4.90	0.25
18	Turkey	84	4.83	0.28
19	Switzerland	77	4.82	0.32
20	United Kingdom	102	4.81	0.28
...	...	...	...	...
29	United States	390	4.53	0.14
30	China	369	4.51	0.13
31	France	128	4.51	0.27
32	Australia	67	4.49	0.41
...	...	...	...	...
38	India	119	4.31	0.27
39	Italy	86	4.24	0.32
45	Brazil	141	4.16	0.23
...	...	...	...	...
67	Japan	111	3.67	0.28
...	...	...	...	...
138	Argentina	96	2.08	0.25
139	Venezuela	38	1.68	0.28

Source: Data from World Economic Forum Executive Opinion Survey, "How would you assess your national government's overall risk management effectiveness of monitoring, preparing for, responding to and mitigating against major global risks (e.g., financial crisis, natural disasters, climate change, pandemics, etc.)?

Scale: 1 = not effective in managing major global risks; 7 = effective in managing major global risks"; World Economic Forum, 2013; see Campbell, 2014.

events had fostered a stronger earthquake culture than found in other nations with less tangible experience, whether that mindset itself has better prepared the country to come back from very different calamities, such as a financial crisis or a disease pandemic, remains an open question.

INSTITUTIONAL EFFECTIVENESS

Some of Chile's present-day readiness can be attributed to practices put in place by Sebastián Piñera and his ministers in the wake of the earthquake, but much of it predates the event and is rooted in Chile's institutional values, which have placed exceptional emphasis on effectiveness, fairness, and implementation by the state, at least since the end of the military dictatorship that held power from 1973 to 1990.

This is evident from an analysis of the question on national government risk-readiness in the 2012 national competitiveness data of the World Economic Forum. We examine whether measures of institutional traditions are predictive of whether countries like Chile gave a high rating to a question on national risk management. We draw on metrics that we believe reflect the extent to which the legitimacy of the state, the subordination of political personality to public purpose, and public policies are fairly and effectively implemented. We find that many of the correlations of the "national government's overall risk management effectiveness" with measures of institutional effectiveness are very high, as seen in Table 11.4, where we include, for the sake of brevity, only those measures with the five highest correlations (on a range of 0 to 1) in the three areas of rule of law, state effectiveness, and management effectiveness. We also see in the table's two right-hand columns that compared with countries worldwide, Chile ranks well above the average; its score is generally about one standard deviation above the average for the 144 countries.

The picture that emerges in Chile is one of institutional practices that, when combined with the country's national leadership, helps account for

Table 11.4. Correlations of National Risk Management Effectiveness with Rule of Law, State Effectiveness, and Management Effectiveness

Country Factor	Corre-lation	Chile Score	All Countries Score
Rule of Law			
How would you characterize business-government relations in your country? (1 = Generally confrontational; 7 = Generally cooperative)	.807	5.17	4.39
How efficient is the legal framework in your country for private businesses in challenging the legality of government actions and/or regulations? (1 = Extremely inefficient; 7 = Highly efficient)	.798	4.63	3.68
How efficient is the legal framework in your country for private businesses in settling disputes? (1 = Extremely inefficient; 7 = Highly efficient)	.790	4.80	3.79
How would you rate the corporate ethics (ethical behavior in interactions with public officials, politicians and other enterprises) of firms in your country? (1 = Among the worst in the world; 7 = Among the best in the world)	.779	5.31	4.15
In your country, how common is it for firms to make undocumented extra payments or bribes connected with […] awarding of public contracts and licenses? (1 = Very common; 7 = Never occurs)	.748	5.04	3.52
State Effectiveness			
In your country, how you would rate the ability of politicians to govern effectively? (1 = Very weak; 7 = Very strong)	.865	4.59	3.37
In your country, to what extent are government reforms implemented efficiently? (1 = Reforms are never implemented; 7 = Reforms are implemented highly efficiently)	.859	4.85	3.76
How would you rate the composition of public spending in your country? (1 = Extremely wasteful; 7 = Highly efficient in providing necessary goods and services)	.825	4.82	3.30

(continued)

Country Factor	Corre-lation	Chile Score	All Countries Score
To what extent does the use of [information and communication technologies] by the government improve the quality of government services to citizens (e.g., speeding-up of delivery time, reducing errors, introducing new online services, enhancing transparency) in your country? (1 = Not at all; 7 = Has generated considerable improvements)	.811	5.17	4.19
To what extent do government officials in your country show favoritism to well-connected firms and individuals when deciding upon policies and contracts? (1 = Always show favoritism; 7 = Never show favoritism)	.804	4.27	3.23

Management Effectiveness

Country Factor	Corre-lation	Chile Score	All Countries Score
How would you characterize corporate governance by investors and boards of directors in your country? (1 = Management has little accountability to investors and boards; 7 = Investors and boards exert strong supervision of management decisions)	.705	4.87	4.51
In your country, who holds senior management positions? (1 = Usually relatives or friends without regard to merit; 7 = Mostly professional managers chosen for merit and qualifications)	.680	4.87	4.32
To what extent is management compensation in your country based on performance rather than fixed salaries? (1 = Not at all—based on fixed salaries; 7 = Heavily—based on performance using bonuses or equity compensation)	.656	4.56	3.86
In your country, how do you assess the willingness to delegate authority to subordinates? (1 = Not willing—top management controls all important decisions; 7 = Very willing—authority is mostly delegated to business unit heads and other lower-level managers)	.642	3.67	3.79
In your country, if someone loses a purse or wallet containing US$ 100 and it is found by a neighbor, how likely is it to be returned with the money in it? (1 = Very unlikely; 7 = Very likely)	.624	4.08	3.84

Source: Data from the World Economic Forum, 2013.
Note: Correlations can range from −1.0 to 1.0.

the country's comeback from the earthquake of 2010. Both proved import-ant, we believe, and neither was sufficient alone.

A country's institutional practices predate any individual's place at the leadership helm. A product of generations of experience and evolution, they are larger and more enduring than the leadership figures who tempo-rarily hold center stage. National leaders nonetheless carry a special respon-sibility for helping to reaffirm and occasionally redefine those principles. We offer a leadership checklist for sustaining and evolving institutional practices for those who may one day have to confront calamities as a senior official or a top manager:

Leadership Checklist for Building Institutional Practices for National Resilience

1. *Rule of Law.* Build cooperative relations between government and business; ensure that business can legally challenge government regulations and actions; strengthen the legal framework for settling business disputes.

2. *State Effectiveness.* Improve the capacity of politicians to govern effectively; expand the ability of ministries to execute government reforms; focus on efficient use of public funds.

3. *Local Effectiveness.* Develop a culture where local decision-makers can institute measures to reduce the risks of fatalities and damage during a catastrophe.

3. *Management Effectiveness.* Fortify executive accountability to directors and investors; increase use of professionally trained managers; make management compensation more dependent on performance.

Chile's comeback also depended much on the leadership of those in nei-ther the public life nor the private sector. Facilitated by the country's insti-tutional traditions, citizens and nongovernmental organizations (NGOs) of all kinds stepped forward to provide everything from soup kitchens to tent camps to new homes. Some did so entirely on their own, others in partnership with the government. Whatever the approach, they helped provide an infrastructure that neither government nor business was ready or even capable of furnishing. To appreciate their contributions to the recovery, we offer an account of several NGOs that mobilized to fill some of the voids left by F27.

12 CIVIL ACTION

Heroes will emerge here as they always do in times of crisis, but this is real life, and in real life these heroes are often people who seek neither fame nor recognition. They just want to help; they just want to do good.
—Felipe Cubillos, Desafío Levantemos Chile Fundación
(Lift Chile Challenge Foundation)

The state is normally the first responder, the first stabilizer, and the first restorer, a common denominator across many countries. Yet exceptions come to mind.[1]

When the government of Haiti was barely functioning in the wake of its 2010 earthquake, international agencies filled the breach. When local authorities in the United States were caught off guard by the scale of the Hurricane Katrina disaster in 2005, retail companies like Wal-Mart, Home Depot, and Loews jumped in to resupply stranded residents. When the government of Japan had been overwhelmed by the Tōhoku earthquake and Fukushima meltdown in 2011, other retail chains such as Costco and Lawson took it upon themselves to distribute water and other essentials.

Although notable counterpoints, those exceptions still do not negate the more general principle that the state typically takes first responsibility in crisis management and recovery efforts, and as we have already seen, Chile was no exception. President Piñera and his cabinet mobilized swiftly and massively.

Yet in Chile the government was not the only first responder. Volunteers and nonprofit organizations also stepped forward in large numbers, initially providing relief during the emergency period, then engaging in reconstruction to aid the recovery effort. Often at great expense to themselves, they complemented the state's actions, doing what the latter could not. One private group, for instance, assumed sole responsibility for temporary housing in one of Chile's most afflicted regions, and another took complete charge of rebuilding public schools in another region.

To appreciate the drivers of the civil action that also contributed significantly to Chile's comeback, we focus on the impetus and impact of three private groups, drawing on interviews that our research team conducted with the organizers of each.[2]

DESAFÍO: FISHING BOATS IN ILOCA

We begin with Felipe Cubillos, a lawyer, entrepreneur, and sailor. He had gained public prominence for coskippering a forty-foot sailboat, *Desafío Cabo de Hornos—Challenge Cape Horn*—around the world in a regatta for small crews with limited budgets. He then acquired a devoted following from his satellite broadcasts during the circumnavigation and later a book, *Sueños de Alta Mar—Dreams of the High Seas.*

Felipe Cubillos was in Santiago on February 27, safely distant from the event's worst damage. Still, stunned like everybody as the scale of destruction became known, he asked a friend to fly him to the worst of the affected coastline. "Felipe was a Good Samaritan," recalled Cristián Goldberg, a fellow businessman and civil activist. "He firmly believed he had to do something for his country," and for that, Cubillos gravitated to what he knew best.

Cubillos arrived by helicopter in Iloca, a fishing village in the Maule region, and upon arriving, "his first focus was, being a sailor, to help the fishermen repair their boats," recalled Goldberg. Many vessels had been destroyed, a great loss for those in the village, especially because of the timing. Holy Week and Good Friday were just a month away, and more than half of the annual income for many of the captains came from that week alone because of its seafood tradition.

Cubillos vowed on the spot: "Let us fix the boats! Let's get motors for the boats!" But doing so would be difficult. Chile's normal capacity for building fishing craft was just forty boats per month, but since no engines were available to outfit any at the moment, its effective capacity was zero.

Undaunted, just six days after the earthquake, Cubillos appealed to his network of sailing enthusiasts:

> Hello to everyone: we have been for three days now in the coastal zone, at the epicenter of the earthquake, and the situation is heartbreaking. I would say that the tsunami caused far more damage than the earthquake.... In the villages along the coast there is practically nothing left standing.... I am stunned by the look in people's eyes: a combination of shock, sadness, pride and hope [because] they know, and we know, that we are going to get things up and running again, and we know we are going to do it together.[3]

And for that, private generosity would be essential: "Heroes will emerge here as they always do in times of crisis, but this is real life, and in real life these heroes are often people who seek neither fame nor recognition. They just want to help; they just want to do good."[4]

Cubillos appealed to other networks as well, including those connected with the around-the-world regatta: "During the race, we learned a lesson that we will never forget: you are never going to conquer or dominate the forces of nature, but the important thing is to have the strength to get back up when nature's power has beaten you to the ground." And that resilience was just what was now required of his countrymen. "The tremendous earthquake that has whipped our beautiful land reminds us once again that Chile is a country of extremes; a country that is accustomed to the greatest forces of nature and with a population whose enormous heart enables her to keep standing upright with pride and dignity."[5]

The Internet helped. Blogs, Facebook, Twitter, and thousands of messages among volunteers and benefactors gave rise, in the words of one associate, to a "remarkable and infectious spirit of collaboration." But above all, Cubillos served as the personal catalyst, mobilizing a following that he had created during his sailing venture on the *Desafío Cabo de Hornos*. As money and volunteers poured in, Desafío Levantemos Chile Fundación— Lift Chile Challenge Foundation—seemed a natural name for his newest venture.

Desafío could have evolved into a conventional charity, but Cubillos had decided that it should also serve as a catalyst, spurring and not just subsidizing. It would mobilize sweat equity, not just gift equity. One of its volunteers caught the point as he overheard Cubillos with a group of fishermen. A boat captain was saying not to worry because he had learned that someone was going to give them new boats, but Cubillos interjected. "Santa Claus does not exist," he declared, and thus "if they wanted to re-cover their boats, they would have to start working the next day, first thing in the morning." Cubillos's small army of repairers would be arriving early the following day.[6]

Cubillos recruited Rufino Melero, an associate from the yachting fra-ternity, to organize the volunteers. His Volvamos a la Mar—Back to the Ocean—program sought to pair volunteers with boat owners, and in sup-port Melero soon found himself buying motors and fishing gear in bulk, negotiating with government agents and private companies, and appealing to contributors for larger and larger amounts. Both demand and donations soared, and without quite appreciating it at the moment, Melero, like many of the volunteers, had effectively taken a leave-of-absence from his own en-terprise.[7]

Expanding the organization, Cubillos assigned another volunteer, Dan-iel Bravo, to take charge of the repair agenda. At the time of the earthquake, Bravo had been running a shipyard in Santiago where he assembled yachts:

> When I saw how much help was needed, my builders and I left immediately for Iloca. The first thing we did in each bay was to take an inventory of how many boats we could fix. [Then] I would put one boat builder and some ten volunteers into each bay, most of them young people who would learn some task in the process and later help us to advance faster. The fishermen worked a lot, too. Our main job was to train them and give them the materials that we were continually receiving from Santiago.

Bravo and his repair teams worked fourteen-hour days for a month, re-storing 130 of the boats. They had given up most everything in the interim, including income, but, as Bravo explained, it had become a mission: "It was a sacrifice that the fishermen deserved more than anyone. I am a sailor. I have traveled all over the world and I can say that sailors are always there to lend a hand. If you are in the middle of the ocean, they'll change their entire route just to give you directions." And with that, "I felt that everything I have learned in my life was actually being applied to something worthwhile, that my knowledge as a naval engineer had actually been of use."[8]

Cubillos and his volunteers soon attracted $2 million from Antofagasta Minerals; $5 million from another mining company, Freeport; and several million dollars more from the Chilean government. They helped boat owners secure loans from the state bank at modest rates. They corralled forty-four new engines, the entire available stock worldwide, along with fishing nets and diving gear to ultimately send 284 fishing vessels back to sea, the first just eighteen days after the earthquake, in time for Holy Week. They also acquired ten statues of Saint Peter, the fishermen's patron saint, to replace the many effigies that had been swept away with everything else on February 27.

DESAFÍO: SCHOOLS IN MAULE

Cristián Goldberg had been in Canada when the calamity struck. He was founder and chairman of Tecno Fast Atco, a company that made, leased, and sold modular buildings. If a company required workforce camps in remote regions of Chile, Peru, or Argentina, Tecno was ready to install them. Among his customers were some of the world's premier mining companies, including BHP Billiton, Barrick Gold Corporation, and Antofagasta Minerals. Tecno was also in business to assist in emergencies. With a fleet of temporary modular buildings and office trailers, it could deploy temporary shelters on a moment's notice for an army of relief workers.

When Goldberg first learned of the devastation from Canadian television, he called Cubillos, who had already arrived in Iloca, to say that he would join Cubillos and that he could arrange delivery of a five-hundred-bed camp. But when Goldberg arrived soon after the earthquake, the mayor of Iloca pushed back: "No way; we do not need a camp; we need a school!" Instantly, Goldberg responded, "OK, let's do the schools."

Desafío's near instant response in Iloca to restore not only fishing but also schooling led the national government to ask that it take charge of reconstructing not just one school but all damaged schools in the Maule region, an area the size of Belgium and home to more than a million residents. The government would focus its resources on neighboring regions if Desafío could rebuild that one. And, given the president's declaration that all schools across the country would be reopened within six weeks, Desafío would have to have them all up and running by April 26. Asked how soon they would be ready, Goldberg vowed in just two weeks. Locals scoffed, but Goldberg's experience with modular construction told him otherwise.

Cubillos recruited Cristobal Lira to lead the school initiative, and the latter's own account captures the infectious idealism of the moment that had led volunteers like himself to step forward:

> I had just graduated from the university the summer before the earthquake. I had a trip planned for three days after, but when I realized the gravity of the situation, I decided to stay and see if I could help. I had known Felipe Cubillos for some time, through sailing, and when I heard that he was in the coast helping the fishermen, I called him up. Right away he said he needed me, but not for rebuilding boats. He wanted me to take charge of a new project: rebuilding schools. I said yes, though I was not sure what I would be doing. By the next day I was traveling through the region with another volunteer…to see the damage firsthand. From that day onward, we never stopped. We knew that if the students were not back in school by the end of April, at the latest, they would lose the entire school year.

Twelve trucks entered Iloca on March 20 with the school's prefabricated classrooms. There was "nothing more moving" that Saturday, recalled Goldberg, just three weeks after the earthquake. "The trucks entered the town with the school modules on top, adorned with flags. My countrymen and women were there, many crying. We were crying, watching as that community was starting to rise up, with patriotism, pure patriotism in the townspeople's blood." Goldberg and his crew worked day and night on the school. When it opened, Goldberg recalled, "the pride of delivering it will mark us forever."

When a television reporter asked nine-year-old Victor Diaz in Iloca about the devastation, he had intended to say that the early responders had "brought us blankets" and that he then really wanted to get back to school. But Diaz mistakenly used *zafrada* in place of *frazada*—"blanket" in Spanish—and his endearing response on national television gave him the moniker of "Zafrada" and placed Iloca and its devastated school on the national map. President Piñera announced he would come for the reopening of the "Zafrada" school.

Twenty-two days after the earthquake, Desafío inaugurated the new modular school in Iloca with seats for 150 children, the president did attend, and now with children in school during the daytime, parents could focus on recovery more easily. Mining companies that had pledged assistance took the lead in reconstructing schools in still other areas, and within seventy days of the earthquake, Desafío had reopened thirty-one schools and three playgrounds. A public campaign for stuffed animals delivered eight thousand teddy bears to children coming back to their classrooms, and corporate donations funded twenty-two library collections and fifteen library buildings. Completing the details, Desafío arranged for each student to have a box of school supplies upon arriving.

DESAFÍO: BACK TO BUSINESS

The momentum carried Desafío into a third arena. Local businesses, many run out of their operators' homes, had been devastated as well. Felipe Cubillos discovered that larger businesses were turning to their insurers for help, but smaller enterprises were uninsured. Desafío urged the national government and large financial institutions like Banco Santander to cut interest rates and expedite small loans; it asked local wholesalers and distributors to help out as well, since the sooner their customers were back in business, the more quickly they would come back as well.

Again, Desafío's recruitment of a ready organizer proved the foundation. Diego Larraín, the volunteer who would take charge of the business initiative, recalled, "Immediately following the events of February 27, I organized a trip to Pelluhue [a town in the Maule region not far from the epicenter] with some friends to distribute water, clothing, and food. That first week

I ran into Felipe Cubillos; he was working with a team that was repairing the fishermen's boats, and he invited me to come by the bays." Once there, Cubillos persuaded him on the spot to move beyond short-term relief and take charge of the business recovery initiative.[9]

One of Desafío's first business beneficiaries was El Rucaray, a restaurant in the badly damaged city of Cauquenes near Pelluhue. Desafío arranged to deliver two plain modular units to the restaurant owner, and with a creative design from a local architect, the restaurant reopened with a rustic colonial look and room for fifty patrons. A second floor of the modular units became a complete home for the owner and family, with kitchen, full bath, laundry room, living area, two bedrooms, and even a terrace.

Goldberg recalled: "The project was beautiful! You know, the big retail chains do not need help, they have insurance and always survive and thrive. But the small retailers were suffering. By building back the stores and their living quarters in the same building, we were restoring the fabric of the community at a low cost." In all, Desafío helped restore 44 commercial storefronts, 55 small businesses, and 105 other enterprises.

DESAFÍO'S OWN TRAGEDY AND COMEBACK

Many of Desafío's leading figures—including founding director Felipe Cubillos—were aboard a Chilean Air Force flight on September 2, 2011, to Juan Fernández, the offshore archipelago that had been devastated by the F27 tsunami eighteen months earlier. The pilot attempted to land twice but finally crashed into the sea, killing all twenty passengers. Felipe Cubillos, who had given so much of himself to help others, was forty-nine years old.

Cristián Goldberg, the business volunteer whom Cubillos had recruited but who fortunately was not on the flight, felt he had no other option but to step forward. "We had a choice after the accident," he said. "The NGO Desafío could die as well or we could take the foundation and keep it going. We decided to continue." "People do not choose to be poor," he reflected. "People do not choose to be the victims of an earthquake, either," and Desafío under his direction would continue to help surmount both.

Desafío evolved into a multichanneled organization, linking those who could help with those who still needed help in a range of areas. More than a thousand volunteers, including five dozen physicians, came to run more than sixty projects. It moved from recovery to relief, but its working philosophy also became more eclectic. When a group of its volunteers proposed to start a campaign for the homeless, Goldberg countered that the organization does entrepreneurship but not giveaways. Yet the need was great—Chile counted more than ten thousand homeless even before the earthquake—and Desafío came to embrace their cause as well.

The engine of civil recovery, Desafío learned from its experience, was an upward spiral, a set of steps that built on one another: rubble removed, then a shelter, next a school, and finally a business. For those who had lost nearly everything, explained Cristián Goldberg, the restoration of each fostered a virtuous circle as "mothers take their kids to school, parents can go back to fishing or reconstruction work, and the community can start rising up."

TECHO: *MEDIAGUAS* FOR *CAMPAMENTOS*

Rural peasants had migrated in large number to cities for work throughout the Latin region in recent decades, but their marginal and low-paying opportunities often condemned them and their families to campamentos—campsites—of extreme poverty amid urban wealth. Many of the campsites in Chile had been eradicated through government housing initiatives, but not all. By one estimate, at least twenty-seven thousand families still resided in more than six hundred campsites around the time of the earthquake.[10]

Civic groups had had a long tradition of working with such campsites. During the late 1990s, Felipe Berríos, a Catholic priest, had led Fundación de Viviendas Hogar de Cristo—Christ's Home Housing Foundation—a branch of Hogar de Cristo, or Home of Christ. The foundation made and sold mediaguas, small prefabricated homes of wood panels and metal sheets designed to house a family of four. A team of six to eight could assemble a home kit in just two days. By the time of F27, Hogar de Cristo had over the years built more than 400,000 such homes.[11]

To further intensify the home building, Felipe Berríos formed a new foundation in 1997—Un Techo para Chile—A Roof for Chile. It had earlier aided reconstruction in El Salvador after a major earthquake in 2001, and when the F27 event hit Chile a decade later, he put the earlier experience to work. Its director, Juan Pedro Pinochet, who had served as CEO of Parmalat in Chile, a multinational dairy and food corporation, had been in a coastal city north of Santiago, Zapallar, when F27 struck. He was able to reach Santiago the next day, a Sunday.

Even as the president-elect and future finance minister were beginning to work on a plan to pay for the country's comeback, a prominent television host, Don Francisco, was already planning to mount a twenty-four-hour telethon, Chile ayuda a Chile—Chile Helps Chile—to assist financially. The program would be the latest of a series of annual telethons dating back to 1978 that had become a Chilean national event, watched by a larger fraction of the country than any other telethon in the world.

The interior ministry called Pinochet and representatives of other NGOs to meet on Monday, just two days after the quake, to decide how the telethon funds should be spent. They agreed that some of the cash would go to Home of Christ and another NGO to distribute food and clothing, and the rest would go for Techo to build prefabricated homes. Banco de Chile and Santander arranged for four hundred of their branches, staffed with ten thousand volunteers, to receive contributions live over the twenty-four hours of the telethon. The target for the event was audacious—15 billion pesos—about $30 million, but telethon's actual fund-raising far exceeded expectations, with 45 billion pesos pouring in.[12]

The national telethon helped serve as a turning point for the recovery, changing the public mood from despair to action and rallying the country around assisting the most affected. The incoming minister of planning, Felipe Kast, characterized the shift: "We thought we were a very civilized society, but we then had the looting in the first few days. During the telethon, when Bachelet and Piñera were together on stage singing, this was the moment when everything turned and everyone was back to being united to help the country."

Techo received enough from the telethon to construct nearly twenty-four thousand temporary homes, and it decided on a single model for simplicity in manufacturing and speed in delivering. Construction would follow a three-step protocol that it had evolved from experience. Volunteers would visit a town, first confirming the names and addresses of the victims, then establishing a site and construction plan, and then quickly erecting the new houses.

At the same time, Techo would take its cues from the mayors and municipalities that were far better informed of where the homes were needed than outsiders. And it also sought to connect with the grief of the afflicted, helping the emotional healing along with the physical rebuilding. "The most important thing I learned," reported Pinochet, "is that you have to help with the victim's grief," and his organization's work was thus extended far beyond the mediaguas. "Our kids would sit with the old lady and drink tea with her and mourn the loss of her house, the furniture, the photographs, the family," said Pinochet. "It does not sound tangible, but people have to do their mourning," and "our kids did it" with them.

The Chilean Army began constructing prefabricated homes as well, and a friendly rivalry ensued with each vying to outdo the other. In the end, more than 100,000 volunteers joined Techo to build nearly twenty-five thousand of the temporary houses. And they did so at a moment when building anything was hardly straightforward, since even the most basic supplies were hard to come by. An advisor to President Piñera, Francisco Irarrázabal, captured the point: "A Roof for Chile was building emergency houses just two days after the earthquake," he said. "We were amazed, as we couldn't figure out how they were even buying a nail."

FOUNDATION FOR THE ERADICATION OF POVERTY

Rodrigo Jordán is a well-known mountaineer in a country that prizes adventurers. He had led a successful expedition to climb K2, the world's second highest peak after Mount Everest, and he himself had summited Mt. Everest once and led another successful ascent in 2010. And now he served as chairman of one of the nation's most prominent NGOs, the Fundación para la Superación de la Pobreza (FSP)—Foundation for the Eradication of Poverty.

One of the foundation's most successful initiatives, similar in concept to the U.S. Peace Corps, was Servicio País—Country Service—which placed self-starting antipoverty professionals in poor communities nationwide, including a number in the most affected regions. The foundation's regional directors for Maule and Biobío sprang into action when the earthquake hit. Patricio Contreras, the director for Maule, checked his family (all were OK); collected water, turned off the gas, and inventoried his food supply; checked the program office in the regional capital of Talca (the office lay in ruins); and sought confirmation that each of his fellows was alive and well (all were). Verónica Juretic, the FSP director for Biobío, did much the same, finding her office in the regional capital of Concepción, by contrast, relatively intact.

Both of the regional directors grasped that the tsunami had probably inflicted grievous damage along the coastline, and they wanted to witness the destruction for themselves. Contreras managed to reach the coastal area by borrowing a senator's car and driver; Juretic by hitching a ride with a military vehicle. Contreras was horrified by the "smell of death in Constitución," and Juretic was equally shaken, in her own words, by "the cry and tears of the senior police officer in Concepción because he didn't know what to do and where to start to work. Was it controlling the looting? Dealing with the corpses?" Both foundation directors got to work.

Patricio Contreras went on a local radio station in the first hours to pass along emergency messages of distress or reunification. He then turned to recovery, organizing a local emergency committee to coordinate the work of the area's NGOs and public officials, and Verónica Juretic did the same. The emergency committees worked to assign a large influx of volunteers and to resolve conflicts among the outside agencies rushing in to help. Above all, they served as orchestrators of emergency response for nearly a week until regional governments regained their footing.

The damage to roads, electricity, and telecommunications in the most affected areas had made governing in the first days almost impossible. Many of the local officials in the hardest hit towns found their offices un- inhabitable. In the appraisal of Francisco Irarrázabal, the advisor to the in- coming president, the local officials "could do little more than stand in the town center with a cell phone," since their computers had been destroyed, their staffs were scattered, and they could not even access their own bank accounts. One priority for the national government became the provision of mobile offices—complete with computer and checkbook—to help local officials get back on their feet.

In the meantime, information for guiding governmental response remained scarce, preventing precise intervention. As President Piñera's minister of planning, Felipe Kast, would later recall, "Early on, our main challenge was the quality of information. We didn't really know at that time who was in the worst situation, and who needed what in those first two weeks. As a result, we were sending things that were not a good match with the demand."

In the information vacuum, the government turned to local nonprofits both to collect data on immediate local needs and to deliver these urgent services. Here Servicio País's network of fellows played a critical role, as did other NGOs and multilateral agencies, including Oxfam, UNICEF, and the Pan American Health Organization.

As the initial chaos subsided in the hardest-hit regions of Maule and Biobío, offers of help came flooding into the emergency committees. The government created a website to serve as a matchmaker for volunteers and immediate needs, but it was too overwhelmed to match available supply with required demand. The emergency committees thus moved to a triage model, simply identifying those areas and people most in need and then letting volunteers and their organizations decide on their own where to go and what to offer.

By already being in the most earthquake-affected regions, Foundation for the Eradication of Poverty's country-service fellows and regional directors immediately threw their lot in with the recovery, dedicating themselves to helping those most in need. "Civil society played a big part in the reconstruction effort," said Felipe Kast. "It is very important in an emergency like this one. You always need civil society to work with you." And that proved especially important in the early days, when many municipalities were nearly as paralyzed as the population.

VERTICAL: ASSISTING VICTIMS

Rodrigo Jordán had also created Vertical Instituto, a private organization that uses outdoor education for building teamwork and leadership, and Fundación Vertical, a nonprofit branch of the institute. With two thousand miles of Andes along its border with Argentina, Chile has had a long fascination with mountain exploration. One of its universities even offers a degree in mountaineering. Capitalizing on that interest, Vertical Institute ran programs to develop leadership and teamwork through outdoor experience, similar to the goal of the U.S. organizations National Outdoor Leadership School and Outward Bound. Since its founding in 1994, Vertical had guided more than 100,000 individuals through an array of experiential learning programs.[13]

Vertical's mountain guides had repeatedly led teams of inexperienced managers and students into some of the most remote regions on earth. Their norm for outdoor living was no power, no housing, no food, no water, and no Internet. In fact, Vertical's teams learned how to survive and prosper in the most sparse and demanding of circumstances. And now, residents of Maule and Biobío had been forced to cope under similar circumstances. But while national attention was focusing on the largest cities and densest communities, Vertical opted to go for more remote villages. And for those areas, it would bring what it knew best: surviving and even prospering without permanent shelter, indoor plumbing, or a kitchen stove. It dispatched its mountain guides to rural areas of the most affected regions to teach the essentials of living outdoors.

That skill set was in short supply but high demand. VTR, a large telecommunications company in Chile, had arranged with Vertical the year before to guide thirty-six of its managers to climb the Western Hemisphere's highest peak, Argentina's Aconcagua, with a summit at 22,837 feet. Now, just eight days after F27, the company asked Vertical to establish and manage a "base camp" for a group of its technicians who were heading for repair work in Concepción but for whom neither hotels nor food would be available.

Seeking to broaden Vertical's efforts further, Rodrigo Jordán turned his attention to his nonprofit Vertical Foundation, and there the logic pointed toward fundraising. And for this, Jordán drew on a working relationship with Rolex, the Swiss luxury watchmaker. Since 2000 he had served on Rolex's selection committee for its Awards for Enterprise, biannual prizes of SFr 100,000 to individuals who "possess courage and conviction to take on major challenges."[14]

The Vertical Foundation asked Rolex to back a new program that the foundation had created in the crisis: instead of allocating scarce resources to everyone within reach, the new program, Acompañar—Accompany— would identify just four communities with which to work, and it would then commit to a full year of work with each. The foundation would deliver comprehensive and sustained support, including community building and leadership training. Like Vertical itself, the foundation would pick smaller communities that the government and other NGOs might overlook. And then the foundation would accompany the community for the duration. Rolex pledged $80,000, and Vertical reallocated $200,000 from its own operations to work with the most affected regions.

The foundation dispatched a team to the affected region for several days of on-site reconnaissance, and then a second team to identify four communities seen as most in need of what the foundation could provide. The foundation selected the sites through a relationship with Francisco Irarrázabal, the presidential advisor. Vertical had invited him on one of its mountaineering expeditions, but as a coordinator of the presidential campaign of Sebastián Piñera, Irarrázabal's time was too committed at that moment. After the inauguration Piñera asked Irarrázabal to coordinate the National Emergency Committee, and on Vertical's personal request to Irarrázabal, it was this body that singled out four villages in the most affected regions that would be good targets for Accompany.[15]

The foundation assigned Marcelo Cruz to direct the program, and he appreciated that it would have to be bottom-up, both for principled and pragmatic reasons. Accompany called for developing what the community deemed most urgent, but in any case outsiders had no choice but to learn from local residents. "We didn't know how to help," said Cruz, "until they told us." But that turned out to be one of the program's distinctive assets. "We got their empathy," Cruz added, "when they realized we wanted to help with something beyond the material." Drawing "on the emotional needs of the community, we tried to hear them and help with existing resources. The program was flexible and changed with their needs," which even came to include emotional rehabilitation, self-management, and problem solving.

By way of example, one villager kept pressing a team of volunteers to help her retrieve her mobile phone from the rubble of her home before turning to build an emergency shelter. It was initially unclear why a cellular device, likely destroyed during the house's collapse, could be more important than erecting a shelter. The team found the phone, still functioning, and only then did the volunteers appreciate that it was the villager's lifeline to family and friends, and later, a means for mobilizing fellow villagers to restore their community.

The Accompany program had five staff members rotate among the four villages every two weeks. With time in the communities, the staff noticed that villagers lacked a shared meeting space. In response, Accompany erected geodesic-domed tents with 650 square feet of meeting space within, shelters that had been used in the past for mountaineers to strategize and fraternize at Himalayan base camps.

The foundation leveraged its assets in still other ways. It had long organized leadership development programs, and when the National Emergency Committee arranged a training program in Santiago for village leaders from across Chile, Vertical delivered the content. With the backing of a mining company, the foundation also organized a program for children ages six to eighteen in the capital for training in outdoor survival and community leadership.

Vertical's sustained engagement in the villages, above and beyond relief, proved an ingredient for recovery, and its continued presence derived from its prior working experience and general philosophy. "It has been Vertical's view that collaboration with other organizations and institutions is crucial to long-term and robust success in the for-profit and not-for-profit world alike," concluded Rodrigo Jordán, and "this was the least moment to experiment otherwise."

One of the village leaders of the Santa Fe village in the Biobío region summarized her experience. Accompany's staff members, she said, "helped me to develop myself from a new perspective. They have helped me find and leverage my strengths that maybe were there before but I had been unable to develop on my own. They have taught me to be strong, they have made me believe that there are good people out there, and that you can debate and argue in a constructive manner.... You have changed us enormously."

LEADERSHIP DISPATCHES FROM DESAFÍO, TECHO, AND VERTICAL

The experiences of Desafío, Techo, and Vertical in the wake of F27 point to several leadership principles that can serve as guides for civil action in other national settings:

Leadership Principles for Civil Action

1. *Be There.* Direct engagement with those most affected by the catastrophe can be essential for mobilizing the right kinds of response. Desafío's Felipe Cubillos and Cristián Goldberg came to appreciate that the afflicted residents of Iloca most needed their fishing boats repaired, schools rebuilt, and businesses restarted only when they personally visited the devastated areas.

2. *Personalize.* Nongovernmental organizations can personalize in ways that government agencies might not. The thousands working with Techo's Juan Pedro Pinochet mourned with the earthquake's victims at the same time that they were helping them get back on their feet physically.

3. *Manage.* Civil responses are no less in need of oversight than national agencies. Felipe Cubillos took charge, assembled experts, delegated decisions, and then exercised strong management of the emerging enterprise. As Desafío scaled up, Cubillos fleshed out its mission, goals, and architecture, helping to ensure that the organization continued after his untimely death.

4. *Keep It Simple.* When time is short and need is great, simple solutions can sometimes be best. With its sudden infusion of cash from the telethon and thousands needing immediate shelters, Techo opted for a single prefab housing model that could be manufactured quickly and deployed massively.

5. *Mobilize Resources.* Civil action depends entirely on donated time and money, and recruiting volunteers and raising cash are essential functions. Cubillos could create Desafío only by convincing people to step forward; Pinochet could build his nearly twenty-five thousand houses only with the telethon's successful appeal; Rodrigo Jordán could fully mount one of his programs only with Rolex's backing.

6. *Partnership.* When resources are stretched to the extreme in the wake of a catastrophe, public agencies and civil actors can fill in for one another, furnishing more than either can provide alone. Desafío rebuilt schools in one region while the government focused on another; Techo placed temporary homes in some areas while the army did so in others; Vertical served remote villages that others could not reach.

7. *Leverage.* Nongovernmental organizations can draw upon what they already do well to do what others cannot do as well in a crisis. Vertical's outdoor survival programs provided essential services to stricken areas that government and other organizations would themselves have been unable to furnish.

8. *Involve Public Figures.* Prominent public figures can serve as a catalyst for collective action.

9. *Long-term.* Commitment threatens to dwindle when the immediate crisis abates and restoration becomes more important. Vertical's voluntary pledge at the outset to devote itself to a year of community comeback parallels the national government's vow to bring the country back over four years.

Building on this array of civil-action leadership principles and those of earlier chapters, the next chapter offers a more general framing of the leadership decisions that countries, companies, and communities will want to consider in anticipating great setbacks. We suggest that it is useful to classify leadership decisions as either more intuitive or more deliberative, to view both sets of decisions as essential, and then to ensure that the deliberative is not drowned out by the intuitive during an emergency period and beyond. This chapter begins the final section of the book, *What They—And We—Learned.*

Part III

WHAT THEY—AND WE— LEARNED

13 LONG-TERM DISASTER RECOVERY

> Reconstruction is not limited to the replacement of assets lost in the disaster.... It is aimed at restoring livelihoods, habitat, social integration, governance, and sustainability.
> —President Sebastián Piñera

A relatively short window of opportunity is available in the immediate wake of a disaster for public leaders to devise and implement plans for addressing short-run needs. One immediate way to achieve these objectives is specifying short-run achievable goals that reflect intuitive rather than deliberative thinking, the upper left in the choice spectrum in our guiding diagram at the end of Chapter 4. President Piñera's insistence on reopening all schools within six weeks was one of the most visible cases in point.

At the same time, given the heightened public interest in better preparing for future disasters than had been the case before F27, country leaders can also specify measures that have long-term significance, such as more effective early warning systems and better construction standards—the right side of the discretionary choice spectrum. These actions may require significant up-front costs and take time to execute but promise to reduce fatalities and damage when the next disaster strikes. This form of deliberative thinking also characterized the actions of the president and his ministers in the months after the F27 earthquake, as we have noted in earlier chapters.

Ironically, decision-makers, whether local or national, may be more likely just after a catastrophe than in normal times to engage in long-term strategies for dealing with future disasters. The 8.8 earthquake suddenly made national discussions about being even more prepared for the next disaster more salient because the calamity stirred the public to demand that the country take steps now to reduce the damage and loss of lives from the next earthquake and ensuing tsunami. Long-term investments to prepare the country for the next disaster were momentarily judged to be more critical; before, they had been on the back burner. Some in Chile had felt that an earthquake of 8.8 *would not happen to them*, since the country had not experienced such a massive event since 1960. But in the wake of the actual 8.8 event, more were now likely to conclude that *it would happen to them again*.

Yet concern with undertaking these investments has a short window of opportunity, as memories of the F27 disaster recede and normalcy returns. It is thus in the wake of just such an event that public leaders can take advantage of a national mood that allows for the design and delivery of more deliberative long-term measures. That said, intuitively driven measures are essential as well in the immediate aftermath of calamity, and we have seen both in the decisions taken by the nation's leaders after the F27 event.

RECONSTRUCTING HOUSING AND REEMPLOYING VICTIMS

President Piñera set a short-run goal of building forty thousand emergency houses by June 21, 2010, less than four months after the quake and the official start of winter in the Southern Hemisphere. He also set a long-run goal of fully reconstructing all homes by March 11, 2014.

To jump-start the rebuilding process, the president appointed Cristobal Lira to coordinate institutional donations for the rebuilding, and then to serve as executive secretary of the government's emergency committee (and later to head the Interior Ministry's Division of Public Safety, and still later to serve as secretary of Crime Prevention). Lira earlier had had a stint as general manager of the supermarket chain Distribución y Servicio, ensuring that he was personally familiar with the demands of strategic decision-making and large-scale execution.

To address short-run housing needs, Lira and his staff combined intuitive with deliberative thinking to conclude that the best immediate solution was to secure 25,000 tents. China would have been a natural source for the required number of tents, but its own major earthquakes of 2008 and 2009 had absorbed most of its inventory. The government then turned to the

Mormon Church, with half a million members in Chile, to supply 10,000 of the tents. That was still far from sufficient, and the government constructed more than a hundred temporary villages—aldeas—from scratch, giving another 4,500 families provisional shelter.[1]

Although temporary, the villages, some resembling trailer parks, opened opportunities for more deliberative thinking. With residents temporarily located in concentrated areas for one or two years, village leaders soon began to organize community work, enterprise development, and grant applications. Some town mayors and regional governors resisted the national initiative to build temporary housing, fearful that these villages could morph into blighted slums. And some suppliers considered delayed delivery of housing materials in anticipation of rising prices, but the government declared that it would not accept supplies from companies that did not provide materials by May 31, and enforced that cutoff. Most suppliers delivered their materials on time at prevailing prices, saving public monies.[2]

With longer-term recovery also in mind, the national government instituted the Manos a la Obra—Let's Get to Work—program to hire the unemployed to restore damaged homes. That program engaged members of more than 50,000 families with an average payroll of $540 per family. The government added still another employment initiative, Fuerza de Apoyo Humanitario, the Humanitarian Support Force, by hiring some 20,000 disaster victims—60 percent women—to work in collaboration with the army and under the direction of a brigadier general to reconstruct homes. With a staff of officers and civilians skilled in logistics and administration, the Humanitarian Support Force erected more than 70,000 emergency homes, rebuilt damaged roads, and repaired hospitals with a work force that very much needed jobs.[3]

DECENTRALIZATION OF RECOVERY

When President Piñera assumed office, he faced a relatively centralized institutional apparatus for disaster management. But in his view, it delegated too little power to local authorities to make decisions customized around recovery from their specific calamities—in other words, not enough tiered leadership. One Maule official, for instance, complained, "If you do not establish exceptions in the processes associated with public investment, we are going to face a lot of hassle for the approval of reconstruction projects," and he urged the Santiago agencies to find a way of transcending their normal investment hurdles.[4]

With fine-honed deliberative decision-making as the goal, the president sought ways to give community leaders in the most affected regions more latitude for devising both their own emergency responses and longer-term recovery plans. An early plan of the presidential team at La Moneda laid out the rationale:

> The real challenge posed by state-level reconstruction will be to rely on local capacities, municipalities, and regions, since they are more aware of their needs and the identity that only the affected communities can restore. This effort of decentralization suggests that the plan of reconstruction is not homogenous or generic, but rather that each community will own and be co-responsible for its own plan.[5]

When the president signed two bills in September 2010 aimed at further transferring authority to the regional and local governments, he similarly emphasized:

> The reform points in the direction of ending what many consider a suffocating centralism that takes out oxygen from the regions and the Metropolitan region, so as to allow, once and for all, that the economic, cultural, and political life of the country may not be concentrated in Santiago, but find its roots and vitality in each region and in every corner of our country.[6]

BUILDING CODES

Chile has a long history of major earthquakes, and they have brought a cumulative improvement in the country's building codes so that structures can better withstand earthquakes and save lives. The codes are not designed to prevent buildings from suffering any damage from major earthquakes, a prohibitively costly measure. Rather they are intended to thwart building collapse that could doom occupants and those attempting to flee, while at

the same time reducing physical damage. Prior to a magnitude 8.3 earthquake in 1928, Chile had not instituted any building codes for seismic resistance. In the town of Talca, where most buildings were of unreinforced
masonry—stone or brick and mortar—95 percent were destroyed. In the
aftermath, a legislative mandate created a body to develop such codes, and
the government formally implemented them in 1935.[7]

But despite the new codes, a magnitude 8.3 event in 1939 destroyed most
of the city of Chillan and resulted in twenty-eight thousand fatalities. Upon
reviewing its 1935 building code, the government imposed far more stringent limitations on building heights as a function of the construction materials utilized. It prohibited unreinforced masonry structures and tightened
standards for adobe. With the passage of time—and no additional severe
earthquakes, as well as the increased cost of construction—the government
in 1949 lifted its height restrictions on steel and reinforced concrete structures, and allowed some masonry buildings of up to four stories.[8]

In the wake of the magnitude 9.5 Valdivia earthquake in 1960, the code
was further strengthened, and it was toughened yet again after an 8.0 event
in 1985 that centered on Santiago and caused extensive property damage.
Another 8.0 event in 1995 led to still further construction requirements.
The code was revised again to include a provision holding developers and
builders responsible for any damage to their structures for a decade after
completion. That requirement reduced reliance on inspection and enforcement, both subject to bureaucratic problems and corruption.[9]

The new code requirements are a principal reason why damage to buildings from F27 was relatively minor compared with other countries that experienced earthquakes of less severity. Turkey, for instance, experienced a 7.4
magnitude event in 1999 with 125 times less energy than released by the 8.8
event in Chile, but 170,000 houses were severely damaged or destroyed, and
4,000 commercial buildings completely collapsed or were severely damaged
because building codes were less consistently enforced. Similarly, in 2010,
following the Haitian 7.0 earthquake, that released five hundred times less
energy than F27, the government of Haiti estimated that 250,000 residences
and 30,000 commercial buildings had collapsed or were severely damaged,
because the country had no building codes.[10]

CONCLUSION

Leaders of organizations and countries make many important decisions in the wake of a disaster that draw on both intuitive and deliberative styles of thinking. Intuitive thinking is more quick and direct, deliberative thinking more slow and analytic. The first is more tactical, the second more strategic in nature. Both are essential—providing each is deeply informed by past decisions when leading companies or countries.

Although disasters call for a combination of both types of thinking, intuitive decisions tend to dominate in the immediate wake of a calamity because of the need for fast action. In this regard we have seen the president and his cabinet members quickly jump into a host of actions that meet short-term goals, such as reopening the schools within forty-five days, upon taking office. At the same time, deliberative decisions by the top tiers also helped ensure that their actions were not solely guided by short-term thinking, as we have seen in Chile's longer-term comeback, where deliberative thinking played a prominent role in the president's development of a recovery plan. Drawing on these considerations and Chile's actions in the wake of F27, we identify five leadership principles for improved decision-making:

Leadership Principles for Long-Term Decisions

1. *Intuitive vs. Deliberative Decisions*. During the immediate aftermath of a disaster, a time of uncertainty and exigency, it is important that deliberative thinking be incorporated in combination with intuitive thinking to develop a course of action for both the emergency period and long-term recovery.

2. *Recognizing Biases and Simplified Heuristics*. We know from research and experience that decisions by individuals and organizations are often guided by availability biases and simplified decision rules such as maintaining the status quo. Enterprise and country leaders will want to work to

recognize these suboptimal tendencies to ensure that they do not inadvertently misdirect their own decisions or those of subordinates.

3. *Develop Long-term Strategies.* Intuitive responses are essential for leading during the immediate aftermath of a disaster, and more deliberative responses become essential for developing long-term recovery strategies. We have seen the government of Chile respond in both ways by providing temporary housing and classrooms in the first months after F27, but then also building permanent homes and schoolhouses in the four years after F27.

4. *Decentralizing Decisions.* Command and control can be vital for overcoming a crisis, but distributed leadership becomes more vital when the crisis subsides and reconstruction begins. It is then that deliberative decisions become more vital and more informed if they are decentralized so that those most affected by the catastrophe have their voices heard.

5. *Safety Precautions and Protections.* Decisions guided by deliberative thinking become part of a nation's fabric if they are used to design well-enforced regulations and standards, such as building codes, coupled with market-based policies, such as insurance policies that promise to reduce and transfer losses from future disasters, making the organization or the country more resilient physically and economically.

An early application of many of the leadership principles that we have seen in President Piñera and his cabinet ministers in the wake of F27 came less than half a year later, when a mining cave-in trapped thirty-three miners in northern Chile for more than two months. The president, his minister of mines, and the leaders of many private and nongovernmental organizations collaboratively mobilized to rescue the miners, bringing the last person to the surface on October 13, 2010. In the following chapter we examine the roles that intuitive and deliberative thinking played in rescuing these thirty-three miners, and we will see again the importance of acting tactically and strategically during a crisis, whether caused by the earth in motion or a mine's collapse. We also see how leadership lessons from the earthquake recovery of the past months found immediate application in this new crisis.

14 RESCUING THIRTY-THREE MINERS

> You need to collect all the information and then decide on a
> plan, and then get the whole country behind the plan. Accelerate
> the speed of the process; set goals and don't waste time. Ask for
> help. Show that you are in charge. Act specifically. Spread out the
> responsibility.
> —President Sebastián Piñera

An early application of what the nation's leaders had learned from the F27 earthquake came just five months later, when a cave-in trapped thirty-three miners some twenty-three hundred feet below the surface in northern Chile. Sebastián Piñera and his lieutenants would be tested again. With the first months of the F27 recovery under their belts, the leadership team was steeped in strategic thinking and deliberative decision-making even though the nation's full recovery from the earthquake still had more than three years to go.

The new disaster that struck on August 5, 2010, was not nearly as massive as F27, but for the thirty-three trapped miners it was no less a matter of life or death. A cave-in had entombed the workers in a medium-size copper and gold mine beneath the moonlike wilderness of the Atacama Desert near the city of Copiapó, five hundred miles north of Santiago.

Mining Minister Laurence Golborne had just arrived in Ecuador's capital on a state visit with President Piñera. Golborne, an engineer, entrepreneur, and manager, had earlier served as chief executive of a large retail firm, and under his eight-year direction the company had expanded annual sales tenfold. He had been asked by President Piñera to join the cabinet, not because he knew much about mining, but because he understood a lot about managing. Now, at 11 p.m., Golborne's phone came to life with a message whose starkness also conveyed its urgency: "Mine cave-in, Co-piapó; 33 victims."

If Golborne were to attempt a rescue of the miners, he appreciated that his crisis leadership would have to be exercised in tandem with that of the president, and that their tiered leadership in the weeks ahead would make the ultimate difference one way or the other. In what follows, we see a carryover of Golborne's and Piñera's earthquake experience that helped make that difference. We also witness many of the same leadership principles that had accounted for the F27 recovery, further underscoring the importance of taking charge and coming back, whatever the crisis.[1]

TAKING CHARGE

The day after the mine's collapse, Golborne deliberated whether he should travel to the site. "From 5,000 kilometers away," he said, "I didn't know much, but I did understand the magnitude of the problem." He decided that he would have to fly to the calamity, but in doing so he ran the danger of committing the government to resolving the crisis, with all the attendant political risks. Although the disaster was not of the government's making, as soon as Golborne reached the mine, the government would begin to own the rescue—and plenty of the blame if it did not go well. But when Golborne asked the president for permission to return to Chile, Piñera characteristically did not hesitate: "Yes, yes, go!"

Still, Golborne's decision to travel to the mine was not welcomed by others in the administration. His own chief of staff, Luz Granier, an economist and close advisor, initially challenged Golborne's decision to rush to the stricken mine. She had researched prior accidents and reported that no mining minister had ever gone to the site of an accident. "Ministers," she warned "do not show up at accidents right away." Golborne appreciated the downside hazard. "We were not part of the problem" at the start, he recalled, but once he arrived at the scene, he would become "the responsible party."

Aside from the political risks, Golborne himself was in many ways not prepared to lead the rescue. He had majored in civil engineering at one of the nation's premier universities, and later studied business at North-western and Stanford universities. He was attracted more to administra-tion than to the technical side of engineering, and he rose rapidly up the business ranks to become chief executive of Cencosud. When he stepped down as CEO in 2009, the company was employing more than 100,000 and its annual revenue topped $10 billion. A success in the private sector, yes, but he had had no record of public service. Still, the president had sought cabinet members with a proven management record, regardless of technical expertise or political experience, and Golborne fit the bill.

Upon reaching the San José mine at 3:30 a.m. on August 7, Laurence Golborne noted that CNN and other news channels were already broad-casting live, early signs of the media deluge soon to follow. The mining minister briefed the president by satellite phone at dawn and several more times during the morning hours. The news was not encouraging. A res-cue crew had reported that the miners, if still alive, were far below the sur-face—and shafts leading to them were blocked or too unsafe to enter. Any solution seemed far beyond the operator's capacities. Golborne privately concluded that the miners would likely never be found, let alone be found alive.

Still, in going to the site, Golborne drew on a problem-solving style that came with his management background. "I am not knowledgeable in min-ing. I have visited two mines before this. I do not have technical knowledge," he noted. But "what I do know is how to manage challenging projects, lead people, build teams, and provide the necessary resources."

FINDING THE MINERS

Two days after the cave-in, Golborne joined an emergency meeting with the mine owner and found that confusion prevailed. Even elemental facts such as the number of trapped miners—estimates ranged from thirty-three to thirty-seven—could not be verified by the owner. As a result, Mining Minister Golborne gently took control of the emergency meeting and, by unspoken implication, oversight of the rescue plan and the rescue organi-zation that would soon follow.

Then, a tumultuous meeting with the victims' relatives moved the mining minister toward more overt ownership of the rescue. In a state of shock from the rescue crew's bleak appraisal—but following a personal pledge of transparency—Golborne took a megaphone. "I started telling them the bad news," he recalled, "but then I saw, in front of me, two of the daughters of Franklin Lobos, an ex-soccer player who was in the mine. They silently started crying—teardrops on their faces with a profound sadness. I broke down. I could not continue speaking."

One of the relatives, however, shouted out, "Minister, you cannot break down. You have to give us strength!" And "this was a turning point for me," Golborne said. It would be difficult to explain to the relatives, or anybody in Chile, he concluded, if he did not stay composed—and above all, if he did not take charge.

Flying the same day from Colombia back to Chile, Sebastián Piñera called mining officials, foreign companies, even country leaders. Knowing that the presidential aircraft would be passing near the site of the disaster on its way to Santiago, the president ordered an unscheduled stop at Copiapó. His aircraft landed at 10 p.m., against the advice of his own advisors, who felt that he had to stay arm's length from the operation.

Newsweek magazine publicly expressed what many around the president were saying privately. "Disaster and politics make a volatile cocktail, as risky as it is tempting. A successful rescue can create an instant hero, bathing a leader in glory before a global audience. But a bungled operation, an outright tragedy, or even dubious behavior by a national leader while the world is watching can just as quickly cripple a government and bury a political career."[2]

Even Golborne cautioned against the president's visit. "I always thought the president had to stay away," he said, "monitoring from a distance—not directly involved. If there had been a problem, this would have had a direct cost for the president." Despite the prospective downside, President Piñera was of a mind to plunge in: "I was informed that the company that owned the mine was not capable of leading the search operation. I made a simple decision: it was the government or nobody." The president told a senior official who met the aircraft on the ground, "We are not going to rest until we find them and bring them out." Said another official, "Piñera was telling Golborne, once and again: 'You have to find them!' The 'mission impossible' message never got to Piñera."

When the president joined the families later the same day, they complained about the mine owner's tepid response and the failed search so far. Many had come from a mining tradition and knew well the technical issues confronting the rescue. When they demanded that the mine's management be pushed aside, the president agreed and then vowed, "We are going to search for them as if they were our children."

The president's decision to embrace a full-throttled rescue was in keeping with a take-charge temperament that we have already seen in the F27 recovery, and it was well captured in the words of one official: "President Piñera does not appear to have second thoughts. He does not show doubts. Maybe he internally has second thoughts and doubts, but he never shows them." The president became fixed on a goal until new data dictated otherwise. "He looks for information, forms an opinion, and then decides until new information is available," said the observer. In this case, he continued, "it was a clear-cut decision to search for the miners."

President Piñera appreciated the potential perils. "We took a lot of risks," he said. "What if we never found them, or if we found them all dead?" But in his view the opportunity more than offset the risk. "President Piñera was aware of the risks," recalled Golborne. "He is not irresponsible. He weighs every decision, costs and benefits, and then decides."

Having committed themselves to taking full charge of the rescue, Sebastián Piñera and Laurence Golborne turned to the challenge of executing a rapid retrieval. Golborne decided to drill boreholes to try to locate the miners and then winch down supplies. He also told the president that he needed a mining expert to take charge of the effort: "I realized that in the technical issues we did not have the needed leadership. I could not provide that leadership. Although I am an engineer," he confessed, "I do not have any technical knowledge about mining."

The decisions of the president and mining minister point to the leadership value of experience-informed thinking for intuitive decision-making. In weighing every decision and then quickly deciding as the mine crisis unfolded, Sebastián Piñera had drawn on extensive prior experience in running an enterprise, if not a government. Evidently his earlier successes had helped foster a self-confidence in making rapid decisions that served him well in an emergency when tempo proved vital, and he brought a host of implicit heuristics to reach not only fast decisions but also effective ones.

Much the same can be said of the mining minister. Although he came with no background in mining engineering, he assembled a team that more than made up for that. What then proved critical were a set of rapid leadership decisions, and here too the press of time would limit carefully crafted deliberative thinking. But Laurence Golborne's prior experience as a senior business leader had been an important factor in the president's asking him to serve—and the resulting heuristics provided informed guidance under the circumstances.

After his unscheduled visit to the mine, President Piñera flew to Santiago but returned the next day with mining engineer André Sougarret. The president had asked the state copper company for a top-flight mining engineer to direct the rescue's engineering, and the company singled out Sougarret, then manager of El Teniente, one of the largest underground copper mines in the world. Called to La Moneda and then to accompany the president's flight back to the mine, Sougarret was informed by the president that his singular mission was to rescue the miners and that he could count on all state resources.[3]

FINDING AND RESCUING THE MINERS

Sougarret and his team of engineers expected a drilling machine to reach the right depth on August 22—and when it finally did, rescue workers could hear a faint tapping on the drill pipes. Seventeen days after the entrapment, one of the borehole drills had finally reached the miners, 2,257 feet below the surface. When the drill head was retrieved to the surface, it contained a confirming message scrawled in red letters: Estamos Bien En El Refugio, los 33, "We are fine in the shelter, the 33."

Golborne continued to lead the rescue on site in the days that followed, but the president also remained directly engaged, following daily develop-

President Sebastián Piñera with message from trapped miners, August 22, 2010. AP Photo/Hector Retamal.

ments and arranging for additional resources. "Piñera was always saying," recalled one of the rescuers, "the government is *here*." And the president himself was frequently there, making six trips to the mine in the weeks ahead.

The rescuers reached the miners with two more boreholes, creating three umbilical cords to the trapped men. They worked the new lifelines continuously, dropping and retrieving thin, metal cylinders dubbed "carrier pigeons." Requiring an hour for descent, the cylinders were, at first, filled with rehydration tablets and high-energy glucose gels to help the miners restore their digestive systems. Soon they included food, water, clothing, and letters. Later, an electric line, fiber optic cable, and even a water pipe were also sent down the boreholes.

Amid the jubilation, Golborne's attention shifted to the new challenge of retrieving the miners. And, fortunately, a plan for the potential extraction had already been under development under his direction. A much wider shaft would be drilled to the trapped, and for that, the president telephoned several country leaders for technology and assistance, including the U.S. president, Barack Obama. The White House called back an hour later with help. NASA joined the rescue, helping to design a capsule to bring the miners to the surface, along with American companies including Aramark, Center Rock, Schramm, and UPS.[4]

On September 1, however, President Piñera warned: "There is no chance the miners would be freed by Chile's Independence Day celebrations," which began on September 18. He offered a much more distant date for anchoring public expectations. "The government," he offered, "is doing all it can, so we can celebrate Christmas and New Year's with them." Having come under so much criticism for raising unrealistic expectations about the rate of recovery from the earthquake, the president was not planning to make the same error twice. He may have also learned from U.S. president Barack Obama's mistake of expressing overly optimistic timelines in the summer of 2010 for capping the spewing oil well in the Gulf of Mexico, only to see the deadlines repeatedly unmet. The Chilean president finally announced on October 4 that the rescuers hoped to have the miners out within eleven days: "We are very close to rescuing them, and I hope to be able to rescue them before leaving for Europe." He was scheduled to depart on October 15.

In the meantime, under the subterranean leadership of crew foreman Luis Urzúa, the miners had split themselves into three groups of eleven men each, operating on morning, afternoon, and night shifts that mimicked, as best as possible, a miner's daily life. Each group slept, worked, and relaxed separately, but they gathered regularly for shared meals, video conferences, and prayer meetings.

Golborne commenced the miners' extraction at 7 p.m. on October 12. The rescue team dubbed it "Operación San Lorenzo"—Operation St. Lawrence—after the miners' patron saint. Although the rescuers had played down the risks of ascent, they asked that the first four miners brought up the shaft be those who were most fit. After these four, others came up based on their condition, the least healthy first. Coming up one by one, each miner stepped into a global spotlight with live television coverage worldwide. The one Bolivian among the otherwise Chilean crew stepped from the capsule onto the surface, pointed to his own T-shirt with the emblem of a Chilean flag on it, and shouted, "Thank you, Chile!"

The daughters of Franklin Lobos, the former soccer player, were reunited with their father, and at 8:55 p.m. on October 13, shift supervisor Luis Urzúa, the last of the miners, reached the surface, capping off a flawless extraction. His disciplined leadership below was later credited, along with that of others, for organizing and sustaining the thirty-three miners throughout their ordeal. After greeting his son, Urzúa stood with President Piñera and declared, "I've delivered to you this shift of workers, as we agreed I would." Replied the president, "I gladly receive your shift because you completed your duty, leaving last, like a good captain," and then he added, "You are not the same after this, and Chile won't be the same either."

LEARNING FROM CRISIS TIMES TWO

Emergency responders have long followed a protocol of assigning one individual to serve as incident commander, but extreme events, such as the mining cave-in, rarely come with preset templates. In that void, President Piñera built a multitiered leadership team for surmounting the crisis, taking charge where nobody otherwise proved capable of being in charge. He also reached out to many others for help, both nationally and internationally, including several country presidents. In the summary observation of one journalist, "Piñera oversaw the rescue of the 33 miners like a field marshal on the front."[5]

In doing so, the president also depended on the separate exercise of leadership below him. Had the shift-supervisor failed to sustain his fellow miners through their weeks of deprivation, and had Laurence Golborne failed to direct his rescue team through weeks of drilling and extraction, Sebastián Piñera's leadership efforts would have been in vain.[6]

Golborne had come to understand from the nation's F27 recovery experience that underestimating, and then under-reacting to, a crisis can add disaster to disaster. "We learned," he said, "that a government should never underestimate the potential magnitude of a crisis. You have to act fast and deploy all necessary resources anticipating that things can turn bad. You cannot hesitate; you have to act and at full throttle." And as a result, he recalled, "In the case of the Atacama accident, we reacted immediately and deployed all necessary resources." Chile's take-charge management mind-set, ratified and reinforced by the earthquake experience, had found fresh application. In the mining minister's own concluding words:

> I believe the fact that we were not government bureaucrats, but people who had grown in the private sector, helped. Had we been bureaucrats, we probably would not have taken control of the rescue. Legally we did not have the authority to intervene [since] it was an accident in a private mine and the owners were responsible for getting the men out. A bureaucrat would have asked for three quotes for every expense decision. We did not have the time. We just made the decision and hired or purchased whatever item or service was necessary. In short, we moved at fast speed and with the task in mind to bring the men back.

LEADERSHIP IN MICROCOSM

The lives of thirty-three miners in the Atacama desert had been at stake, not the livelihoods of 3 million across F27's most impacted regions. But in witnessing the leadership of President Sebastián Piñera and Laurence Golborne during the miners' rescue, we witnessed in microcosm many of the same leadership actions that had served the president and his cabinet in the country at large over the prior months.

Just as in the days after F27, the president had taken charge. He had authorized the mining minister to effect the rescue at a mine that the government did not own or control; he committed his government to backing the rescue, a risky endeavor opposed by many in his own administration; he recruited technical experts and specialized equipment from home and abroad; and he publicly and privately expressed unvarying support for his mining minister's leadership initiatives throughout the ordeal, all in a race against time.

In seeing those actions played out yet again in the rescue, we are reminded of the most important leadership qualities that can make the difference in a crisis undertaking, whether from a devastating seismic event or a catastrophic cave-in. These are the capacities that appear most valued for the outcome of both:

Leadership Principles Most Vital for Crises Small and Large

1. Take charge even if you are not fully in charge—if you are best positioned to make a difference.

2. Bring a management mindset to bear, with execution at the top of the agenda.

3. Act fast, take risks, build partnerships.

4. Collaborate across the several echelons of leadership, supporting, guiding, and reinforcing all tiers along with your own.

5. Secure the expertise you lack.

6. Hold down overly optimistic expectations.

Chile's recovery from the F27 earthquake and its rescue of the thirty-three miners offer insight into the human condition and our ability to overcome great adversity. Considering the decisions of the mining minister and the president, and drawing on both contemporaneous and historical incidents of similar magnitude, our final chapter seeks to identify what country and company leaders can best learn from Chile's experience so that they can incorporate it into their leadership without themselves having to go through a massive remake of a devastated country or an urgent extraction of stranded miners.

15 LEADERSHIP DISPATCHES

I do what is humanly possible to do.
—President Sebastián Piñera

Our book has been intended to serve as an after-action review of one nation's experience in the wake of its greatest disaster in a generation. It has drawn on the specific leadership actions of Chile's president and others to suggest guiding principles for national leaders elsewhere when misfortune strikes their country, and even company leaders if their firm is hit hard as well. Our purpose has been neither to celebrate nor to criticize what Chile's leaders did—but rather to learn from what they did in ways that during extraordinary times can instruct others.[1]

In this concluding chapter we identify for national leaders elsewhere several final lessons from Chile's extraordinary comeback. We also briefly draw on the experiences of others who were forced to confront their own disasters, not always successfully, to extract a set of final principles for leadership in the wake of a great calamity, whether a product of nature's whims or human foibles.

"To withstand and recover from natural and human-caused disasters," concluded the U.S. Geological Survey (USGS) and the American Red Cross in their review of the F27 earthquake, "it is essential for citizens and communities to work together to anticipate threats, limit effects, and rapidly restore functionality after a crisis." The USGS and Red Cross then identified "ten commandments" from Chile's experience for those potentially subject to a future earthquake in California:

**Recommendations by the U.S. Geological Survey
and American Red Cross for California from Chile's
Experience with the F27 Earthquake:**

1. Conduct comprehensive exercises (including joint government, private sector, NGO, emergency responder, and community exercises) before the event.

2. Empower people to be prepared.

3. Educate the population, comprehensively and continually, about what will happen during the event.

4. Emergency and earthquake professionals should work with representatives of print and broadcast media before the disaster to determine how to best serve the community.

5. Emergency plans need to be redundant, flexible, and detailed to handle the unexpected in very large disasters.

6. Recognize the competing personal and professional demands that will be made on staff after a disaster and include these in emergency plans.

7. Organizations need to plan for nonstructural damage and the potential need to evacuate even without structural damage.

8. Recognize vulnerabilities in our communications systems and make comprehensive backup plans to avoid complete communication collapse.

9. Explore mechanisms to encourage building owners to adhere rigorously to existing building codes.

10. Collect all possible data about each disaster when it happens.[2]

While the recommendations do not explicitly reference public officials or leaders in the private and nonprofit sectors responsible for preparing for and responding to a major California earthquake, they are implicitly targeted at those who will make the greatest difference. In referencing "empower people to be prepared"—the second prescription in the list above—

the recommendation points at state and local officials in California who have the resources and maybe even a mandate to arrange for large-scale earthquake preparedness campaigns. Recommendations such as the above "ten commandments" can serve as a field-tested template for leadership decisions when new calamities strike.[3]

Yet if they are only learned and not actually applied, they remain just that: "lessons collected." This was the apt characterization by a participant in a recent conference on risk and resilience in Washington, DC, organized by the U.S. National Academies and the World Economic Forum. Too often, the participant lamented, history has repeated itself when the last disaster's invaluable lessons unfortunately just sat on a shelf.

In moving from *reported* lessons to *learned* lessons to *applied* lessons, we seek leadership dispatches that offer specific guidance to those who should take action, what they should do, and when they should do so. We also want the dispatches to be compelling and linked to specific events and contexts so they are likely to be adopted by others for dealing with concrete problems that they face. That is why we have delved into the tangible actions taken by the president, cabinet members, company executives, civic leaders, and others in the wake of F27. They offer memorable guidance that, it can be hoped, will be internalized by leaders who can resurrect them when they face catastrophic events in the future.

CAN LEADERSHIP REALLY MAKE A DIFFERENCE?

Leaders of some companies or countries might be immobilized after a calamitous event by inertia or the status quo bias, unable to respond proactively. Even in times of relative peace, leaders may feel as though the scope of their influence is limited. Yet scholarly findings prove much the opposite.

By tracking the same company in the same market with no ongoing changes other than bringing in a new chief executive, researchers have pinpointed the impact of the top executive on a firm's financial performance. According to several such studies, the CEO of a large corporation can move the firm's earnings up or down by as much as 10 to 15 percent within just several years, depending on his or her capabilities. Other research has compared the impact of the CEO on company performance when the firm is facing changing and uncertain conditions versus more fixed and predictable markets. Here the research reveals that the chief executive's leadership is most consequential when the firm is weathering changing and uncertain times—precisely the conditions that confront a country or company in the wake of a catastrophe. Still other studies compare the impact of the leadership capabilities of the chief executive with the leadership abilities of the entire top team, and this research stream confirms that a company performance depends much upon the actions of not only the top executive but also the top team.[4]

Chile's experience is consistent with these conclusions. In the wake of the 8.8 magnitude event on February 27—a moment when the uncertainties were overwhelming and when a path to swift recovery without sacrificing economic growth was not obvious—the country's leaders faced critical choices and they took advantage of the opportunity to make them. The president, cabinet ministers, and leaders of private and nonprofit organizations stepped forward, opting to lead the recovery rather than remaining paralyzed in the palace.

AFTER-ACTION REVIEW
FOR BETTER FUTURE ACTIONS

After-action reviews, a long-standing tradition in the U.S. military, entails looking back on major leadership actions just taken, asking what worked, what did not, and how one's leadership could be strengthened in the future. Public agencies have often relied upon such reviews as well. Whatever the venue, they provide a disciplined method for learning directly from past leadership actions about the specific ways for improving one's future leadership.[5]

One of the authors arranged to witness an after-action review in real time, similar in purpose to our personally joining Chile's president during his visit to the new housing project. A wilderness fire crew was combating a raging blaze in California's Yosemite National Park in 2004, and the crew met at the end of every afternoon to improve the leadership actions during its many days on the fireline. The incident commander, operations director, safety officer, planning chief, and a dozen senior firefighters gathered to review the present day's decisions and decide on the next day's actions, asking what had been planned for the day, what actually happened, and how the officers should consequentially lead their crew differently the next day. In analogous fashion, the New York City Fire Department conducted an after-action review of its experience during Hurricane Sandy in 2012, finding, for instance, that the city's varied agencies should strengthen their coordination in calm times for its more effective application during turbulent times.[6]

Such reviews have long been employed in the private sector as well. At the end of every week since the founding of China's computer maker Lenovo in 1984, for example, Chief Executive Liu Chuanzhi and his top aides have reviewed their decisions of the past five days, looking to identify what they had done well and not done well. Through that weekly learning experience, they built the company into the world's largest maker of personal computers. Similarly, Deutsche Bank, headquartered in Germany, looks back on its own crisis moments to better lead through the next, seeking fresh insights for strengthening the firm's leadership from each. With some seven thousand employees in the New York City region when Hurricane Sandy struck in 2012, for instance, one of the largest storms ever to assault the East Coast, the bank concluded that the provision of emergency housing, fuel, and transportation to stranded employees during the storm was beyond what the bank's separate business lines were capable of providing. The after-action review urged that the bank centralize its crisis command to expedite employee assistance during a future calamity.[7]

A distinctive value of after-action reviews of disasters is that they draw upon the actual experiences of leaders in prior calamities to extract improved directions for leaders in future calamities. Consider, for instance, what the consulting firm McKinsey & Co. brought to Chile just after F27. The company had had recent experience in advising public officials in the wake of eight major disasters during the 2000s, including the terrorist attack of 9/11 in New York City, the 8.6 earthquake and tsunami of 2005 off the coast of Indonesia's Sumatra, the 7.9 earthquake of 2008 in China's Sichuan province, and the 7.0 earthquake of 2010 in Haiti.

McKinsey had found from its work with the City of New York that better preparedness for future large-scale disasters was essential for the fire and police agencies; from its work with Indonesia that building back *better* was essential, not just restoring what had been; from its work with China that government can fruitfully complement its own recovery efforts with corporate and nonprofit contributions; and from its work with Haiti that streamlining and coordinating relief supply chains is essential for their effective delivery. Drawing on its after-action review of a host of recent calamities worldwide, McKinsey thus formulated experience-based recommendations for guiding Chile's own leadership decisions after F27.[8]

In referencing one's own past experience with disasters, or those of others, however, we recognize that a host of barriers can still prevent the ready conversion of experience-based insights into actual leadership behavior. By way of illustration, consider the disaster brought on by the explosion of one of BP's drilling platforms in the Gulf of Mexico on April 20, 2010. The general public and scientific experts were perplexed at the inability of the British energy firm to stop the resulting oil spill that would dump more than 200 million gallons of crude oil into the Gulf of Mexico over the next three months, more than thirty times the volume of the *Exxon Valdez*'s oil spill in 1984. What was also surprising was that BP had had several disastrous experiences of its own in previous years from which one might have expected the firm to have strengthened its risk leadership in ways that might have prevented the oil spill in the first place.

An explosion at BP's Texas City plant on March 23, 2005, for instance, had killed 15 people and injured more than 170 others, one of America's worst industrial accidents in a generation. The U.S. government later found more than three hundred safety violations at that plant, and BP agreed to pay $21 million in fines. Similarly, a BP oil platform 150 miles southeast of New Orleans nearly sank on July 11, 2005, during Hurricane Dennis when a valve installed backward had allowed surging water to flood the platform. Poorly inspected pipes in BP's operation in Prudhoe Bay, Alaska, had led to a crude oil spill of more than 200,000 gallons in 2006, resulting in another fine of $20 million.[9]

Despite those accidents, it appears that BP was behaving as if another catastrophe would not happen, focusing attention not on learning from its own recurrent setbacks but on other priorities, including short-term cost savings from its drilling operations. The failure of BP to draw upon its own experiences—to its great detriment, costing more than $20 billion in restitution and lasting damage to its brand—can be traced to a host of learning barriers that are found in many companies and countries. In our view, recognizing the barriers is a first step to overcoming them, and drawing on research reported elsewhere, we briefly identify several of the most important:[10]

Barriers to After-action Learning from Extreme Events

1. *Misperception of Risk.* Like us all, leaders often underestimate the likelihood and consequences of extreme events in their own backyard by not recognizing scenarios in which they may occur. This bias is frequently reinforced by the absence of historical data on prior disasters; disagreements among experts on their estimates of probability and severity add further to leaders' misperceptions of risk.

2. *It Will Not Happen to Us.* Decision-makers frequently view the low likelihood of an extreme event as falling below their threshold of immediate concern. There are only so many priorities on which national and corporate leaders can concentrate at a given time, and with a range of more proximate challenges always at hand, their ignoring unlikely but high-impact events is not surprising.

3. *Short-term Horizons for Evaluating Protective Measures.* Decision-makers are often under enormous pressure to quickly recoup upfront costs in any mitigation measures. Everyday myopia is thus likely to inhibit investment in protective measures seen as costly.

4. *Status Quo Bias.* Many decision-makers are reluctant to move away from the here-and-now because of the upfront time

and costs entailed even when the strategic case for building resilience before it is needed may be compelling.

5. *Projection Bias.* Some decision-makers tend to project the future from the calm of the moment, and thus may be reluctant to invest in preventive measures that do not seem necessary prior to a disaster.

6. *Declining Attention Spans.* Decision-makers' engagements can be intense during a crisis, but as soon as the immediate crisis recedes, their gaze may soon turn elsewhere.

7. *Procrastination.* Decision-makers agree that something needs to be done and have good intentions to do so, but they repeatedly postpone action, a get-to-it-next-year syndrome.

The importance of surmounting these learning barriers is perhaps nowhere better illustrated than in the aftermath of Japan's Tōhoku earthquake on Friday, March 11, 2011. At 9.0 magnitude, it was the fourth largest earthquake to occur anywhere on Earth within the past century. During the six-minute earthquake more than two hundred miles of the Japan coastline dropped two feet, but far more devastating was the resulting tsunami that overwhelmed the coastline less than twenty minutes later.

Just forty-five miles off the peninsula of Tōhoku, a ten-foot upward thrust of the sea floor had created an enormous outflow of water in all directions. The resulting wave front rose thirty feet above normal sea level in many coastal regions, sweeping inland as much as six miles along Japan's northeast shoreline, destroying almost everything in its path. It also overwhelmed the Fukushima Daiichi nuclear power plant, one of the world's fifteen largest atomic power complexes with six reactors at water's edge.

Under regulatory oversight, Tokyo Electric Power Company Incorporated (TEPCO), the plant's owner/operator, had constructed a water barrier to defend against a tsunami resulting from an 8.0 magnitude event. But this 9.0 earthquake sent a forty-five-foot wave crashing over the plant's twenty-foot barrier, flooding a set of backup generators that were programmed to kick in if the plant's power supply was interrupted and if several hours of reserve battery power were also exhausted. The tsunami cut off external power to the plant, however, and although the reserve batteries worked as designed, they quickly reached their time limit, and without the backup generators, the plant's main water pumps were soon without power to cool the reactors' cores and spent fuel rods nearby.

In the ensuing days, three of the Fukushima plant's reactor cores melted, three sets of spent fuel rods exploded, and blasts ripped off two of the reactors' outer containment structures, resulting in the spewing of significant amounts of radiation that would linger for a long time into the air and water. The government first ordered evacuation of all residents within twelve miles of the reactors and then expanded the evacuation zone out to eighteen miles. As the crisis continued and seemed to worsen, a voluntary or even mandatory evacuation seemed conceivable for a much larger region.

Although the disaster at Fukushima had been triggered by a greater natural event than had been imagined by most, a postdisaster parliamentary report also found that its meltdown "was a profoundly man-made disaster—that could and should have been foreseen and prevented. And its effects could have been mitigated by a more effective human response." Mincing no words, the report concluded that government agencies and the Tokyo Electric Power Company had "effectively betrayed the nation's right to be safe from nuclear accidents," and it attributed the betrayal to a "multitude" of human errors and "willful negligence" deriving from the nation's mindset of "reflexive obedience" and "groupism." At its root cause, the report pointed to the country's insularity, which had prevented its public and private leaders from absorbing the lessons of the earlier accidents in America's Three Mile Island in 1979 and Ukraine's Chernobyl in 1986. In other words, learning barriers had prevented the nation's leaders from appreciating what was already publicly available from other countries' calamitous experiences with nuclear accidents.[11]

Of course, an after-action review for improved leadership actions is only as good as a nation's willingness to surmount its learning barriers, to transform lessons *reported* to lessons *learned* to lessons actually *applied*. Chile's experience has given us many fresh leadership lessons for absorption and application. It is now up to those most responsible for country and company resilience to ensure that Chile's lessons are absorbed and applied.

LONG-TERM INCENTIVES

The experiences of Chile, Japan, BP, and other countries and companies highlight the need to redirect our thinking and actions so that future catastrophes receive our leadership attention now. We need to appreciate that the human impact of catastrophes has been growing in recent years and is likely to accelerate in the future as more people and their settlements become subject to calamities. If more countries and their citizens lie in harm's way but their leadership's attention still remains unfocused, we are certain to experience even greater setbacks from future disasters.

Appreciating that myopia is a common human shortcoming, we believe that leaders concerned with managing extreme events need to recognize the importance of providing short-term economic incentives to encourage long-term planning. We offer two suggestions to that end:

Incentive 1: Extend financial responsibility over a multiyear period. That will give decision-makers an economic incentive to undertake preventive measures today knowing that they will reap long-term benefits from the near-term investment. This could take the form of multiyear contracts, contingent bonuses or options, and tax reductions or subsidies.

Incentive 2: The public sector can help level the playing field. Government agencies and legislative bodies can develop and enforce regulations and standards coupled with economic incentives to encourage individuals and companies to adopt cost-effective risk management strategies. *All* firms in a given industry will then have an even-handed financial incentive to adopt catastrophe risk management practices without becoming less competitive in the short run.

TAKING CHARGE FOR LEADING A COMEBACK

In inaugurating work on a new building for the national emergency office, Chile's president had said, "We cannot control nature," but "we do have to be able to be well prepared when nature strikes." Drawing on his experience and that of his cabinet and a host of other national leaders after the F27 event, we conclude with a final checklist of just five major principles for those who carry responsibility for leading in the wake of a catastrophic event.[12]

The Leadership Checklist for Comeback

1. Draw on existing institutions for reconstruction and bouncing back.

2. Invest citizens or employees with voice and influence on the recovery's specifics.

3. Set specific objectives and deadlines and hold lower tiers responsible for execution.

4. Think and act strategically and deliberatively, transcending the predictable reactions that can fix leaders more on System-1 than System-2 actions.

5. Take charge.

In reflecting on taking charge for leading a comeback, President Piñera characterized his legacy as one of proactive mobilization. "This government was able to get the best out of the people," he believed, and "the best out of the civil society to really unleash the forces of freedom and private initiative and innovation." And much of that had come through a team that he had created from those who had managed and led large organizations in the past. "We were able to engage in public service a lot of people who were very successful in the private sector," and they "came with this new attitude, with new standards."

One of the most important functions of his leadership, concluded the president, was "to motivate people and to have them really committed and motivated all the time." Many had accepted large cuts in personal income, but it was, he said, "very important to engage and motivate people to get involved and to get really committed to the huge task of undertaking simultaneously a reconstruction process and a construction of the country." In the end, reflected the president, "We were able to create a team that was extremely committed, and with a sense of urgency, transparency, efficiency and excellence."

Moreover, the president and his lieutenants appreciated that their public service was only temporary, a four-year opportunity to restore and improve their country with no immediately succeeding term in the cards. That alone likely contributed to their round-the-clock dedication to the tasks at hand rather than any political calculus.

Sebastián Piñera gathered all of his cabinet members twice annually for each to learn what all the others had been accomplishing. Ministers serially reported what they had achieved, what they planned for the next six months, and how they would pay for it. "They get a big clear picture of the goal of the government as a whole," said the president. And with that better appreciation for the "whole picture," a nation's improbable comeback from such a colossal calamity, came a calling to achieve it.

DÉJÀ VU ALL OVER AGAIN

President Sebastián Piñera passed the presidential sash to Michelle Bachelet on March 11, 2014, as she reentered the office she had four years earlier yielded to him. Just three weeks later—at 8:46 p.m. on April 1— Chile suffered another massive earthquake, this time a magnitude 8.2 located along the northern rather than southern coastline. A tsunami followed, and though fainter than that after F27, it came with enough potential for official warnings to be issued far to the north. That evening, one of the authors, attending a conference at a coastal hotel in Panama, received a tsunami "watch" from conference organizers, cautioning the possibility of a seven-foot surge.

Chile's revamped National Emergency Office, ONEMI, was far better prepared this time, a product of the remake of Chile's early warning system that the new president's predecessor had instituted as part of his deliberate commitment to go well beyond simple recovery from F27. ONEMI managers, regional governors, and national ministers now carried satellite telephones. A public awareness program, Chile Preparado—Chile Prepared— had been running tsunami drills and had widely distributed evacuation protocols. The agency had installed regional offices throughout the country, dozens of seismic stations along the coastline, and $40 million worth of sirens in vulnerable areas. And ONEMI no longer required preapproval by the Chilean Navy before issuing an evacuation order, a bureaucratic cobweb that had significantly slowed the national tsunami warning after F27. As a result, Chile required just three minutes to announce the magnitude and location of its major earthquake this time, down from twenty minutes in 2010, and it declared a coastal evacuation less than a minute later.[13]

Although the April 1 earthquake was significantly less powerful than F27, with a tenth of the released energy, the new event, at 8.2 Mw, was still among the world's ten most powerful earthquakes in populated regions during the past half-century. Nonetheless, the total loss of life—just six dead—in 2014 was a fraction of the nation's toll in 2010. And that was partly a result of ONEMI's evacuation of Chile's northern coast, quickly moving more than 925,000 people to higher ground.

"The 2010 earthquake provided us with an enormous learning opportunity," said an official of ONEMI, and a story in the April 3 edition of the *New York Times* headlined the same point: "Responding to Quake, Chile Uses Lessons of the Past."[14]

EPILOGUE: A QUIET SUMMER AFTERNOON

What is past is prologue.
—William Shakespeare, *The Tempest*

Labor Day is an honored tradition in many countries. In the United States, the first Monday in September has been the recognized holiday since 1887, a nation's annual tribute to its workers. But it has also come to signal the end of summer, a joyful but poignant reminder that school days and office meetings are just ahead.

The Labor Day tradition was in full swing as the summer came to its unofficial close. Chefs were grilling on their barbecues, testing new recipes or improving old ones. Friends and relatives dropped by, and so did neighbors with family photos and travel stories. The weather in San Francisco was picture perfect on this final day of summer, though some assert that it is always summer in the Golden State.

California's more than 40 million residents have made it the nation's most populous state—and largest economy. If considered a stand-alone country, California's $2 trillion GDP would rank it among the ten largest economies in the world, ahead of Brazil and Spain. Still, state borrowing has long been a vexing concern. An earlier governor, Jerry Brown, had signed a balanced-budget bill in 2013, but the state's continuing indebtedness of more than $100 billion had remained a financial threat.

California faced an even greater threat from its topographical location. Like Chile, its vertical dimension was aligned almost precisely along the great ring of fire, making it highly susceptible to earthquakes even though no major event has occurred since the Northridge earthquake of 1994. Northridge and the San Francisco earthquake of 1906 were in the back of many minds, but most had learned to live with the chance that "the big one" could hit during their lifetime. Despite the known risks, many blue-chip corporations continued to build their headquarters near San Francisco: Apple, Chevron, Cisco, Facebook, Google, Häagen-Dazs, Hewlett-Packard, Netflix, Visa, and Wells Fargo. And nine out of ten California residents had still not purchased earthquake insurance.

Gubernatorial candidate Isadora Pender that Monday afternoon was sharing her optimistic vision of the state's future with the many politicians and supporters she had invited to her backyard barbecue, with its unequaled view across the San Francisco Bay. Voters had picked her in the June primary to stand in the general election that was now just two months away. She had received more votes in the primary than had her opponent, the incumbent governor, and polls were giving her a comfortable 12-point margin over him. If all went well, Pender was likely to be elected the next governor of California, the first woman to serve.

Then at 3:34 p.m. it hit. When the glassware started to vibrate, most thought it just another of the mild tremors that they had so often felt before. The silverware rattled a little, a few glasses cracked, but then it stopped. When it returned twenty minutes later, however, it came in full force, a monster earthquake that shook the barbecue violently.

As the shaking finally subsided after nearly three minutes, some of the younger children were crying, and as their terrified parents scanned the horizon, they could sense destruction everywhere. They would later learn that California had just suffered the most powerful earthquake in its history, many times more powerful than the 1906 disaster.

All power and telecommunications were down, and the candidate for the governorship turned her thoughts to San Francisco's high rises. Had any collapsed? How many people might have been injured or worse? Could a tsunami wash over the Monterey Peninsula and Half Moon Bay? Were other parts of the state—Sonoma Valley in the north or Los Angeles in the south—devastated as well? And what about Silicon Valley, a high-octane engine for the state's economy.

The shock had thrown Isadora Pender to the ground, and as she pulled herself up, she appreciated that what had just happened would change her future and that of millions of others. Californians had been warned for years that this could happen, but had its residents, business leaders, and public officials, she wondered, taken the threat seriously enough to really prepare for it?

The November election, something Pender had worked so long to win, would have to wait. It was now about working with thousands of other private citizens to save the trapped and injured who might still be rescued in the coming hours. And if she won in the Fall, her governorship was sure to take her into uncharted territory. She would have to orchestrate a swift and complete recovery for one of the largest states in the country and one of the largest economies in the world.

Few prior experiences on which to develop her strategy came to mind. But then she remembered the story of how a Latin American president and his country, perched along the same ring of fire, had come back. It was possible.

LIST OF TABLES, FIGURES, AND PHOTOGRAPHS

Photographs

NOTES

Preface

Note: Unless otherwise indicated, direct quotations are from personal interviews conducted by the authors. A roster of all those interviewed is available at the end of the book.

1. Sources of information on the scale and impact of Chile's earthquake and other disasters can be found in the following chapter.

2. We assembled a research team from the United States and Chile. The team included the three authors, Wharton doctoral-candidate Luis Ballesteros, and Santiago-based Matko Koljatic, professor of strategic management at Catholic University, and Aldo Boitano, former chief executive of Vertical Institute. The research was undertaken in collaboration with several initiatives of the World Economic Forum, including its Global Agenda Council on Catastrophic Risks, of which the three of us have been members (www.weforum. org/content/global-agenda-council-catastrophic-risks-2012–2014), with Elaine Dezenski serving as a liaison with the World Economic Forum. The research has also been informed by our ongoing work with the Forum's annual *Global Risk Report* since its inception in 2006 (www.weforum.org/issues/global-risks). Our team members, identified at the book's end, bring their experience with risk management, disaster response, finance, insurance, decision processes, organizational leadership, company strategy—and even direct involvement with the F27 earthquake itself. One of our team members personally experienced the earthquake and later volunteered several months of his time and his organization's resources to assist in Chile's recovery.

Detailed study of leaders in the act of making decisions, however, has often proven unusually elusive—like the Higgs boson. Organizational leaders communicate in public, but much of what they decide is done in private. As a consequence, in the words of one inside observer, like another elusive particle of physics, the neutrino, "most executive decisions produce no direct evidence of themselves" (Barnard, 1968, p. 193; see also Jordán, 2009; Useem, Cook, and Sutton, 2005). We have accordingly sought to identify the most useful practices from Chile's experience through not only public sources but also private interviews with a host of key decision-makers identified at book's end. The public sources include a number of reports on the earthquake by both the government of Chile and independent institutions such as the International Monetary Fund, the Organisation for Economic Co-operation and Development, the U.S. Geological Survey, the American Red Cross, financial institutions, and research universities in Chile and elsewhere. The private interviews include a range of senior officials. The government of Chile opened its offices and records to our research team, and the president, cabinet ministers, and others gave time to numerous discussions and information requests. We interviewed President Sebastián Piñera, Health Minister Jaime Mañalich, Housing Minister Rodrigo Pérez, Finance Minister Felipe Larraín, Public Works Minister Hernán de Solminihac, Planning Minister Felipe Kast, their staffs and advisors; many others in government, businesses, not-for-profit organizations, and academia; and still others who were directly familiar with the nation's actions in the months that followed the catastrophic event of February 27, 2010.

We ask readers to join the dialogue on the leading practices that are evident from Chile's experience or other catastrophic events by going to our website, constructed in collaboration with the World Economic Forum's Global Agenda Council on Catastrophic Risks. We believe that countries, companies, and communities can best overcome what is unnatural in catastrophic risk management by learning from what others have devised through their own experience. We are especially grateful to the government of Chile for opening its doors so that others can learn from its leaders' actions.

Chapter 1

1. NBC Universal Archives, 2010.
2. NBC News, 2010.
3. Guzman, 2010.
4. Einhorn, 2010.

Chapter 2

Epigraph: U.S. National Aeronautics and Space Administration (NASA), 2010; Ohio State University, 2010.

1. American Red Cross and U.S. Geological Survey (USGS), 2011; special issue of *Earthquake Spectra* on the F27 earthquake, June, 2012.

2. Emol, 2010; Superintendency of Securities and Insurance, 2012; see www.reuters.com/article/2010/02/27/us-quake-chile-idUSTRE61Q0S920100227.

3. See www.interior.gob.cl/filesapp/listado_fallecidos_desapareci-dos_27Feb.pdf; www.reuters.com/article/2010/02/27/us-quake-chile-idUS-TRE61Q0S920100227.

4. Desafío Levantemos Chile, 2012.

5. *People's Daily*, 2011.

6. Cheng Song et al., 2012; American Red Cross and USGS, 2011.

7. Mitrani-Reiser et al., 2012; see also Kirsch et al., 2010.

8. Mitrani-Reiser et al., 2012.

9. Government of Chile, Subsecretaría del Interior de Chile, 2011.

10. Data provided by the Ministry of Finance; Government of Chile, Programa de Reconstrucción y Materemoto del 27 de febrero de 2010, 2010; Ministry of Finance, 2010; Pan American Health Organization, 2010; Michel-Kerjan and Slovic, 2010.

Chapter 3

Epigraph: International Monetary Fund, 2013.

1. CIGRE, 2010; Compañía Chilena de Electricidad, 2010a, 2010b; CEPAL, 2010; Pan American Health Organization, 2010.

2. Barrionuevo, 2010a, 2010b; Bresciani, 2010; Camara de Diputados, 2010, 2012; Diario Financiero, 2012a, 2012b; *El Mostrador*, 2010; Government of Chile, Ministerio de Planificación, 2010; Mella Polanco, 2012; Pan American Health Organization, 2010; Pujol, 2010; Ramirez and Sandoval, 2012; Servicio Sismológico de Chile, 2010.

3. American Red Cross and USGS, 2011.

4. Siembieda et al., 2010.; see also Benfield, 2011.

5. Webber, 2010.

6. International Monetary Fund, 2010, 3, 11, 57.

7. International Monetary Fund, 2011.

8. Organisation for Economic Co-operation and Development, 2011.

9. Siembieda, 2012.

10. International Monetary Fund, Article IV, 2011, 4.

11. Dacy and Kunreuther, 1969.

12. Ministry of Economy, Development and Tourism, 2011.

13. See www.dailymail.co.uk/news/article-1366676/Japan-tsunami-Global-stock-markets-tumble-amid-fears-nuclear-disaster.html; Trading Economics, 2013.

14. Yahoo Finance, 2013.

15. Government of Chile, 2013.

16. Ministry of Housing, 2013.

17. American Red Cross and USGS, 2011.

18. Michel-Kerjan, 2012.

19. International Monetary Fund, Chile, 2013, 4; Comerio, 2013, 1.

Chapter 4

Epigraph: See Prada, 2010; Webber, 2010; Jude, 2012.

1. Munich Re, 2013; World Bank, 2013a, 2013b; see also Loayza and Otker-Robe, 2014.

2. U.S. Global Change Research Program, 2014; Goldin and Mariathasan, 2014.

3. See, for instance, National Academies, 2012.

4. World Economic Forum, 2014a, 2014b; G20 and OECD, 2012. We have actively worked with the OECD, World Economic Forum, and World Bank on these risk-related initiatives, and the present study has its roots in our continuing collaboration with those organizations. The authors are also completing a separate study of leadership and governance in catastrophic risk management among America's five hundred largest publicly traded companies in collaboration with the Travelers Companies (Wharton Risk Management and Decision Processes Center, 2014).

5. Useem, 2006; Yukl, 1989.

6. Waldman et al., 2001.

7. House et al., 2004; Tilcsik and Marquis, 2013.

8. National Academies, 2012.

9. McCauley et al., 2013.

10. Waldman et al., 2001.

11. Michel-Kerjan and Slovic, 2011; Kunreuther and Weber, 2014; Rosenzweig, 2014.

12. James, 1878; Friedrich Nietzsche, 1872/2008; Martin Heidegger, 1962; Kahneman, 2003; 2011.

13. Weber and Johnson, 2009; Kahneman, 2011; see also Fiske and Taylor, 2013; and Camerer, Loewenstein and Rabin, 2004.

14. Simon, 1957; Kunreuther et al., 2013; Cyert and March, 1963; Cohen et al., 1972; Barreto and Patient, 2013.

15. Feltovich et al., 2006; Weber, 2011; Samuelson and Zeckhauser, 1988.

16. Tversky and Kahneman, 1973.

17. Kunreuther et al., 2013; Krantz and Kunreuther, 2007.

18. Charlesworth and Okereke, 2010; Kunreuther, Heal, et al., 2013.

19. Klein, 2003.

20. Weick and Sutcliffe, 2001.

21. Klein et al., 2006; March and Simon, 1958; Thompson, 1967, 56. In the same conceptual vein, Küpers and Weibler (2008) have argued for viewing leadership as less "person-centered" and more a "relational" and "collective phenomenon" that entails "multiple levels" of working collaboration. Other have similarly pressed for appreciating that leadership is often exercised through the collaboration of several levels, including Berson et al., 2006; Hannah and Lester, 2009; Yammarino et al., 2005; and Yukl, 2012.

22. Schein, 2010; Hall and Hall, 1960; Reilly, 1989.

23. Javidan et al., 2006; House et al., 2004.

24. Kunreuther and Useem, 2010.

Chapter 5

Epigraph: Quoted in Moffett, 2010.

1. El19, 2010; BBC News, 2010; Barrionuevo and Lacey, 2010.

2. Barrionuevo, 2010a, 2010b.

3. The cabinet members and their political affiliations are available on the book's webpage at http://wlp.wharton.upenn.edu/the-leadership-center/leadership-dispatches.cfm.

4. Pica, 2010; OECD Observer, 2010.

5. Bresciani, 2012.

6. Government of Chile, 2013.

7. Ibid.

8. Ibid.

Chapter 6

1. U.S. Army, 2012; Dempsey, 2012; Heath and Heath, 2007; Kolditz, 2007.

2. When one of this book's authors met with President Piñera for an hour in connection with the project, the president sat down with an article and an earlier book coauthored by the visitor, and it was evident from the marked-up copies and pointed questions that he had done his homework.

3. Warren, 2010.

4. American Red Cross and USGS, 2011, 31.

5. Jiji Press, 2011, 2.

6. Peters and Waterman, 1982.

7. Ministry of Housing and Urbanization, 2010a.

8. Bossidy and Charan, 2002.

9. Centro de Políticas Públicas, 2012.

10. Collins and Hansen, 2011.

11. Isaacson, 2011, 2012.

12. Ramirez and Sandoval, 2012; Pan American Health Organization, 2010.

13. Siembieda et al., 2010.

14. Comerio, 2013, 9–11.

15. Ibid., 23–26.

16. Ibid., 28–29.

Chapter 7

1. The World Bank valued the current GDP in 2010 in the United States at $14.96 trillion and Japan at $5.50 trillion; World Bank, 2014; Government of People's Republic of China, 2011.

2. Cutter, 2006.

3. Ministry of Housing, 2010.

4. Monti, 2011.

5. Central Bank of Chile, 2010; Monti, 2011; See also Kovacs, 2010.

6. Risk Management Solutions, 2011; Rabobank, 2010.

7. World Bank, 2011.

8. The ESSF fund replaces the original Copper Stabilization Fund and receives fiscal surpluses above 1 percent of GDP. It was started with an initial payment of approximately $2.5 billion (resulting from of the closure of the original Copper Stabilization Fund), and it accumulates copper revenues when the price of copper is high to support the government budget when the price of copper is low. By April 2013, the fund held $15 billion (Ministry of Finance, 2013a).

9. Government of Chile, 2013.

10. Moody's, 2010.

11. Bradley, 2010.

Chapter 8

1. Alberto Monti (2011) indicated that "the indemnity, for instance, is often limited by contract to the outstanding amount of the loan. If the loan is almost completely repaid by the borrower at the time of occurrence of the damaging event and the earthquake destroys the house, the debtor is basically left without any financial protection, notwithstanding the insurance policy. Also, the quantification of the indemnity may take into account depreciation of the insured building, instead of being based on its replacement value. The costs associated with the inhabitability of the house (i.e., living expenses) are seldom covered and can be a significant burden for the debtor.... A system fully relying on earthquake insurance mandated by banks or other credit institutions, therefore, may prove to be unable to provide a sufficient degree of protection to householders." Insurance coverage varies geographically, of course, higher (at about 31 percent) in the Santiago metropolitan region but only 15 percent in the Biobío region, where the city of Concepción is located.

2. Muir-Wood, 2011; Mideplan, 2011; Ministry of Housing, 2010.

3. Superintendency of Securities and Insurance, 2010.

4. Munich Re, 2011; Centro de Políticas Públicas, 2012.

5. Aon Benfield, 2011: "The settlement of mortgage related claims was a relatively smooth process as the insureds were the banking institutions. Once a property was inspected and damages established, the payments were made directly by the insurance company to the banking institution and not the mortgagees directly."

6. Michel-Kerjan et al., 2011; Claude, 2011.

7. Norma de Carácter General 139, 2002; Carvallo Pardo, 2012; Superintendency of Securities and Insurance, 2012; Centro de Políticas Públicas, 2012.

8. ONEMI, 2013; Superintendency of Securities and Insurance, 2010; Asociación de Aseguradores de Chile, A.G., 2012.

9. Data provided by Superintendency of Securities and Insurance, 2013. The authors thank Ernesto Rios, head of the Insurance Regulation Division of Superintendency of Securities and Insurance, for data and discussions. See BCI Seguros, 2013; Superintendency of Securities and Insurance, 2012; and Schmidt, 2013. See also www.sigweb.cl/biblioteca/SegurosContraSismos. pdf; and http://diario.latercera.com/2012/02/28/01/contenido/negocios/10-102066-9-precios-de-seguros-contra-sismos-han-aumentado-30-promedio-tras-el-27f.shtml.

10. Muir-Wood, 2011.

Chapter 9

1. Unidad Presidencial de Gestión del Cumplimiento, 2013; Rindiendo Cuenta: Balance de Tres Años de Gobierno del President Sebastián Piñera, 2013; Larraín, 2011; Ministry of Finance, 2013a, 2013b; Diario Financiero, 2012a; Mella, 2012; Centro de Investigación Periodística, 2013.

2. AmCham Chile, 2010; Anglo American, 2010.

Chapter 10

1. See Mella, 2012.

2. Adimark GfK, 2013.

3. Cooperativa.cl, "Sebastián Piñera: En 20 días hemos avanzado más que otros en 20 años," April 1, 2010, www.cooperativa.cl/sebastian-pinera--en-20-dias-hemos-avanzado-mas-que-otros-en-20-anos/prontus_nots/2010-04-01/133613.html.

4. Government of Chile, www.gob.cl/destacados/2012/05/21/mensaje-presidencial-21-de-mayo-2012-chile-cumple-y-avanza-hacia-el-desarrollo.htm.

5. Sweeney, Matthews, and Lester, 2011.

6. Centro de Estudios Públicos, 2012.

Chapter 11

1. UN University Institute, 2012, 16.
2. Marshall and Cole, 2011.
3. A host of other country ratings are summarized at http://libguides.princeton.edu/content.php?pid=14421&sid=1187293.
4. Skidmore et al., 2009.
5. American Red Cross and USGS, 2011, 1–2. Skidmore et al., 2010.
6. American Red Cross and USGS, 2011, 33.
7. Ibid., 3 and 17.
8. Ibid., 17.

Chapter 12

1. The authors wrote this chapter in collaboration with research-team members Aldo Boitano and Matko Koljatic.
2. Identified in Individuals Interviewed.
3. Desafío Levantemos Chile, 2012.
4. Ibid.
5. See http://globaloceanrace.com/?page=news&news_id=386.
6. Desafío Levantemos Chile, 2012.
7. Ibid.
8. Ibid.
9. Ibid.
10. See www.uahurtado.cl/noticias-universitarias/2012/05/seminario-analizo-realidad-de-los-campamentos-en-chile; Martinez et al., 2003.
11. Martinez et al., 2003.
12. See www.untechoparachile.cl/?page_id=1229.
13. See www.vertical.cl/home/quienessomos.php?Lang=en.
14. See www.rolexawards.com/about/awards.
15. Acompañar Program, 2013; Penny Bamber, Vertical Instituto, personal communication.

Chapter 13

1. Brain and Mora, 2012.
2. Ministry of Housing, 2010; Brain and Mora, 2012; Pan American Health Organization, 2010.

3. Government of Chile, Ministerio de Planificación, 2010; Government of Chile, Plan de Reconstrucción, 2010; Pan American Health Organization, 2010; Ministry of Housing and Urbanization, 2011a, 2011b.

4. Mella Polanco, 2012.

5. Gobierno de Chile, 2010, 10.

6. Subsecretaría de Desarrollo Regional y Administrativo, 2011.

7. Risk Management Solutions, 2011.

8. Wood et al., 1987.

9. Renois. 2010.

10. Ibid.

Chapter 14

1. Publicly available accounts of the rescue steps serve as a valuable source for this chapter. Much of the president's leadership and that of the mining minister would be conducted behind closed doors, however, and we have of necessity also completed more than fifteen hours of interviews and meetings with those directly involved in the top and middle tiers of the rescue. While some of these private sources requested anonymity, those that did not are identified in the list of Individuals Interviewed. Except where otherwise indicated, quoted materials are drawn from these interviews.

2. Margolis, 2010.

3. Rojas, 2010.

4. Government of Chile, 2010.

5. Margolis, 2010.

6. Taleb, 2010; Bostrom and Ćirković, 2008; Collins and Hansen, 2011; Hammond, 2000; James, 2010; Kunreuther and Useem, 2010; Perrow, 2011.

Chapter 15

1. See, for example, Gad-el-Hak, 2008; and Amaratunga and Haigh, 2001.

2. American Red Cross and USGS, 2011.

3. For a sampling of book accounts, see Barton, 2008; Blythe, 2002; Bostrom and Ćirković, 2008; Diacu, 2010; James, 2010; Kolditz, 2007; Kunreuther and Michel-Kerjan, 2011; Perrow, 1999; Posner, 2004; Redlener, 2006; and Weick and Sutcliffe, 2001.

4. Cannella, Finkelstein, and Hambrick, 2008; Lieberson and O'Connor, 1972; Thomas, 1988; Waldman, Ramirez, House, and Puranan, 2001.

5. Henshaw, 2012; Campbell and Dardis, 2004; Morris and Moore, 2000.

6. Useem, 2006; New York City Fire Department, 2013.

7. Useem, 2006; private communication with Deutsche Bank, 2013.

8. See, for instance, McMahon, Nyheim, and Schwarz, 2006.

9. BP U.S. Refineries Independent Safety Review Panel, 2007; National Commission on the BP Deepwater Horizon Oil Spill and Offshore Drilling, 2011.

10. Michel-Kerjan and Slovic, 2010; Kunreuther and Heal, 2003; Kunreuther, 2009; Kunreuther, Meyer, and Michel-Kerjan, 2012; Kunreuther and Useem, 2010; Michel-Kerjan et al., 2014.

11. National Diet of Japan, 2012; Asahi Shimbun, 2012; Tabuchi, 2012.

12. See also Ernesto Ayala's (2013) account of the president's leadership of the recovery.

13. Opazo Santis, 2014; ONEMI, 2013; Medina, 2014.

14. Bonnefoy and Romero, 2014; Sanchez, 2014.

Epilogue

Epigraph: William Shakespeare, Act 2, Scene I, *The Tempest,* a line inscribed on the base of "The Future" statue near the entrance to the U.S. National Archives in Washington, DC.

REFERENCES

Acompañar Program, "Executive Summary, Fundación Vertical," 2013, www.fundacionvertical.cl/acompanar/acompanar/03_description_INGLES_files/Acompanar%20Executive%20Report.pdf.

Adimark GfK, Encuesta: Evaluación Gestión del Gobierno, June 2013, Adimark, 2013.

Adimark GfK, Encuesta: Evaluación Gestión del Gobierno, February 2014, Adimark, 2014.

Adimark GfK, Encuesta: Evaluación del Gobierno Post Terremoto, Adimark, 2010.

Allison, Graham T., and Philip Zelikow, *Essence of Decision: Explaining the Cuban Missile Crisis,* Longman, 1999.

Amaratunga, Dilanthi, and Richard Haigh, eds., *Post-Disaster Reconstruction of the Built Environment: Rebuilding for Resilience,* Wiley, 2001.

AmCham Chile, "Anglo American inaugura seis escuela modulares," *Revista Business Chile,* July 2010, http://businesschile.cl/es/amcham/novedades-socios/anglo-american-inaugura-seis-escuela-modulares.

American Red Cross and U.S. Geological Survey, "Report on the 2010 Chilean Earthquake and Tsunami Response," U.S. Geological Survey, 2011, http://pubs.usgs.gov/of/2011/1053.

Anglo American, "Nuevas escuelas para reconstruir Chile: Compromiso con los afectados por el terremoto," 2010, http://anglo-american-chile.production.investis.com/sustainable-development/case-studies/rebuilding-schools-following-the-earthquake.aspx?sc_lang=es-ES.

Aon Benfield, Chile: One Year On, 2011, http://www.aon.com/attachments/reinsurance/201102_chile_one_year_on_report.pdf.

Apostol, Gina, "Surrender, Oblivion, Survival," *New York Times,* November 14, 2013.

Asahi Shimbun, "Final Report (I): TEPCO, NISA's Dilly-Dalying Caused Man-Made Disaster," July 6, 2012.

Asociación de Aseguradores de Chile, A.G., "Defensor del asegurado recibe 52 casos por cada millón de siniestros," 2012, http://portal.aach.cl/Contenido.aspx?P=117.

Auerswald, Philip, Lew Branscomb, Todd La Porte and Erwann Michel-Kerjan,, eds., *Seeds of Disaster, Roots of Response: How Private Action Can Reduce Public Vulnerability*, Cambridge University Press, 2006.

Ayala, Ernesto, *The Reconstruction of Chile*, Presidential Report Collection, Colección Memoria Presidencial del Gobierno, 2013.

Balaisyte, Jurgita, and Luk N. Van Wassenhove, "Why the Japan Disaster Is So Different from the Other Disasters," INSEAD Humanitarian Research Group, 2011, www.insead.edu/facultyresearch/centres/isic/humanitarian/EarthquakeTsunamiJapanDifferences.cfm.

Ballesteros, Luis, "Financing Catastrophe Relief and Recovery in Developing Countries: Are Global Financial Markets the Answer? The Case of Haiti," prepared for the Latin American and Caribbean Region, Sustainable Development Unit, World Bank; Wharton School, University of Pennsylvania, 2010.

Ballesteros, Luis, "Drivers of Corporate Philanthropic Disaster Response," Wharton School, University of Pennsylvania, 2013.

Barnard, Chester I., *The Functions of the Executive*, Harvard University Press, 1968.

Barreto, Ilídio, and David Patient, "Toward a Theory of Intraorganizational Attention Based on Desirability and Feasibility Factors," *Strategic Management Journal* 34, 2013: 687–703.

Barrionuevo, Alexei, and Marc Lacey, "Chile Officials Call for Aid as Devastation Sinks In," *New York Times*, March 1, 2010, www.nytimes.com/2010/03/02/world/americas/02chile.html.

Barrionuevo, Alexei, "Chile Leader Enters Changed Political Landscape," *New York Times*, March 10, 2010a.

Barrionuevo, Alexei, "Aftershocks Jolt Chile as New President Is Sworn In," *New York Times*, March 11, 2010b.

Barton, Laurence, *Crisis Leadership Now: A Real-World Guide to Preparing for Threats, Disaster, Sabotage, and Scandal*, McGraw Hill, 2008.

BBC News, "Massive Earthquake Strikes Chile," 2010, http://news.bbc.co.uk/2/hi/americas/8540289.stm.

BCI Seguros Generales, S.A., Informe de Cambio de Clasificación, 2013.

Berson, Yair, Louise A. Nemanich, David A. Waldman, Benjamin M. Galvin, and Robert T. Keller, "Leadership and Organizational Learning: A Multiple Levels Perspective," *Leadership Quarterly* 17, 2006: 577–94.

Blythe, Bruce, *Blindsided: A Manager's Guide to Catastrophic Incidents in the Workplace*, Portfolio, 2002.

Boin, Arjen, Paul 't Hart, Eric Stern, and Bengt Sundelius, *The Politics of Crisis Management: Public Leadership under Pressure*, Cambridge University Press, 2005.

Bonnefoy, Pascale, and Simon Romero, "Responding to Quake, Chile Uses Lessons of Past," *New York Times*, April 3, 2014.

Bossidy, Larry, and Ram Charan, *Execution: The Discipline of Getting Things Done*, Crown Business/Random House, 2002.

Bostrom, Nick, and Milan M. Ćirković, *Global Catastrophic Risks*, Oxford University Press, 2008.

Boyd, Roddy, *Fatal Risk: A Cautionary Tale of AIG's Corporate Suicide*, Wiley, 2011.

BP U.S. Refineries Independent Safety Review Panel, Report, 2007.

Bradley, Ruth, "Finance Minister of the Year for Latin America 2010," *Emerging Markets*, September 10, 2010, www.emergingmarkets.org/Article/2690726/Finance-Minister-of-the-Year-for-Latin-America-2010.html.

Brain, Isabel, and Pia Mora, *Before and After the Earthquake and 27F Tsunami in Chile: Learning in Housing, Urban, and Insurance*, Institute for Security Studies, Center for Public Policy, Pontificia Universidad Católica de Chile, Santiago, 2012.

Bresciani, Luis E., "Chile 27F 2010: la catástrofe de la falta de planificación," *Revista EURE* 36, 2010: 151–53.

Bresciani, Luis E., "De la emergencia a la política de gestión de desastres: la urgencia de institucionalidad pública para la reconstrucción," in *Emergencia y reconstrucción: el antes y después del terremoto y tsunami del 27F en Chile*, ed. I. Brain and P. Mora, Pontificia Universidad Católica de Chile, Santiago, 2012.

Buckner, Randy L., and Daniel C. Carroll, "Self-Projection and the Brain," *Trends in Cognitive Sciences* 11, 2007: 49–57.

Business Chile, "Las Aseguradoras de Chile Saldan las Cuentas," 2010, www.businesschile.cl/es/noticia/terremoto/las-aseguradoras-de-chile-saldan-las-cuentas.

Caldera Sánchez, A., "Building Blocks for a Better Functioning Housing Market in Chile," OECD Economics Department Working Papers, no. 943, OECD Publishing, Paris, 2012.

Camara de Diputados de Chile, Comision Especial Investigadora del Estado de la Institucionalidad, Informe de la Comision en relacion a su capacidad de respuesta frente a desastres naturales, 2010.

Camara de Diputados, Comision de Gobierno Interior y Regionalizacion, "Informe sobre Proyecto de Ley que Establece el Sistema Nacional de Emergencia y Protección Civil y Crea La Agencia Nacional de Protección Civil," 2012, http://sil.congreso.cl.

Camerer, Colin, George Loewenstein, and Matthew Rabin, *Advances in Behavioral Economics,* Princeton University Press, 2004.

Campbell, Donald J., and Gregory J. Dardis, "The 'Be, Know, Do' Model of Leader Development," *Human Resource Planning* 27, 2004: 26–39.

Campbell, Karen, "Can Effective Risk Management Signal Virtue-Based Leadership?" *Journal of Business Ethics,* 2014: 1-16.

Cannella, Bert, Sydney Finkelstein, and Donald C. Hambrick, *Strategic Leadership: Theory and Research on Executives, Top Management Teams, and Boards,* Oxford University Press, 2008.

Carvallo Pardo, Javier, "El sismo y la industria aseguradora: balance final, lecciones y tareas pendientes," in *Emergencia y reconstrucción: el antes y después del terremoto y tsunami del 27F en Chile,* ed. I. Brain and P. Mora, Santiago de Chile: Pontificia Universidad Católica de Chile, 2012.

CBS News, "Chile Controls Message on Miner Rescue Timeline," September 2, 2010, www.cbsnews.com/news/chile-controls-message-on-miner-rescue-timeline.

Central Bank of Chile, "Informe de Política Monetaria, Marzo, 2010" 2010, www.bcentral.cl/publicaciones/politicas/pdf/ipm032010.pdf.

Centre for Research on the Epidemiology of Disasters, the International Disaster Database, Emergency Events Database, 2014, www.emdat.be.

Centro de Estudios Públicos, Estudio Nacional de Opinión Pública No. 68, 2012.

Centro de Investigación Periodística, "Donaciones al Fondo Nacional de Reconstrucción por el 27/F solo suman 25% del total que espera Hacienda," 2013, http://ciperchile.cl/radar/donaciones-al-fondo-nacional-de-reconstruccion-por-el-27f-suman-25-del-total-que-espera-hacienda.

Centro de Políticas Públicas, *Emergencia y reconstrucción: el antes y después del terremoto y tsunami del 27F en Chile*, ed. I. Brain and P. Mora, Santiago de Chile: Pontificia Universidad Católica de Chile, 2012.

CEPAL, *Especial terremoto Chile: banda ancha, una plataforma para la prevención y la reconstrucción*, ed. A. García, 2010a.

CEPAL, "Terremoto en Chile. Una primera mirada al 10 de marzo de 2010," 2010b, www.eclac.cl/noticias/paginas/4/35494/2010–193-Terremoto-Rev1.pdf.

Charlesworth, Mark, and Chukwumerije Okereke, "Policy Responses to Rapid Climate Change: An Epistemological Critique of Dominant Approaches," *Global Environmental Change* 20, 1, 2010: 121–29.

CIGRE, *Experencias y desafíos en el sistema eléctrico de CGE. Distribución a raíz del terremoto 27 de febrero*, 2010.

Claude, Jorge, 2010 Chile Earthquake, presentation at the High-Level Roundtable on the Financial Management of Earthquakes, OECD, Paris, June 23–24, 2011.

Cohen, Michael D., James G. March, and Johan P. Olsen, "A Garbage Can Model of Organizational Choice," *Administrative Science Quarterly* 17, 1972: 1–25.

Collins, Jim, *Good to Great: Why Some Companies Make the Leap...and Others Don't*, HarperBusiness, 2001.

Collins, Jim, and Morten T. Hansen, *Great by Choice: Uncertainty, Chaos, and Luck—Why Some Companies Thrive Despite Them All*, HarperCollins, 2011.

Comerio, Mary C. "Housing Recovery in Chile: A Qualitative Mid-program Review," Pacific Earthquake Engineering Research Center, February, 2013, http://peer.berkeley.edu/publications/peer_reports/reports_2013/web-PEER-2013-01-Comerio.pdf.

Comisión de Gobierno Interior y Regionalización, Cámara de Diputados, "Informe sobre Proyecto de Ley que Establece el Sistema Nacional de Emergencia y Protección Civil y Crea La Agencia Nacional de Protección Civil. Boletín No. 7550-06-1," 2012, http://sil.congreso.cl.

Compañía Chilena de Electricidad, Experiencia de Chilectra en la recuperación del servicio. Terremoto 27 de febrero 2010, 2010.

Consejo Nacional de Normalización de la Construcción (CNNC), "Constitución, objetivos y funciones del CNNC," 2012, www.iconstruccion.cl/files/CNNC%20Doc%20acuerdo%20final.pdf.

Cutter, Susan, "The Geography of Social Vulnerability: Race, Class, and Catastrophe," Understanding Katrina, Social Science Research Council, 2006, understandingkatrina.ssrc.org/Cutter.

Cyert, Richard M., and James G. March, *A Behavioral Theory of the Firm*, Wiley, 1992 (1963).

Dacy, Douglas, and Howard Kunreuther, *The Economics of Natural Disasters*, Free Press, 1969.

Dempsey, Martin E., Mission Command White Paper, Chairman of the Joint Chiefs of Staff, 2012.

Desafío Levantemos Chile, "What Is Your Challenge?" (¿Cuál es tu Desafío?), 2012, Desafío Levantemos Chile, www.desafiolevantemoschile.cl.

De Solminihac, Hernán, Management in Emergency Conditions: 27/F Earthquake's Lessons, Ministry of Mines, 2012a.

De Solminihac, Hernán, Chile: Many Times Hurt by Natural Disasters, Permanently Blessed by Natural Resources, Minister of Mining, Republic of Chile, 2012b.

Diacu, Florin, *Mega Disasters: The Science of Predicting the New Catastrophe*, Princeton University Press, 2010.

Diario Financiero, "Grupos económicos y grandes empresas invirtieron US$ 70 millones en reconstrucción. Edición del 27 de febrero," 2012a, www.df.cl/grupoeconomicos-y-grandes-empresas-invirtieron-us-70-millones-en-reconstruccion/prontus_df/2012-02-26/210815.html.

Diario Financiero, "Fondo Nacional de la Reconstrucción consiguió recaudar más de US$100 millones desde su instauración," 2012b, www.df.cl/fondo-nacional-de-la-reconstruccion-consiguio-recaudar-mas-de-us-100-millones-desde-su-instauracion/prontus_df/2012-02-26/210814.html.

Diermeier, Daniel, *Reputation Rules: Strategies for Building Your Company's Most Valuable Asset*, McGraw-Hill, 2011.

Division of Inter-ministerial Coordination, Ministry General Secretariat of the Presidency of Chile, "Summary of Progress: Reconstruction Following the Earthquake of February 27, 2010."

Division of Inter-ministerial Coordination, Ministry General Secretariat of the Presidency of Chile, "Progress Report on Reconstruction, February 27 to July 31, 2012," Division of Inter-ministerial Coordination, Ministry General Secretariat of the Presidency of Chile, August 28, 2012.

Economist, The, "Typhoon Haiyan: Worse Than Hell," and "Typhoon Haiyan and the Philippines: Stress Test," November 16, 2013.

Einhorn, Catrin, "A Survivor's Tale from Chile," *New York Times*, March 3, 2010, http://thelede.blogs.nytimes.com/2010/03/03/a-survivors-tale-from-chile/?_php=true&_type=blogs&_r=0.

El19, Digital.com, "Masivo Terremoto de Magnitud 8,8 Sacude Chile: 122 Muertos," 2010, www.el19digital.com/index.php?option=com_content&view=article&catid=24:internacionales&id=10559:urgente-masivo-terremoto-de-magnitud-88-sacude-chile&Itemid=15.

El Mostrador, "Tsunami en el Shoa: destituyen a su Director y se anuncia su restructuración," 2010, www.elmostrador.cl/noticias/pais/2010/03/06/tsunami-en-el-shoa-destituyen-a-su-director-y-se-anunciareestructuracion.

El Tiempo, "Empresarios colombianos no deben temerle a la competencia: Piñera," November 27, 2010.

Emol, "Aeropuerto de Santiago recibe primeros vuelos comerciales tras el terremoto," 2010, www.emol.com/noticias/nacional/2010/02/28/400904/aeropuerto-de-santiago-recibe-primeros-vuelos-comerciales-tras-el-terremoto.html.

Erikson, Kai, and Lori Peek, "Hurricane Katrina Research Bibliography," Task Force on Katrina and Rebuilding the Gulf Coast, Social Science Research Council, 2010, http://katrinaresearchhub.ssrc.org/KatrinaBibliography.pdf.

Feltovich, Nick, Atsushi Iwasaki, and Sobei H. Oda, "Payoff Levels, Loss Avoidance, and Equilibrium Selection in the Stag Hunt: An Experimental Study," Group Decision and Negotiation, Karlsruhe, Germany, June 25–28, 2006, conference proceedings, KIT Scientific Publishing, 2006.

Fiske, Susan, and Shelley E. Taylor, *Social Cognition: From Brains to Culture*, 2nd ed., Sage, 2013.

Flynn, Stephen, *The Edge of Disaster: Rebuilding a Resilient Nation*, Random House, 2007.

Franklin, Jonathan, *33 Men: Inside the Miraculous Survival and Dramatic Rescue of the Chilean Miners*, Putnam, 2011.

G20 and OECD, "Disaster Risk Assessment and Risk Financing," 2012, www.oecd.org/gov/risk/G20disasterriskmanagement.pdf.

Gad-el-Hak, Mohamed, ed., *Large-Scale Disasters: Prediction, Control, and Mitigation*, Cambridge University Press, 2008.

Gawande, Atul, *The Checklist Manifesto: How to Get Things Right*, Holt, 2009.

Global Adaptation Institute, GAIN Vulnerability Index 2011, 2012, http://index.gain.org/ranking/vulnerability.

Global Adaptation Institute, GAIN Readiness Index 2011, 2012, http://index.gain.org/ranking/readiness.

Goldin, Ian, and Mike Mariathasan, *The Butterfly Defect: How Globalization Creates Systemic Risks, and What to Do About It*, Princeton University Press, 2014.

Government of Chile, Ministerio de Planificación, "Programa de las Naciones Unidas para el Desarrollo," 2010, www.pnud.cl/prensa/noticias-2011/Encuesta%20Post%20Terremoto_Minuta.pdf.

Government of Chile, Plan de Reconstrucción. "Terremoto y Maremoto del 27 de Febrero de 2010," 2010, www.ministeriodesarrollosocial.gob.cl/pdf/e60b893eb66a10139bfe68d2c6005636.pdf.

Government of Chile, Subsecretaría del Interior de Chile, "Informe final de fallecidos y desaparecidos por comuna," January 31, 2011.

Government of Chile, 2010, www.gobiernodechile.cl/cronologia-los-hitos-del-rescate-de-los-33-mineros.

Government of Chile, October 12, 2010, www.gobiernodechile.cl/cronologia-los-hitos-del-rescate-de-los-33-mineros.

Government of Chile, *Reporte de Cumplimiento de la Reconstrucción del Terremoto del 27 de Febrero de 2010* ("Reconstruction Progress Report Following the Earthquake of February 27, 2010"), February 2013.

Government of People's Republic of China, China's 12th Five-Year Plan (2011–15), March 2011.

Guzman, Juan Andres, "Chile Earthquake: A Survivor's Tale," *Miami Herald*, March 2, 2010, www.mcclatchydc.com/2010/03/02/89648/chile-earthquake-a-survivors-tale.html.

Hall, Edward T., and Mildred Reed Hall, *Understanding Cultural Differences*, Nicholas Brealey Publishing, 1960.

Hammond, Kenneth R., *Judgment under Stress*, Oxford University Press, 2000.

Hannah, Sean T., and Paul B. Lester, "A Multilevel Approach to Building and Leading Learning Organizations," *Leadership Quarterly* 20, 2009: 34–48.

Heath, Chip, and Dan Heath, *Made to Stick: Why Some Ideas Survive and Others Die*, Random House, 2007.

Heidegger, Martin, "Being and Time," trans. John Macquarrie and Edward Robinson, Harper & Row, 1962.

Henshaw, Todd, "After Action Reviews," Nano Tools for Leaders, Wharton Leadership Program, University of Pennsylvania, March–April 2012, http://

wlp.wharton.upenn.edu/LeadershipDigest/nano-tool-after-action-reviews.cfm.

House, Robert J., Paul J. Hanges, Mansour Javidan, Peter W. Dorfman, and Vipin Gupta, *Culture, Leadership, and Organizations*, Sage Publications, 2004.

Iacobeli, Andrés, Plan de Reconstrucción y Nueva Política Habitacional, 2010.

Inter-American Development Bank, "Governance Indicators Database," 2013, www.iadb.org/datagob.

International Monetary Fund, *Chile, 2011 Article IV Consultation*. International Monetary Fund, 2011.

International Monetary Fund, *Chile: Financial System Stability Assessment*, International Monetary Fund, 2011.

International Monetary Fund, *Chile, Selected Issues*, International Monetary Fund, 2012.

International Monetary Fund, *IMF Country Report, Chile, 2010*, 2010.

International Monetary Fund, *World Economic Outlook, October, 2012, Coping with High Debt and Sluggish Growth*, International Monetary Fund, 2012.

International Monetary Fund, *World Economic Outlook, October, 2013, Transitions and Tensions*, International Monetary Fund, 2013.

International Monetary Fund, *Chile, 2013 Article IV Consultation*, International Monetary Fund, 2013.

Isaacson, Walter, *Steve Jobs*, Simon and Schuster, 2011.

Isaacson, Walter, "The Real Leadership Lessons of Steve Jobs," *Harvard Business Review*, April 2012.

Jacobs, Andrew, "Philippines' President Faces Growing Anger," *New York Times*, November 13, 2013.

James, Erika Hayes, *Leading under Pressure: From Surviving to Thriving before, during, and after a Crisis*, Routledge, 2010.

James, William, "Remarks on Spencer's Definition of Mind as Correspondence," *Journal of Speculative Philosophy* 12, 1878, 1–18.

Javidan, Mansour, Peter W. Dorfman, Mary Sully du Luque, and Robert J. House, "In the Eye of the Beholder: Cross Cultural Lessons in Leadership from Project GLOBE," *Academy of Management Perspectives* 20, 2006, 67–90.

Jiji Press, "42% Didn't Immediately Flee Tsunami," *Japan Times*, August 18, 2011.

Jordán, Rodrigo, *Real Leadership: From Theory to Practice*, Pearson Education, 2009.

Kahneman, Daniel, "A Psychological Perspective on Economics," *American Economic Review* 93, 2003: 162–68.

Kahneman, Daniel, *Thinking, Fast and Slow*, Farrar, Straus and Giroux, 2011.

Kirsch, Thomas D., Judith Mitrani-Reiser, Reuben Bissell, L. M. Sauer, Michael Mahoney, Willian T. Holmes, Nicolás Santa Cruz, and Francisco de la Maza, "Impact on Hospital Functions following the 2010 Chilean Earthquake," *Journal of Disaster Medicine and Public Health Preparedness* 4, 2010: 122–28.

Klein, Gary, *Intuition at Work: Why Developing Your Gut Instincts Will Make You Better at What You Do,* Currency Doubleday, 2003.

Klein, Katherine, Jonathan C. Ziegert, Andrew P. Knight, and Yan Xiao, "Dynamic Delegation: Hierarchical, Shared, and Deindividualized Leadership in Extreme Action Teams," *Administrative Science Quarterly* 51, 2006: 590–621.

Kluger, Jeffrey, and James Lovell, *Lost Moon: The Perilous Voyage of Apollo 13*, Houghton Mifflin, 1994.

Kolditz, Thomas A., *In Extremis Leadership: Leading as if Your Life Depended on It*, Jossey-Bass/Wiley, 2007.

Kovacs, Paul, "Reducing the risk of earthquake damage in Canada: Lessons from Haiti and Chile," Institute for Catastrophic Loss Reduction, Canada, 2010.

Krantz, David, and Howard Kunreuther, "Goals and Plans in Protective Decision Making," *Judgment and Decision Making* 2, 3, 2007: 137–68.

Kranz, Eugene, *Failure Is Not an Option: Mission Control from Mercury to Apollo 13 and Beyond*, Simon and Schuster, 2009.

Kunreuther, Howard, "The Weakest Link: Managing Risk through Interdependent Strategies," in *Network Challenge: Strategy, Profit and Risk in an Interlinked World,* ed. Paul R. Kleindorfer and Yoram Wind, Wharton School Publishing, 2009.

Kunreuther, Howard, and Geoffrey Heal, "Interdependent Security," *Journal of Risk and Uncertainty* 26, 2003: 231–49.

Kunreuther, Howard, Geoffrey Heal, Myles Allen, Ottmar Edenhofer, Chris B. Field, and Gary Yohe, "Risk Management and Climate Change," *Nature Climate Change* 3, 2013: 447–50.

Kunreuther, Howard, Robert J. Meyer, and Erwann Michel-Kerjan, "Overcoming Decision Biases to Reduce Losses from Natural Catastrophes," in *Behavioral Foundations of Policy*, ed. E. Shafir, Princeton University Press, 2012.

Kunreuther, Howard, and Erwann Michel-Kerjan, *At War with the Weather*, MIT Press, 2011.

Kunreuther, Howard C., Mark V. Pauly, and Stacey McMorrow, *Insurance and Behavioral Economics: Improving Decisions in the Most Misunderstood Industry,* Cambridge University Press, 2013.

Kunreuther, Howard, and Michael Useem, eds., *Learning from Catastrophes: Strategies for Reaction and Response,* prepared in collaboration with the World Economic Forum's Global Agenda Council on the Mitigation of Natural Disasters. Pearson, 2010.

Kunreuther, Howard, and Elke U. Weber, "Aiding Decision Making to Reduce the Impacts of Climate Change," *Journal of Consumer Policy,* 37, 2014: 397–411.

Küpers, Wendelin, and Jürgen Weibler, "Inter-leadership: Why and How Should We Think of Leadership and Followership Integrally?" *Leadership* 4, 2008: 443–75.

Lagadec, Patrick, *Preventing Chaos in a Crisis—Strategies for Prevention, Control and Damage Limitation,* McGraw Hill, 1993.

Lagadec, Patrick, *Unconventional Crises, Unconventional Responses: Reforming Leadership in the Age of Catastrophic Crises and Hypercomplexity,* Center for Transatlantic Relations, School of Advanced International Studies, Johns Hopkins University, 2008.

Larraín, Felipe B., *Desafíos del Terremoto: reconstrucción y su Financiamiento.* Ministerio de Hacienda, Gobierno de Chile, 2011.

Lieberson, Stanley and James F. O'Connor, "Leadership and Organizational Performance: A Study of Large Corporations," *American Sociological Review* 37, 1972: 117-130.

Loayza, Norman, and Inci Otker-Robe, "World Development Report 2014, Risk and Opportunity—Managing Risk for Development," World Bank, 2014, http://documents.worldbank.org/curated/en/2013/10/18376450/world-development-report-2014-risk-opportunity-managing-risk-development-overview.

Mapfre Global Risks, "8.8, the Maule Earthquake, Chile, 27F 2010," www.mapfre.com/portal/global-risks/docs/documento_terremoto_chile_en.pdf.

Maps of the World, "Chile Political Map," 2013, www.mapsofworld.com.

March, James G., and Herbert Alexander Simon, *Organizations,* Wiley, 1958.

Margolis, Marc, "Chilean President Grabs Limelight in Miners' Rescue," *Newsweek,* October 13, 2010, www.newsweek.com/chilean-president-grabs-limelight-miners-rescue-74163.

Marquis, Christopher, and Matthew Lee, "Who Is Governing Whom? Executives, Governance and the Structure of Generosity in Large US Firms." *Strategic Management Journal* 34, 2013: 483–97.

Marshall, Monty G., and Benjamin R. Cole, *Global Report 2011: Conflict, Governance, and State Fragility*, Center for Systemic Peace, 2011.

Martinez, José Luis, Carlos Simón, and Ana Agüero, *Caso Un Techo para Chile*, Capitulo 3, La acción Social de la Empresa, Pearson, 2003.

McCauley, Cynthia D., Scott DeRue, Paul Yost, and Sylvester Taylor, *Experience-driven Leader Development: Models, Tools, Best Practices, and Advice for On-the-Job Development*, Jossey-Bass/Wiley, 2013.

McMahon, Paul, Thomas Nyheim, and Adam Schwarz, "After the Tsunami: Lessons from Reconstruction," *McKinsey Quarterly*, 2006: 94–105.

Medina, María Belén, "El manejo de la Presidenta Bachelet: las diferencias entre el 27/F y el terremoto y tsunami del norte," *La Tercera*, April 2, 2014, www.latercera.com/noticia/politica/2014/04/674-572266-9-el-manejo-de-la-presidenta-bachelet-las-diferencias-entre-el-27f-y-el-terremoto.shtml.

Mella Polanco, M., "Efectos sociales del terremoto en Chile y gestión política de la reconstrucción durante el gobierno de Sebastián Piñera," *Revista Enfoques* 2012, 19–46.

Michel-Kerjan, Erwann, "How Resilient Is Your Country?" *Nature* 491, 2012: 497.

Michel-Kerjan, Erwann, and Howard Kunreuther, "Paying for Future Catastrophes," *New York Times* (Sunday Review), November 24, 2012.

Michel-Kerjan, Erwann, and Paul Slovic, "The Collapse of Compassion," *Huffington Post*, October 7, 2010.

Michel-Kerjan, Erwann, and Paul Slovic, eds., *The Irrational Economist: Making Decisions in a Dangerous World*, PublicAffairs, 2011.

Michel-Kerjan, Erwann, Ivan Zelenko, Victor Cardenas, and Daniel Turgel, "Catastrophe Financing for Governments: Learning from the 2009–2012 MultiCat Program in Mexico," OECD Working Papers on Finance, Insurance and Private Pensions, no. 9, OECD Publishing, 2011.

Michel-Kerjan, Erwann, Charles Scawthorn, Axel E. N. Baeumler, Aditi Banerjee, Pierre Rondot, Mohamed Medouar, Olivier Mahul, Laura Boudreau, Antonia Davila-Bonazzi, and Julie Dana. 2014. *Building Morocco's resilience: inputs for an integrated risk management strategy*. Washington DC : World Bank Group. http://documents.worldbank.org/curated/en/2014/01/19226575/building-moroccos-resilience-inputs-integrated-risk-management-strategy.

Mideplan, "Encuesta Post-terremoto: principales resultados, efectos en la calidad de vida de la población afectada por el tsunami y el terremoto," 2011.

Ministry of Economy, Development and Tourism, Turismo: Informe Anual, 2011.

Ministry of Finance, Plan de Financiamiento para la Reconstrucción, 2010.

Ministry of Finance, Fondo Nacional de Reconstrucción, 2013a, http://donaciones.hacienda.cl.

Ministry of Finance, Ministro Felipe Larraín: "Logramos reconstruir el país creciendo, creando empleos y sin dejar de lado nuestro programa de Gobierno," 2013b, www.hacienda.cl/sala-de-prensa/noticias/historico/ministro-felipe-Larraín-logramos.html.

Ministry of Housing and Urbanization, "Plan de Reconstrucción," 2010a, www.minvu.cl/opensite_20111122105648.aspx.

Ministry of Housing and Urbanization, "Plan de Reconstrucción, Programa de Gobierno y Financiamiento 2010–13," 2010b.

Ministry of Housing and Urbanization, "Reconstruction Plan: Chile United for Better Reconstruction, October 2010," 2010c."

Ministry of Housing and Urbanization, "Plan de Reconstrucción: Chile Unido reconstruye Mejor, Vivienda, Barrio y Ciudad," 2011a.

Ministry of Housing and Urbanization, "Informe: Avance en la entregade soluciones habitacionales, Programa de Reconstrucción en Vivienda," 2011b.

Ministry of Housing and Urbanization, "Informe de Avance Programa de Reconstrucción," 2012.

Ministry of Housing and Urbanization, "Informe de Avance Programa de Reconstrucción," 2013.

Ministry of the Interior, "Gobierno firmó acuerdo con cuerpo militar del trabajo para agilizar tareas de reconstrucción en las zonas afectadas por el terremoto," 2010, www.interior.gob.cl/n5400_12-04-2010.html.

Ministry of the Interior, General Secretariat of the Presidency, "Balance de Reconstrucción: un año del 27-F," 2011, www.minsegpres.gob.cl/wp-content/uploads/files/informeReconstruccion.pdf.

Ministry of Planning, "Encuesta Post Terremoto: principales resultados efectos en la calidad de vida de la población afectada por el terremoto/tsunami," 2010, www.ministeriodesarrollosocial.gob.cl/encuesta-post-terremoto/documentos/informe-encuesta-post-terremoto.pdf.

Mitrani-Reiser, Judith, Michael Mahoney, William T. Holmes, Juan Carlos de la Llera, Rick Bissell, and Thomas Kirsch, "A Functional Loss Assessment of a Hospital System in the Biobío Province," *Earthquake Spectra* 28, 2012, S473–S502.

Mitroff, Ian, *Crisis Leadership: Planning for the Unthinkable*, Wiley, 2003.

Moehle, Jack P., and J. David Frost, "Preface" to special issue of *Earthquake Spectra*, 28, 2012: vii–viii.

Moffett, Matt, "Chile's Inauguration Jolted by Aftershock," *Wall Street Journal*, March 12, 2010.

Monti, Alberto, Policy Framework for the Improvement of Financial Management Strategies to Cope with Large-scale catastrophes in Chile, OECD, 2011.

Moody's, "Moody's Upgrades Chile to Aa3 from A1," Moody's Investors Service, June 16, 2010.

Morris, Michael W., and Paul C. Moore, "The Lessons We (Don't) Learn: Counterfactual Thinking and Organizational Accountability after a Close Call," *Administrative Science Quarterly* 45, 2000: 737–65.

Muir-Wood, Robert, "Designing Optimal Risk Mitigation and Risk Transfer Mechanisms to Improve the Management of Earthquake Risk in Chile," OECD Working Papers on Finance, Insurance and Private Pensions, October 2011.

Muller, Alan, and Gail Whiteman, "Exploring the Geography of Corporate Philanthropic Disaster Response: A Study of Fortune Global 500 Firms," *Journal of Business Ethics* 84, 2009: 589–603.

Munich Re, "Natural Catastrophes 2010," Munich Re, 2011.

Munich Re, "Natural Catastrophes 2012," Munich Re, 2013.

National Academies, *Disaster Resilience: A National Imperative*, National Academies Press, 2012.

National Aeronautics and Space Administration, "Chilean Quake May Have Shortened Earth Days," 2010, www.nasa.gov/topics/earth/features/earth-20100301.html.

National Commission on the BP Deepwater Horizon Oil Spill and Offshore Drilling, "Report to the President," 2001, www.oilspillcommission.gov/sites/default/files/documents/DEEPWATER_ReporttothePresident_FINAL.pdf.

National Diet of Japan, "The Fukushima Nuclear Accident Independent Investigation Commission," 2012, http://warp.da.ndl.go.jp/info:ndljp/pid/3856371/naiic.go.jp/wp-content/uploads/2012/09/NAIIC_report_lo_res10.pdf.

National Oceanic and Atmospheric Administration, Center for Tsunami Research, 2010, http://nctr.pmel.noaa.gov.

NBC News, Chile Earthquake, February 27, 2010, www.nbcnews.com/id/35616563/ns/world_news-chile_earthquake/#.U2Ox_k1OU-U.

NBC Universal Archives, "Telephone Interview with 'Time' Magazine's Eben Harrell," February 27, 2010, www.nbcuniversalarchives.com/nbcuni/clip/51112251528_s14.do.

Neff, Thomas J., and James M. Citrin, *You're in Charge: Now What?* Crown Business, 2007.

New York City Fire Department Incident Management Team, "Sandy Support Executive Summary, November 24, 2012—December 29, 2012," 2013. A report prepared by the New York City Department Incident Management Team.

New York City Fire Department Incident Management Team, "Executive Summary: Hurricane Sandy, October 28, 2012—November 10, 2012," 2013.

Nietzsche, Friedrich, *The Birth of Tragedy* (1872), Oxford University Press, 2008.

Norma de Carácter General, "Imparte Normas Sobre Activos Representativos . . . ," 2002, www.svs.cl/institucional/mercados/ver_archivo.php?archivo=/web/compendio/ncg/ncg_152_2002.pdf.

OECD Observer, "Interview Chile's Economy," Organisation for Economic Co-operation and Development, May, 2010, www.oecdobserver.org/news/fullstory.php/aid/3246/ Interview_Chile_92s_economy.html.

Ohio State University, "Researchers Show How Far South American Cities Moved in Quake," Research Communications, March 8, 2010, http://researchnews.osu.edu/archive/chilemoves.htm.

ONEMI, Decreto Supremo No 38/2011 del Ministerio del Interior, Comité Nacional de Operaciones de Emergencia, 2013.

Opazo Santis, Hector, "Terremoto de abril de 2014 en Chile," Disaster Recovery Institute, 2014.

O'Reilly, Charles "Corporations, Culture, and Commitment: Motivation and Social Control in Organizations," *California Management Review* 1989: 9–25.

Organisation for Economic Co-operation and Development, *High-Level Roundtable on the Financial Management of Earthquakes*, 2011, www.oecd.org/pensions/insurance/high-levelroundtableonthefinancialmanagementofearthquakes.htm.

Pan American Health Organization, "El terremoto y tsunami del 27 de febrero en Chile: crónica y lecciones aprendidas en el sector salud," 2010, http://reliefweb.int/report/chile/el-terremoto-y-tsunami-del-27-de-febrero-en-chile-cr%C3%B3nica-y-lecciones-aprendidas-en-el.

People's Daily, "Collapse of Alto Río, Chile's Painful Lesson from Megaquake," February 23, 2011.

Perrow, Charles, Normal Accidents: Living with High-Risk Technologies, Princeton University Press, 1999.

Perrow, Charles, The Next Catastrophe: Reducing Our Vulnerabilities to Natural, Industrial, and Terrorist Disasters, Princeton University Press, 2011.

Peters, Thomas J., and Robert H. Waterman, In Search of Excellence: Lessons from America's Best-Run Companies, HarperCollins, 1982.

Pica, Carolina, "Chile's Piñera Plans Bond Issue for Quaker Costs," Wall Street Journal, April 9, 2010.

Pino Toro, Manuel, Buried Alive: The True Story of the Chilean Mining Disaster and the Extraordinary Rescue at Camp Hope, Palgrave, 2011.

Posner, Richard A., Catastrophe: Risk and Response, Oxford University Press, 2004.

Povoledo, Elisabetta, and Henry Fountain, "Italy Orders Jail Terms for 7 Who Didn't Warn of Deadly Earthquake," New York Times, October 22, 2012.

Prada, Paulo, "Quake Jolts Chile's President-elect from His Agenda," Wall Street Journal, March 4, 2010.

Pujol, Francesc, "Los beneficios del rescate de los 33 mineros irán a la marca Chile," 2010, www.emol.com.

Rabobank, "Chilean Wine Industry after the Earthquake: Shaken up but Still in the Race," 2010, unpublished.

Ramírez, N., "Los buses-escuela y otros curiosos recintos para volver a clases tras el terremoto," 2010, www.emol.com/noticias/nacional/2010/04/15/408331/los-buses-escuela-y-otros-curiosos-recintos-para-volver-a-clases-tras-el-terremoto.html.

Ramirez, Pedro, and Jorge Sandoval, "Tsunami paso a paso: los escandalosos errorores y omisiones del SHOA y la ONEMI," 2012, http://ciperchile.cl/2012/01/18/tsunami-paso-a-paso-los-escandalosos-errores-y-omisiones-del-shoa-y-la-onemi.

Redlener, Irwin, Americans at Risk: Why We Are Not Prepared for Megadisasters and What We Can Do About It, Knopf, 2006.

Renois, Clarens, "Haitians Angry over Slow Aid," *The Age* (Melbourne), February 5, 2010.

Risk Management Solutions, *The 2010 Maule, Chile Earthquake: Lessons and Future Challenges*, 2011, http://static.rms.com/email/documents/liferisks/reports/2010-chile-earthquake-lessons-and-future-challenges.pdf.

Rojas, Rocío Montes, "Chile—rescate de mineros: entrevista a André Sougarret—rescate de mineros," *El Mercurio*, October 17, 2010.

Rosenzweig, Phil, *Left Brain, Right Stuff: How Leaders Make Winning Decisions*, Public Affairs, 2014.

Samuelson, William, and Richard Zeckhauser, "Status Quo Bias in Decision Making," *Journal of Risk and Uncertainty* 1, 1988: 7–59.

Sanchez, Ray, "Strict Building Codes Saved Lives in Powerful Chile Earthquake, CNN, April 3, 2014, www.cnn.com/2014/04/02/world/americas/chile-earthquake.

Santa María, Hernán, Pablo Allard, Carl Lüders, and Martín Santa María, "Plan de protección civil: sistema de evaluación estructural rápida post-sismo de edificios e infraestructura," in *Camino al Bicentenario: propuestas para Chile 2010*, ed. I. Irarrázaval and E. Puga, Pontificia Universidad Católica de Chile, Santiago, 2010.

Schein, Edgar, *Organizational Culture and Leadership*, Jossey-Bass, 2010.

Schmidt, Alfredo, "Chile Earthquake 3 Years On: The Dust Has Finally Settled," Willis Wire, April 2, 2013, http://blog.willis.com/2013/04/chile-earthquake-3-years-on-the-dust-has-finally-settled/#sthash.rPUKvcTl.dpuf.

Servicio Sismológico de Chile, Universidad de Chile, Informe técnico, terremoto Cauquenes, febrero 27, 2010, www.sismologia.cl/informes/informe_technico.pdf.

Shear, Michael D., "Health Law Rollout's Stumbles Draw Parallels to Bush's Hurricane Response," *New York Times*, November 14, 2013.

Siembieda, William, "Multi Location Disaster in Three Countries: Comparing the Recovery Process in Japan, Chile and New Zealand," *Focus: Journal of the City and Regional Planning Department* 9, 1, 2012.

Siembieda, William, Laurie Johnson, and Guillermo Franco, "Rebuild Fast but Rebuild Better: Chile's Initial Recovery following the 27 February 2010 Earthquake and Tsunami," *Earthquake Spectra* 28, 2012: S621–41.

Simon, Herbert, "A Behavioral Model of Rational Choice," in *Models of Man, Social and Rational: Mathematical Essays on Rational Human Behavior in a Social Setting*, Wiley, 1957.

Skidmore, Thomas, Peter Smith, and James Green, *Modern Latin America*, Oxford University Press, 2009.

Song, Cheng, Santiago Pujol, and Andrés Lepage, "The Collapse of the Alto Río Building during the 27 February 2010 Maule, Chile, Earthquake," *Earthquake Spectra* 28, 2012, S301–34.

Subsecretaría de Desarrollo Regional y Administrativo, "Documentos de la reconstrucción," 2011, http://ciperchile.cl/2011/05/12/subsecretaria-de-desarrollo-regional-y-administrativo.

Superintendency of Securities and Insurance, "Preguntas Frecuentes Terremoto," 2010, www.svs.cl/sitio/faq/preguntas_frecuentes_terremoto.php.

Superintendency of Securities and Insurance, "President Piñera firma proyectos que impulsan la decentralización del país," 2011, www.subdere.gov.cl/sala-de-prensa/presidente-pi%C3%B1era-firma-proyectos-que-impulsan-la-descentralizaci%C3%B3n-del-pa%C3%ADs-1.

Superintendency of Securities and Insurance, "Terremoto 2010: análisis en Impacto del 27-F en el Mercado Asegurado," 2012.

Sweeney, Patrick J., Michael D. Matthews, and Paul B. Lester, eds., *Leadership in Dangerous Situations*, Naval Institute Press, 2011.

Swiss Reinsurance Company, Ltd., "Sigma N3/2013, World Insurance in 2012," Swiss Re, 2013, www.swissre.com/clients/Sigma_3_2013_World_insurance_in_2012.html.

Swiss Reinsurance Company, Ltd., "Sigma: Natural Catastrophes and Man-Made Disasters in 2012," Swiss Re, 2013, http://www.biztositasiszemle.hu/files/201303/sigma2_2013_en.pdf.

Swiss Re Foundation, "Swiss Re Foundation Partners with the Global Earthquake Model Foundation to Mitigate Earthquake Risk in Latin America," 2013.

Tabuchi, Hiroko, "Inquiry Declares Fukushima Crisis a Man-Made Disaster," *New York Times*, July 5, 2012.

Taleb, Nassim Nicholas, *The Black Swan: The Impact of the Highly Improbable*, Random House, 2010.

Thomas, Alan Berkeley, "Does Leadership Make a Difference to Organizational Performance?" *Administrative Science Quarterly* 33, 1988: 388–400.

Thompson, James D., *Organizations in Action, Social Science Bases of Administrative Theory*, McGraw-Hill, 1967.

Tilcsik, András, and Christopher Marquis, "Punctuated Generosity: How

Mega-events and Natural Disasters Affect Corporate Philanthropy in U.S. Communities," *Administrative Science Quarterly* 58, 2013: 111–48.

Trading Economics, "Monthly Value of Chilean Exports, December, 2009 to January, 2011," 2013a, www.tradingeconomics.com.

Trading Economics, "IGPA Stock Market Index in Chile, 2009–2011," 2013b, www.tradingeconomics.com.

Tversky, Amos, and Daniel Kahneman, "Availability: A Heuristic for Judging Frequency and Probability," *Cognitive Psychology* 5, 1973: 207–32.

Undersecretary for Regional and Administrative Development, "President Piñera firma proyectos que impulsan la decentralización del país," 2011, www. subdere.gov.cl/sala-de-prensa/presidente-pi%C3%B1era-firma-proyec-tos-que-impulsan-la-descentralizaci%C3%B3n-del-pa%C3%ADs-1.

Undersecretary of the Interior, "Informe final de falleciods y desaparecidos por comuna," January 31, 2011.

Unidad Presidencial de Gestión del Cumplimiento, "Rindiendo Cuenta: balance de Tres Años de Gobierno del President Sebastián Piñera." Ministerio Secretaría General de la Presidencia, División de Coordinación Interministerial, 2013.

United Nations Office for Coordination of Humanitarian Affairs, Financial Tracking Service. "Tracking Global Humanitarian Aid Flows, 2013," http:// fts.unocha.org.

United Nations University Institute for Environment and Human Security and The Nature Conservancy, with Alliance Development Works, "World Risk Report," 2012, 16.

Urbana E&D, "Plan de Reconstrucción Sustentable de Curicó, Informe Final," 2011, http://prescurico.cl/sites/default/files/presCURIC%C3%93_In-forme%203_Plan%20de%20Implementaci%C3%B3n_3.pdf.

U.S. Army, Mission Command, Army Doctrine Publication no. 6-0, 2012, https://armypubs.us.army.mil/doctrine/index.html.

U.S. Geological Survey, "Earthquake Hazards Program: Magnitude 8.8—Offshore Biobío, Chile," 2010, http://earthquake.usgs.gov/earthquakes/eqinthe-news/2010/us2010tfan.

U.S. Geological Survey, "Earthquake Hazards Program: Largest Earthquakes in the World since 1900," 2013, http://earthquake.usgs.gov/earthquakes/ world/10_largest_world.php.

U.S. Geological Survey, "Earthquake Hazards Program, Measuring the Size of an Earthquake," 2014, http://earthquake.usgs.gov/learn/topics/measure.php.

U.S. Global Change Research Program, "National Climate Assessment," 2014, http://nca2014.globalchange.gov.

Useem, Michael, *The Leadership Moment*, Random House, 1998.

Useem, Michael, *The Go Point: When It's Time to Decide*, Random House, 2006.

Useem, Michael, *The Leader's Checklist: Fifteen Mission-critical Principles*, Wharton Digital Press, 2011.

Useem, Michael, James Cook, and Larry Sutton, "Developing Leaders for Decision Making under Duress: Wildland Firefighters in the South Canyon Fire and Its Aftermath," *Academy of Management Learning and Education* 4, 2005: 461–85.

Useem, Michael, Rodrigo Jordán, and Matko Koljatic, "How to Lead during a Crisis: Lessons from the Rescue of the Chilean Miners," *MIT Sloan Management Review* 53, Fall 2011: 1–7.

Useem, Michael, Rodrigo Jordán, and Matko Koljatic, "Leading the Rescue of the Miners in Chile," Case, Wharton School, University of Pennsylvania, and School of Business Administration, Pontifical Catholic University of Chile, 2011, http://kw.wharton.upenn.edu/wdp/files/2011/07/Leading-the-Miners-Rescue.pdf.

Useem, Michael, Rodrigo Jordán and Matko Koljatic, "Bringing back the Thirty-Three: Emergent Principles in Multi-Tiered Leadership," in *Extreme Leadership: Leaders, Teams and Situations outside the Norm*, ed. Cristina M. Giannantonio and Amy E. Hurley-Hanson, Edward Elgar Publishing, 2014.

Waldman, D. A., G. G. Ramirez, R. J. House, and P. Puranan, "Does Leadership Matter: CEO Leadership Attributes and Profitability under Conditions of Perceived Environmental Uncertainty," *Academy of Management Journal* 44, 2001: 134–43.

Warren, Michael, "Chile Earthquake March 11: 7.2-Magnitude Quake Hits Chile during Inauguration," *World Post*, March 11, 2010, www.huffingtonpost.com/2010/03/11/72-magnitude-quake-hits-c_n_494779.html.

Weber, Elke U., "Climate Change Hits Home," *Nature Climate Change* 1, 2011: 25–26.

Weber, Elke U., and Eric J. Johnson, "Decisions under Uncertainty: Psychological, Economic, and Neuroeconomic Explanations of Risk Preference," in *Neuroeconomics: Decision Making and the Brain*, ed. P. Glimcher, C. F. Camerer, E. Fehr, and R. Poldrack, Elsevier, 2009: 127–44.

Webber, Jude, "Economic Tremors Unlikely to be Felt in the Long Term," *Financial Times*, March 1, 2010.

Webber, Jude, "Piñera's Term Given Urgency by Chile Quake," *Financial Times*, March 12, 2012.

Weick, Karl E., and Kathleen E. Sutcliffe, *Managing the Unexpected: Assuring High Performance in an Age of Complexity*, Jossey-Bass/Wiley, 2001.

Wharton School Risk Management and Decision Processes Center, Project on Effective Leadership Practices in Catastrophic Risk Management, 2014, www.wharton.upenn.edu/riskcenter/effectiveriskmgmt.cfm.

White House, "Economic Report of the President," 2007, http://www.gpo.gov/fdsys/pkg/ERP-2007/pdf/ERP-2007.pdf.

Witze, Alexandra, "Chile Quake Defies Expectations," *Nature* 508, 2014: 440–41.

Wood, Sharon L., James K. Wight, and Jack P. Moehle. "The 1985 Chile Earthquake: Observations on Earthquake-resistant Construction in Viña del Mar," Department of Civil Engineering, University of Illinois at Urbana-Champaign, 1987.

World Bank, "Natural Hazards, UnNatural Disasters," 2011, https://openknowledge.worldbank.org/handle/10986/2512.

World Bank, "Building Resilience: Integrating Climate and Disaster Risk into Development," 2013a, www.worldbank.org/content/dam/Worldbank/document/SDN/Full_Report_Building_Resilience_Integrating_Climate_Disaster_Risk_Development.pdf

World Bank, "Global Facility for Disaster Reduction and Recovery, Annual Report 2012," 2013b, http://reliefweb.int/report/world/global-facility-disaster-reduction-and-recovery-annual-report-2012.

World Bank, "Worldwide Governance Indicators 2010," 2013c, http://info.worldbank.org/governance/wgi/index.asp.

World Bank, GDP Data by Country, 2014, http://data.worldbank.org/indicator/NY.GDP.MKTP.KD.ZG/countries.

World Economic Forum, "Engineering & Construction Disaster Resource Partnership: A New Private-Public Partnership Model for Disaster Response," November, 2010, http://www3.weforum.org/docs/WEF_EN_DisasterResourcePartnership_Report_2010.pdf.

World Economic Forum, "Global Competitiveness Report, 2012–2013," 2012, http://www3.weforum.org/docs/WEF_GlobalCompetitivenessReport_2012-13.pdf.

World Economic Forum, "Global Risks Report," 2006–2013, www.weforum.org/issues/global-risks.

World Economic Forum, "Global Risks Report," 2014a, www.weforum.org/issues/global-risks.

World Economic Forum, "Global Agenda Council on Catastrophic Risks," 2014b, www.weforum.org/content/global-agenda-council-catastrophic-risks-2012–2014.

Yahoo Finance, "Major Stock Market Index for Chile, Japan, and the U.S., mid-2008 to mid-2012," 2013, http://finance.yahoo.com.

Yahoo Finance, "Nikkei 225 Stock Market Index in Japan, 2010–2011," 2013, http://finance.yahoo.com.

Yammarino, Francis J., Shelley D. Dionne, Jae Uk Chun, and Fred Dansereau, "Leadership and Levels of Analysis: A State-of-the-Science Review," *Leadership Quarterly* 16, 2005: 879–919.

Yukl, Gary, "Managerial Leadership: A Review of Theory and Research," *Journal of Management Development* 15, 1989: 251–89.

Yukl, Gary, "Effective Leadership Behavior: What We Know and What Questions Need More Attention," *Academy of Management Perspectives* 26, 2012: 66–85.

INDIVIDUALS INTERVIEWED

Individual	Position	Date
René Aguilar	Head of Safety, El Teniente mine, Codelco; Deputy Chief of Rescue	Dec. 22, 2010; Mar. 14, 2012
María Ignacia Arrasate	Reconstruction Research Team, Ministry of Housing	Oct. 17, 2012
Ernesto Ayala	Content Advisor, Presidency	July 19, 2013
Penny Bamber	International Relations, Vertical S.A.	Dec. 15, 2010
Nicolás Bar	Cultural Attaché, Embassy of Chile, Washington, DC	Various dates, 2012–2014
Benito Baranda	Director América Solidaria.	Oct. 18, 2012
Cristián Barra	Cabinet Chief, Ministry of the Interior	Jan. 5, 2011
Javiera Blanco	Peace Citizen Minister under President Bachelet	Oct. 18, 2012
Ignacio Briones	International Finance Coordinator, Ministry of Finance	Oct. 19, 2012
Cristián del Campo	Board Chair, Techo para Chile	Oct. 18, 2012
Benjamín Chacana	Director, ONEMI (Civil Protection Agency)	Oct. 17, 2012
Mary Comerio	ICARE Forum: Catastrophic Risk Management	Oct. 18, 2012
José Ignacio Concha	Lift Chile Challenge	Oct. 18, 2012

Individual	Position	Date
Patricio Contreras Uribe	Regional Director Maule, Foundation for Overcoming Poverty	June 26, 2013
Marcelo Cruz	Project Coordinator, Vertical Instituto	July 3, 2013
Hernán de Solminihac	Minister of Mining; former Minister of Public Works	Oct. 17, 2012; Dec. 12, 2012
Pedro Egaña	Undersecretary of Education, Ministry of Education	Mar. 10, 2013
Laurence Golborne	Minister of Mines; Chief of Rescue	Nov. 1, 2010; June 22, 2011, and June 2013
Cristián Goldberg	Director, Tecno Fast Atco; President, Lift Chile Challenge	June 23, 2013
Luz Granier	Chief of Staff, Minister of Mines	Nov. 1, 2010
Rodrigo Hinzpeter	Former Minister of Interior; Minister of Defense	July 19, 2013
Rodrigo Jordán	Founder and Chair of Vertical Instituto, Adjunct Professor of Leadership and Innovation, School of Business Administration, Pontifical Catholic University of Chile,	Numerous dates from 2010 to 2013
Francisco Irarrázabal	Advisor to President Piñera and Director National Emergency Committee	Dec. 7, 2010
Pablo Ivelic Zulueta	National Coordinator, Housing Reconstruction Program, Ministry of Housing	Mar. 15 and Aug. 28, 2012
Verónica Juretic	Regional Manager, Biobío, Foundation for Overcoming Poverty	June 26, 2013

Individual	Position	Date
Felipe Kast	Minister of Planning; Presidential Delegate to Villages and Camps; former Minister of Social Development	Dec. 3, 2010; Oct. 19, 2012; July 18, 2013
Eduardo Katz Gaudlitz	Manager of Protected Forests Direction, National Forest Service	Mar. 15, 2012
Diego Larraín	Project Coordinator, Lift Chile Challenge	Oct. 18, 2012
Felipe Larraín	Minister of Finance	Oct. 19, 2012
Minister Laveleze	ICARE Forum: Catastrophic Risk Management	Oct. 18, 2012
Joaquín Lavín	Minister of Education	Oct. 2012
Cristóbal Lira	Undersecretary, Crime Prevention; former Minister of Emergency	Oct. 17, 2012
Mauricio Löb	Director of Communications, La Moneda	Oct. 17, 2012
Jaime Mañalich	Minister of Health	July 18, 2013
Carlos Marsh	Desafío Levantemos Chile	2013
Roberto Matus	Deputy Chief of Mission, Embassy of Chile, Washington, DC	Feb. 23, 2012
María Inés Mendieta	Interministerial Coordinator, Ministry General Secretariat of Government	Oct. 17, 2012
Leonardo Moreno	Executive Director, Foundation for Overcoming Poverty	June 26, 2013
Emil Namur	Secretario Regional Ministerial	Oct. 17, 2012
Guillermo Parra	Program Coordinator, Vertical S.A.	Dec. 13, 2010
Rodrigo Pérez	Minister of Housing and Urban Development	Aug. 28, Oct. 17 and 19, Nov. 13 and 14, 2012; July 19 and Sept. 5, 11, and 12, 2013

Individual	Position	Date
Ramón del Piano	Chief of Staff of the Minister, Ministry of Finance	Oct. 19, 2012
Sebastián Piñera	President, Republic of Chile	Mar. 15 and Aug. 28, 2012; July 19, 2013; July 28, 2014
Juan Pedro Pinochet	Executive Director, A Roof for Chile	June 27, 2013
Felipe Purcell	Vice President for Corporate Affairs, Anglo American plc	Sept. 27, 2013
Ernesto Ríos	Head, Insurance Regulation Division, Superintendencia de Valores y Seguros	May 2013
Francisco Rodríguez	Interministerial Coordination Division, General Secretariat of the Presidency	July 18 and 19, 2013
Fernando Rojas	Undersecretary of Education	Oct. 19, 2012
Andrés Salgado	ONEMI (Civil Protection Agency)	Oct. 17, 2012
Claudio Seebach	Head of Division, Interministerial Coordination	Mar. 15 and Aug. 28, 2012; July 18 and 19, 2013
André Sougarret	Manager, El Teniente mine, Codelco; Chief Engineer for the Rescue	Jan. 5, 2011
Francisco Vidal	Former Minister of Defense, Government of Michelle Bachelet	Oct. 19, 2012
Askaan Wohlt	Lift Chile Challenge	Oct. 18, 2012

ACKNOWLEDGMENTS

We thank the following organizations and individuals (with titles at the time that we interacted with them):

Government of Chile

María Ignacia Arrasate Rawlins, Reconstruction Research Team, Ministry of Housing and Urban Development

Nicolás Bär, Cultural Attaché, Embassy of Chile, Washington, DC

Javiera Blanco Suárez, Executive Director, Citizen Peace Foundation

Ignacio Briones, Coordinator of International Finances

Cristián del Campo, Chairman of the Board, Techo para Chile

Constanza Cea Sánchez, International Image Consultant, Office of the President

Rodrigo Cerda, Ministry of Finance

Benjamín Chacana, National Director, ONEMI

María Irene Chadwick, Head of Programming

José Ignacio Conchas, Desafío

Hernán de Solminihac, Minister of Mining

Juan Pedro Egaña, Head, Department of Infrastructure, Ministry of Education

Tomás Tagle Galilea, Head Office of Ministry of Housing and Urban

Eduardo Katz Gaudlitz, Manager of Protected Areas Direction, National Forest Service

Javier Irarrázabal, Office of the President

Pablo Ivelic Zulueta, Director, Reconstruction Team of Chile, Ministry of Housing and Urban Development

Felipe Kast, Minister of Planning

Felipe Larraín, Minister of Finance

Cristián Larroulet Vignau, Minister Secretary General of the Presidency

Cristóbal Lira, Undersecretary for Crime Prevention, Ministry of the Interior

Mauricio Löb, Director of Communication, President's Office

Roberto Matus, Deputy Director, Embassy of Chile, Washington, DC

María Inés Mendieta, Chief Minister's Press Secretary General of Government

Emil Namut, Mining Engineer

Rodrigo Pérez Mackenna, Minister of Housing and Urban Development

Ramón del Piano, Minister's Chief of Staff, Finance

Sebastián Piñera, President

Jacqueline Plass Wähling, Undersecretary of Tourism, Ministry of Economy, Development and Tourism

Juan Domingo Riesco Urrejola, Advisor General Secretariat of the Presidency

Ernesto Ríos, Head of Insurance Regulation Division, Securities and Exchange Commission

Francisco Rodríguez Landeta, Division of Interministerial Coordination, General Secretariat of the Presidency

Fernando Rojas, Undersecretary of Education

Felipe Sáez, Director of International Relations, Ministry of Education

Andrés Salgado, Regional Director ONEMI, La Araucania

Claudio Seebach Speiser, Director, Division of Interministerial Coordination, General Secretariat of the Presidency

Francisco Vidal, Former Minister of Defense for President Michelle Bachelet

Wharton School, University of Pennsylvania

Karen Campbell, Fellow, Wharton Risk Center; Senior Economist, World Economic Forum

Preston Cline, Associate Director for Leadership Ventures in the Graduate Leadership Program

Mark Hanna, independent researcher, former doctoral student, Department of Management

Carol Heller, Communications Manager, Wharton Risk Center

Richard Hong, Undergraduate Research Assistant, Wharton Risk Center

Jeff Klein, Director, Wharton Leadership Program

Ann Miller, Administrative Assistant, Wharton Risk Center

World Economic Forum

Marisol Argueta de Barillas, Senior Director, Head of Latin America

Andrew Andrea, Manager, Global Agenda Council on Catastrophic Risks

Elaine Dezenski, Senior Director and Head of Partnering Against Corruption Initiative

Chiemi Hayashi, Head of Research, Risk Response Network

W. Lee Howell, Managing Director, Centre for Global Events and Risk Response Network

Gilbert Probst, Managing Director and Dean, Leadership Office and Academic Affairs

Klaus Schwab, Founder and Executive Chairman

Wessel van Kampen, Project Manager, Risk Response Network

Saadia Zahidi, Senior Director, Head of Gender Parity and Human Capital

World Economic Forum Global Agenda Council on Catastrophic Risks, 2013–14

Baroness Valerie Amos, Undersecretary-General for Humanitarian Affairs and Emergency Relief Coordinator, United Nations, USA

Lauren Alexander Augustine, Director, Office of Special Projects on Risk, Resilience, and Extreme Events, National Academy of Sciences, USA

Shaun Donovan, Secretary of Housing and Urban Development, U.S. Department of Housing and Urban Development, USA

Bekele Geleta, Secretary-General, International Federation of Red Cross and Red Crescent Societies, Switzerland

Peter Guthrie, Professor, University of Cambridge, United Kingdom

Randolph Kent, Director, Humanitarian Futures Programme, King's College, London, United Kingdom

Eduardo Martinez, President, The UPS Foundation, USA

Victor Meyer, Global Head, Corporate Security and Business Continuity, Deutsche Bank, United Kingdom

Kirstjen Nielsen, Senior Fellow, Homeland Security Policy Institute, USA

Satoru Nishikawa, Director-General, Japan Water Agency, Japan

Yuichi Ono, Professor, International Research Institute of Disaster Science, Tohoku University, Japan

Andrin Oswald, Division Head, Novartis Vaccines, Novartis AG, Switzerland

Sara Pantuliano, Head, Humanitarian Policy Group, Overseas Development Institute, United Kingdom

Rodrigo Pérez Mackenna, Minister of Housing and Urbanism and Minister of National Property, Ministry of Housing and Urban Development of Chile, ChileNiyati Sareen, General Manager, Corporate Social Responsibility, Hindustan Construction Company, India

Michael Useem, Professor of Management and Director, Center for Leadership and Change, Wharton School, University of Pennsylvania, USA

Margareta Wahlström, UN Special Representative of the Secretary-General for Disaster Risk Reduction, United Nations International Strategy for Disaster Reduction, Switzerland

Nick Wildgoose, Global Corporate Leader, Supply Chain Product, Zurich Insurance Group, United Kingdom

World Economic Forum Global Agenda Council on Catastrophic Risks, 2012–13

Baroness Valerie Amos, Undersecretary-General for Humanitarian Affairs and Emergency Relief Coordinator, UN Office for the Coordination of Humanitarian Affairs

Lauren Alexander Augustine, Director, Disasters Roundtable, National Academy of Sciences

Bekele Geleta, Secretary-General, International Federation of Red Cross and Red Crescent Societies

Ian Goldin, Director and Professor, Oxford Martin School

Peter Guthrie, Professor, University of Cambridge

Randolph Kent, Director, Humanitarian Futures Programme, King's College London

Eduardo Martinez, President, The UPS Foundation

Victor Meyer, Global Head, Corporate Security and Business Continuity, Deutsche Bank AG

Kirstjen Nielsen, President, Sunesis Consulting LLC

Yuichi Ono, Chief, Disaster Risk Reduction Section, United Nations Economic and Social Commission for Asia and the Pacific

Andrin Oswald, President, Vaccines and Diagnostics, Novartis

Sara Pantuliano, Head, Humanitarian Policy Group, Overseas Development Institute

Rodrigo Pérez Mackenna, Minister of Housing and Urbanism of Chile

William Saito, Commissioner, National Policy Unit, Cabinet Office of Japan

Niyati Sareen, General Manager, Corporate Social Responsibility, Hindustan Construction Company, Ltd.

Nishikawa Satoru, Director, Land and Property Market, Ministry of Land, Infrastructure, Transport and Tourism of Japan

Margareta Wahlström, UN Special Representative of the Secretary-General for Disaster Risk Reduction, United Nations

Nick Wildgoose, Global Corporate Leader, Supply Chain Product, Zurich Insurance Group

ABOUT THE AUTHORS

Howard Kunreuther is James G. Dinan Professor of Decision Sciences and Public Policy, and Co-Director, Center for Risk Management and Decision Processes, Wharton School, University of Pennsylvania, USA. He has a long-standing interest in ways that society can better manage low-probability, high-consequence events related to technological and natural hazards. He is a Coordinating Lead Author on the Intergovernmental Panel on Climate Change (5th Assessment Report), a member of the OECD's High Level Advisory Board on Financial Management of Catastrophes, a fellow of the American Association for the Advancement of Science (AAAS), and distinguished fellow of the Society for Risk Analysis, receiving the Society's Distinguished Achievement Award in 2001. He is the recipient of the Elizur Wright Award for the publication that makes the most significant contribution to the literature of insurance. His most recent book is *Insurance and Behavioral Economics* (with M. Pauly and S. McMorrow; Cambridge University Press). See https://opimweb.wharton.upenn.edu/profile/37.

Erwann O. Michel-Kerjan is Executive Director, Center for Risk Management and Decision Processes, Wharton School, University of Pennsylvania, USA. He teaches in both the Wharton MBA and executive programs. An authority on the financing of extreme events, he was named a Young Global Leader (YGL) by the World Economic Forum in 2007, recognizing the "most extraordinary leaders of the world under the age of forty." Since 2008 he has served as chairman of the OECD Secretary-General High Level Advisory Board on Financial Management of Catastrophes, which advises governments of its thirty-four member countries on these issues. He gave the opening keynote of the G20 on disaster risk management in 2012. Author of more than one hundred publications, his views regularly appear in popular outlets, including the BBC, CNN, the *Economist*, the *Los Angeles Times*, the *New York Times*, the *Wall*

Street Journal, Nature and *Science.* He has edited or written several books, including *The Irrational Economist* (with P. Slovic, PublicAffairs) and *At War with the Weather* (with H. Kunreuther, MIT Press), which received the Kulp-Wright award for the most significant contribution to risk management. See http://opim.wharton.upenn.edu/risk/faculty/michel-kerjan.htm.

Michael Useem is William and Jaclyn Egan Professor of Management and Director of the Center for Leadership and Change Management at the Wharton School of the University of Pennsylvania, USA. His university teaching includes MBA and executive-MBA courses on leadership and change, and he offers programs on leadership, governance, and decision-making for managers in the United States, Asia, Europe, and Latin America. He also works on leadership development and governance with many companies and organizations in the private, public, and nonprofit sectors. He is the author of *The Leadership Moment, Investor Capitalism, The Go Point,* and *The Leader's Checklist.* He is also coauthor and coeditor with Howard Kunreuther of *Learning from Catastrophes,* and coauthor of *The India Way* and *Boards That Lead.* See http://leadership.wharton.upenn.edu/l_change/Useem_Biosketch.shtml.

Research Team

Luis Ballesteros is a researcher and doctoral candidate in the management program of the Wharton School of the University of Pennsylvania. His research interests include competitive strategy and international business, and he is particularly focused on the business drivers behind the provision of collective goods, such as disaster relief, by commercial firms and the impact of their giving on social welfare and economic redistribution. Luis has worked for JP Morgan Chase, the World Bank, and the United Nations Development Program, and he holds degrees from the Massachusetts Institute of Technology and the Mexican Autonomous Institute of Technology.

Aldo Boitano had served during our study as Chief Executive Officer of Vertical, a Chile-based adventure-focused education organization with consulting in human capital and programs in wilderness travel and mountaineering expeditions, and Dean of Instituto Profesional Vertical, an accredited college in Santiago. He serves on the board of Fundacion Vertical, an enterprise devoted to providing opportunities to those who do not have the financial means for outdoor learning programs. He is a guest professor at the University of Chile and the Catholic University of Chile, and formerly Associate Professor on International Business at the University of North Carolina-Charlotte Belk School. He is also an active mountaineer, and served as a member of the 1996 Chilean expedition that summited K2. See http://www.linkedin.com/pub/aldo-boitano/1/128/662.

Matko Koljatic is Professor of Strategic Management at the School of Business Administration of the Catholic University of Chile. A former chief executive for international subsidiaries of Gillette and Johnson and Johnson, he serves on several boards in private and public companies in Chile, including Quiñenco, one of Chile's largest business conglomerates. His university teaching includes executive education, MBA and undergraduate courses on strategy and general management, which he has offered in Argentina, Central America, Chile, Germany, Peru, and the United States. He also serves as editor of *Revista de Administración y Economía UC,* and he edited the book *La Nueva Empresa Chilena.* See http://www.zoominfo.com/#!search/profile/person?personId=565587607&targetid=profile.

World Economic Forum

Elaine Dezenski is Senior Director and Head of Partnering against Corruption Initiative at World Economic Forum, Geneva, Switzerland. She previously served as Senior Director and Deputy Head, Risk Response Network of the World Economic Forum; Managing Director, Global Security Initiative, Interpol; Acting Assistant Secretary for Policy Development, and Deputy Assistant Secretary for Border and Transportation Security Policy, U.S. Department of Homeland Security; and Director, Maritime, Cargo, and Trade Policy, Border and Transportation Security Directorate, U.S. Department of Transportation. She has also served with the Transportation Division, Siemens Corporation, and as a Legis Fellow, Brookings Institution. See http://www.weforum.org/contributors/elaine-k-dezenski.

INDEX